AUSTRALIAN ARTISTS
BOOKS

B
R
B
R
4
2
2
4

AUSTRALIAN ARTISTS
BOOKS

Alex Selenitsch

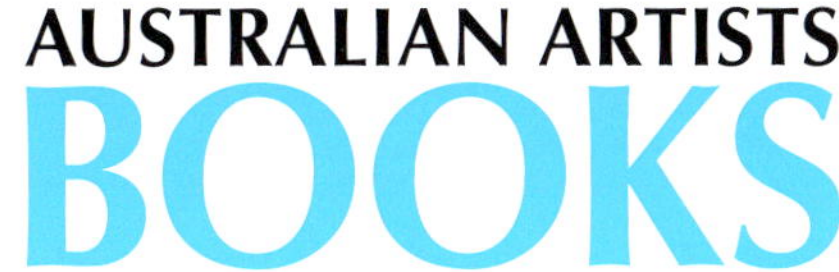

national gallery of **australia**

Produced by NGA Publishing
National Gallery of Australia
nga.gov.au
The National Gallery of Australia is an Australian
Government Agency

Editing: Theresa Willsteed
Design: ZOO Design
Printing: Blue Star Print, Canberra

Cataloguing-in-publication-data
    Selenitsch, Alex.
    Australian artists books.

    Bibliography.

    Includes index.
    ISBN 9780642541864.
    ISBN 0 642 54186 8.

    1. Artists' books – Australia. I. National Gallery
    of Australia. II. Title. (Series: The printed image.
    Australia – Asia – Pacific; 2).

    700.994

The printed image: Australia, Asia, Pacific
Series editor: Roger Butler

printsandprintmaking.gov.au

(front cover)
Christopher CROFT *Sketch-of-book* 1983 (see pp 68–69)

(frontispiece)
Bea MADDOCK *Colour* 1979 (see p 117)

(back cover)
Bea MADDOCK *Impressions of forty working days* 1985
(see pp 42–43)

This publication was supported by the
Gordon Darling Australia Pacific Print Fund.

Acknowledgments
'I cannot rightly tell how I entered it', writes Dante
at the start of *The Divine Comedy*: it echoes my
memory of this project. Roger Butler somehow
put the Gordon Darling Fellowship and I together,
perhaps with the help of Anne McDonald; in any
case I feel they need to be thanked for my entry
into this project, and also the Gordon Darling
Australia Pacific Print Fund, which financed it.

I spent six intensive weeks in the works-on-paper
storage rooms of the Gallery. My thanks to Fiona
Hinton and Jeremy Russell for locating works,
Emma Fowler-Thomason for her company. Every
day, Anne and Roger patiently listened to me over
coffee as I gave wide-eyed descriptions of what
I had just seen.

Dorothy and Petr Herel had me stay with them and
their wonderful cross-kelpie Agnes over those six
weeks: I am grateful for their hospitality and their
introduction to the beauty of daily life in Canberra.

Parts of this work were presented at the Second
Artists Books Conference in Mackay in 2005, and
I thank Robert Heather for that opportunity.

Sarina Noordhuis-Fairfax and Theresa Willsteed
have been my connection to the many people who
have worked to produce this book. My thanks go to
them, and to all of the production team, for getting
the intricacy and detail right.

Alex Selenitsch, 2007

CONTENTS

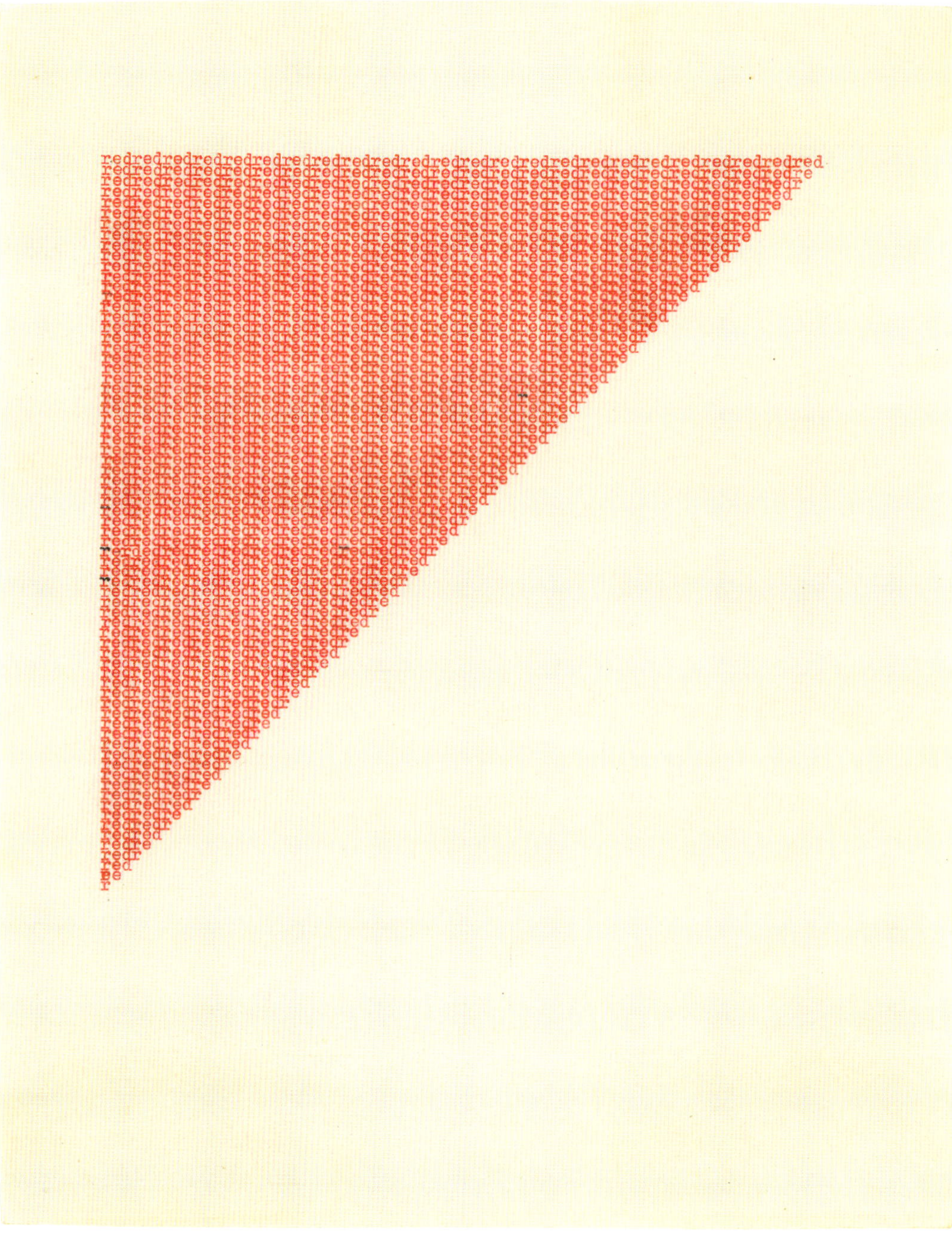

DIRECTOR'S FOREWORD

The publication of *Australian Artists Books* coincides with the National Gallery of Australia's twenty-fifth birthday celebrations which focus on the Gallery's permanent collection. The collection of Australian Prints, Posters and Illustrated Books, assembled by curatorial staff and supported by the Gallery's previous directors, Council, artists and donors, is the most comprehensive holding of Australian prints held anywhere – with more than 40,000 works from the Australia-Pacific region.

This publication draws on the Gallery's collection of more than 1000 artists books produced from the 1960s to the present. The author, Alex Selenitsch, was the second recipient of the Gordon Darling Fellowship, and spent the summer of 2001/2002 in white cotton gloves, folding and unfolding some of the National Gallery of Australia's extraordinary collection of Australian artists books. The Gallery has collected artists books since the late 1970s, initially under the curatorship of Michael Desmond, and the holdings have been greatly expanded since the appointment of Roger Butler as Senior Curator, Australian Prints and Drawings in 1981. The collection has also benefited immensely from generous donations from artists, their relatives and friends, dealers and collectors.

As an architect and poet, Selenitsch is known for his elegant, analytical approach, and here he has produced an engaging and considered narrative which explores the interplay of content and form in a range of artists books from the collection. This publication is the second in the series *The printed image*, which publishes the wide-ranging research of Gordon Darling Fellows, with projects including the history of printmaking in Papua New Guinea and the posters produced by Redback Graphix during the 1980s. Since its inception in 1999, the Fellowship has supported the study of prints and printmaking in Australia and the Pacific region. It is an access initiative of the Gordon Darling Australia Pacific Print Fund, which has also enabled the acquisition of many significant works on paper since its establishment in 1989 by the then Chairman of the Gallery Council, philanthropist Gordon Darling.

I congratulate Alex Selenitsch on his thoughtful examination of this diverse, tactile area of contemporary printmaking. His work makes a significant contribution to understanding the significance of the artists book format as an inventive oeuvre within printmaking in Australian art. I thank Brenton McGeachie and Eleni Kypridis for the accompanying photographs, which show great sensitivity towards the complicated nuances of the artists book.

Ron Radford AM
Director
National Gallery of Australia

Mike PARR
Word situations 1 & 2 1970–71

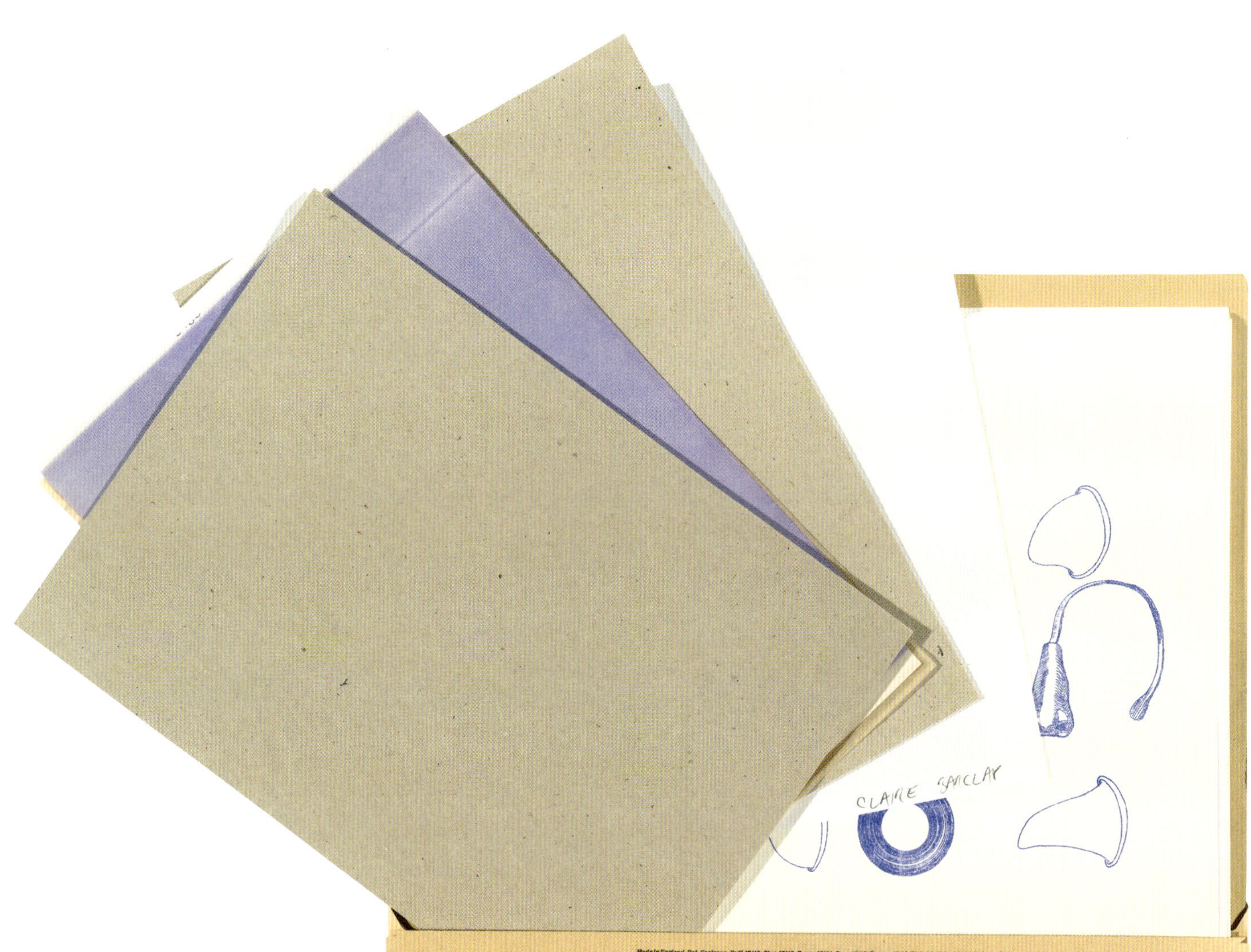

CLAIRE BARCLAY
Made in England. Ref. Foolscap. Buff 45112. Blue 45113. Green 45114. Grey 45115. Orange 45116. Pink 45117. Red 45118. Yellow 45119.
Slimpick Wallet
CLAIRE BARCLAY; ANNE BRENNAN; BARBARA CAMPBELL; LINDSAY
DUNBAR; FIONA HALL; STEVEN HOLLAND; TESS HORWITZ,
STEPHANIE JONES; NIGEL LENDON; KATE LOHSE; eX de MEDICI;
GEORGE POPPERWELL; NEIL ROBERTS; PAUL SAINT; CHRISTOPHER
SNEE; CHRISTINE TARKOWSKI.

INTRODUCTION

Defining artists books

An artists book is a book made by an artist, and is meant as an artwork. This is the most consensual definition and appears in many texts on artists books. Some writers then go on to further categorise the activity in terms of print runs, distribution, production techniques and even subject matter – in most cases these discriminations describe the author's position rather than the activity that is 'artists books'. This survey is no exception as it attempts to be as inclusive as possible, wishing to delay definition until all artists books of every kind can be inspected and related to each other. As the artists book is a living, changing discipline, a specific definition would appear to be impossible from this point of view. But there are good reasons for such a cautious approach.

Firstly, there are many ways of making a book. A book may be designed or conceived by an artist and then mass-produced; it may be printed using craft and fine art print techniques in editions; or it may be a single copy or individual work made by hand. All of these techniques allow the artist to exercise control over the product. There is also the possibility of combining these production methods in any given artists book. Books can also be made out of non-standard book materials (such as bronze, lead and glass), and may have no connection to print at all.

Secondly, the book is a complex artefact. The standard pile of pages, bound together on one side to form a hinge and protected by stiff board covers is only one way that sheets of paper can be collected and fixed together. A book can also take the form of an accordion fold, or a continuous scroll, or a packaged set of loose papers. All are ways of fixing sequences of information. But a book is also a cultural sign and object. It connects to issues of materials, especially paper, and now also to electronics. Through printing, the book highlights issues of standardisation and identity. Through authorship, it relates to issues of experience, truth and individuality. Through its portability, the book relates to issues of social and economic patterns of distribution. Through its use as a container, a book promotes collections. Through its narrative forms, it relates to the metaphysics of time.

Neil ROBERTS (coordinator), Claire BARCLAY, Anne BRENNAN, Barbara CAMPBELL, Lindsay DUNBAR, Fiona HALL, Steven HOLLAND, Tess HORWITZ, Stephanie JONES, Nigel LENDON, Kate LOHSE, eX de MEDICI, George POPPERWELL, Neil ROBERTS, Paul SAINT, Christopher SNEE, Christine TARKOWSKI *Multiple Constantinoples* 1995

Thirdly, there are many different kinds of artists who make books. Different artists choose to do different things with books, taking advantage of the disparate and sometimes contradictory range of techniques and issues mentioned above, and will often bring something idiosyncratic and new to the activity. Anytime a definition is established, someone will create a book that contradicts it. In this sense, an artists book might be thought of as a book that expands our ideas of what an artists book might be.

Alternative names

Artists books can also be thought of as 'book art', 'books as artwork', 'bookwork' or 'book objects'. More names will probably emerge as more artists produce these kind of works and more critics and scholars ponder their significance. 'Artists books' (without an apostrophe) has, in some circles, become the standard name for this activity, and is the name used throughout this text.

Related books

Art books and illustrated books are essentially different to artists books. Art books are books about artists or artworks. Illustrated books, most typically those in which an artist illustrates a text by someone else, can sometimes merge into the arena of artists books. In both cases, the test is whether the text and illustrations could be reformatted in another way without loss of information. In other words, most illustrated books and art books are texts that use the book as a neutral format. Similarly, books written by artists, such as autobiographies, notes, letters and interviews, are not artists books, but artists' texts.

A very brief history

Artists books began to appear in the art world in the 1960s. There are various reasons for this. The following speculations, while not a true causal description, give an idea of the ambience that has helped the artists book to flourish.

Firstly, communications and culture began to merge in the post–Second World War recovery, to the extent that they can now stand for each other. Electronic media, notably television and

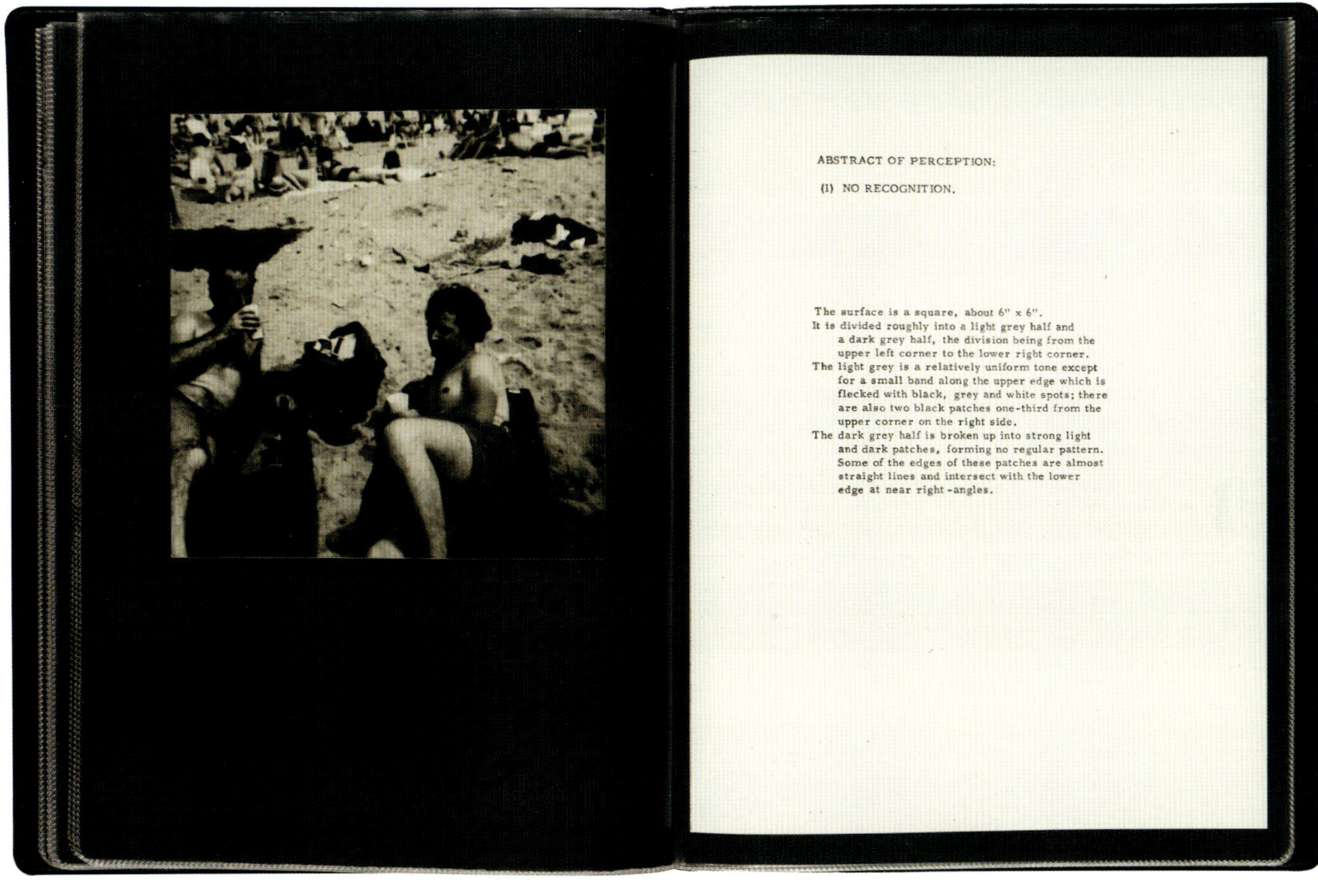

early versions of the computer, began to shift the primary purpose and cutting edge of data collection and storage away from printed paper. Although predictions of a paper-less future have not materialised, the book has lost its prime position as a database, but gained a hold as a cultural artefact, rather like the horse or sailing boat.

Secondly, the professional role of the artist changed from that of a specialist to a generalist. Before the Second World War, artists were easily identified through roles such as painter, sculptor, printmaker, working with prescribed images and media. The realisation that art can be defined through its ideas or through its interaction with an audience, and that this could be done in many different ways, opened up a variety of new forms and techniques for artists to exploit. The growth of art schools associated with a tertiary level of education canonised this attitude to making art.

Ian BURN
Abstracts of perception #2 1968–69

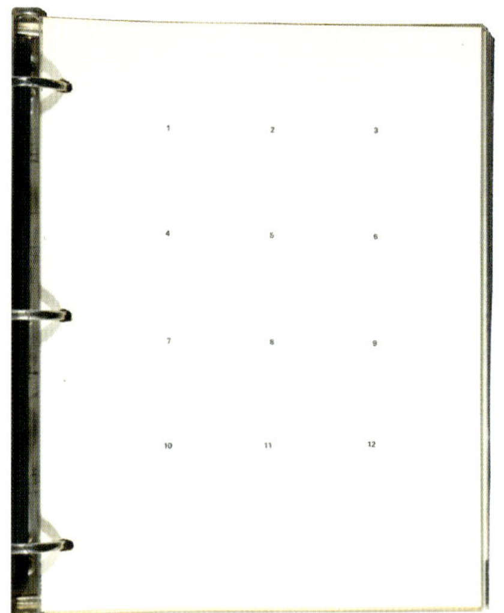 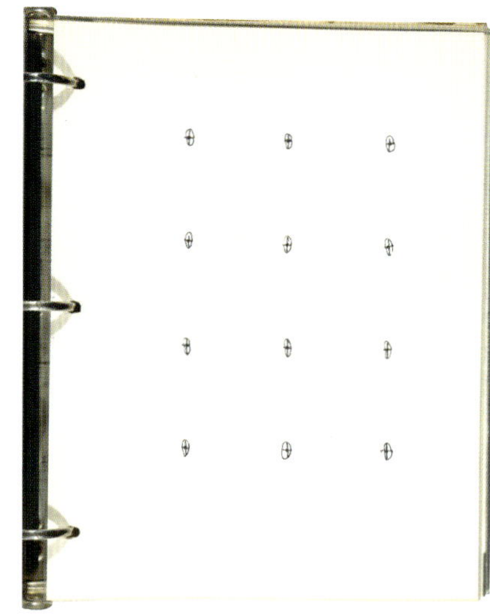 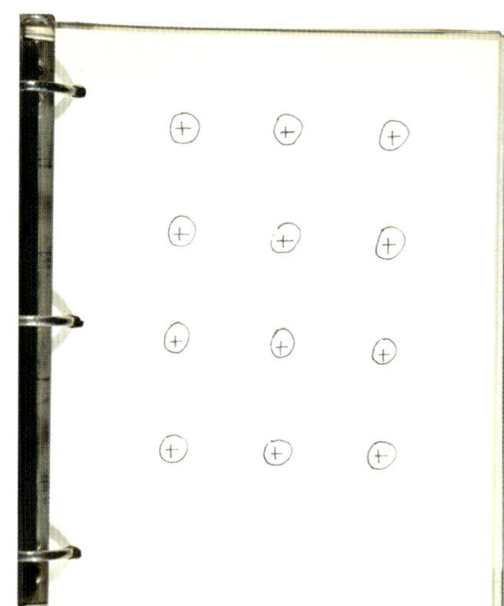

But artists books also have a history as products, and their blossoming in the 1960s was, in some senses, already prepared by works that had been produced over the previous eighty years. Two large groups of works give a sense of this preparation: the French *livre de peintre* and the Russian avant-garde book.

The *livre de peintre* is characterised by luxury. Typically, a visual artist and a poet are brought together to make a fine book of interrelated text and image. Everything about the book – size, weight, paper, binding, printing techniques – is carefully designed. At its most conventional, this method produced a beautiful, if expensive, illustrated book; but it also resulted in such works as Joan Miró and Paul Eluard's *A toute épreuve* 1948–58 and Iliazd's *Pirosmanachvili 1914* 1972.

The Russian avant-garde book is characterised by exploration and creativity. Often, these books were made of meagre materials, using primitive printing technology. Sometimes they incorporated hand-marks or were made entirely by hand. The creativity extended to visual narratives using geometric forms, colours and startling typography. New stories about ordinary life, or of the new industrial utopian city, were combined with intentions to mass-produce and mass-distribute what we now recognise as works of art.

While Paris and Moscow were not the only places that produced *livres de peintre* and avant-garde books, these two tendencies were exhaustively worked out from those cities. Both tendencies not only continue in contemporary artists books practice but also persist as influences in standard book design and production.

Robert JACKS
An unfinished work Volume II 1966–71

The National Gallery of Australia's collection
of Australian artists books

At the time of publication, there were over 1000 Australian artists books in the National Gallery of Australia's collection (depending on your definition). Most of these are held in the Prints and Drawings collection, but some are also kept in the Library, some in the Photography collection and some in the Sculpture collection. This dispersal echoes the leakiness of any definition of these objects. Over ninety per cent of the collection is held in Prints and Drawings, which identifies the strong link that artists books have with graphic art in general, and printmaking in particular.

The collection in Prints and Drawings begins with a few works from the first half of the twentieth century in the *livre de peintre* mode. After a batch of works by Ian Burn and Mel Ramsden from the late 1960s, the collection expands from 1970 onwards in a number of ways.

Firstly, almost immediately a wide range of book types is evident. Some are books that research and collect images relevant to the artist's practice. Others are documents that record an action or performance, sometimes in deliberately deadpan or objective ways, sometimes in creative, interpretive ways. There are proposals for installations and performances. There are stories taken from the artist's experience, often using preset narrative structures such as the seven days of the week, or a walk through a specific place. There are reports and political documents. Finally, there are collections and anthologies that bring together disparate images or groups of artists into the one publication.

Secondly, there are many styles and methods of production. There are 'Multiples', which are mass-produced and identical, with no trace of the artist's touch. There are 'Limited editions', which are books and folios in small print runs using both fine art techniques and commercial and even old-fashioned or obsolete office copying techniques. There are one-off, 'Unique Copies', sometimes made of exquisite and fine materials, sometimes of waste and stuff.

Thirdly, the subject matter of the books varies from subjective notes to objective records, from individual and domestic narratives to social, political and cultural commentary.

All artists books discussed in this book are from the National Gallery's collection. They have been chosen to give a specific sense to the generalisations covered in the preceding paragraphs.

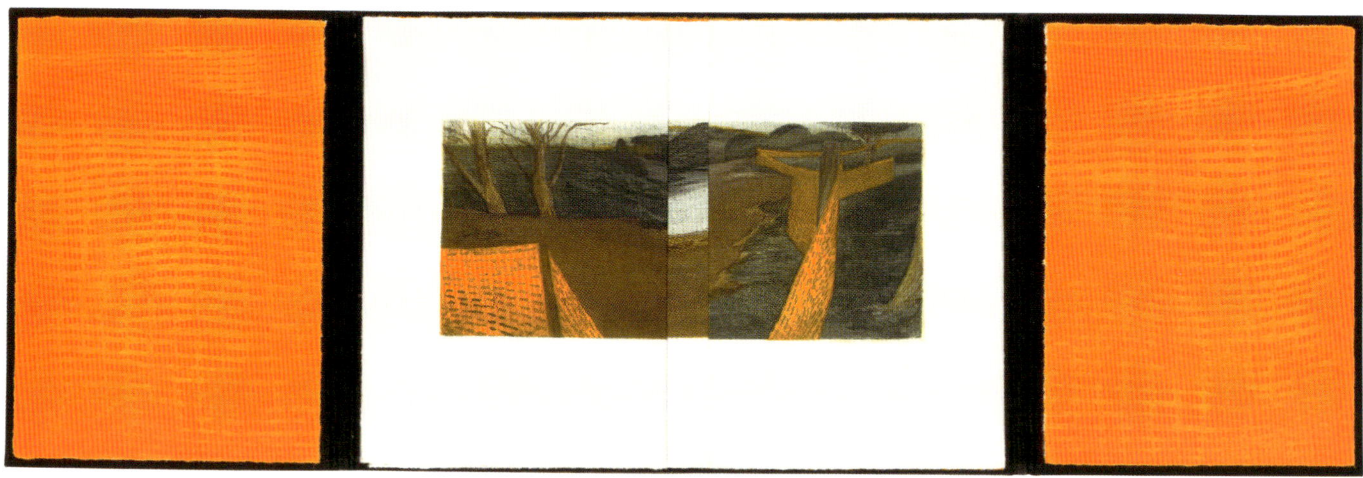

Artists who make books

Many different artists have made books and, while some have made a substantial number, very few artists in Australasia are specialist 'book artists'.

Just as our understanding of artists books gains from an overview of many books, our understanding of the artists books by a particular artist will be enriched when they are considered in relation to other works by that artist. And just as an individual artist's vision may influence what a book could be, the book form can also reveal aspects of that artist's vision which might not be fully realisable in other forms. Taking this point of view, four essays follow, examining the artists books by Ian Burn, Robert Jacks, Bea Maddock and Mike Parr.

Performing the artists book

Typically, an artists book is a work that becomes evident as you hold it, open it up, go back and forth and then close it up again. Often there is a controlled narrative built into the physicality of the book, so that size, weight, texture, stiffness and binding are foregrounded. Nearly always, a tangible experience of the book is necessary to absorb it totally.

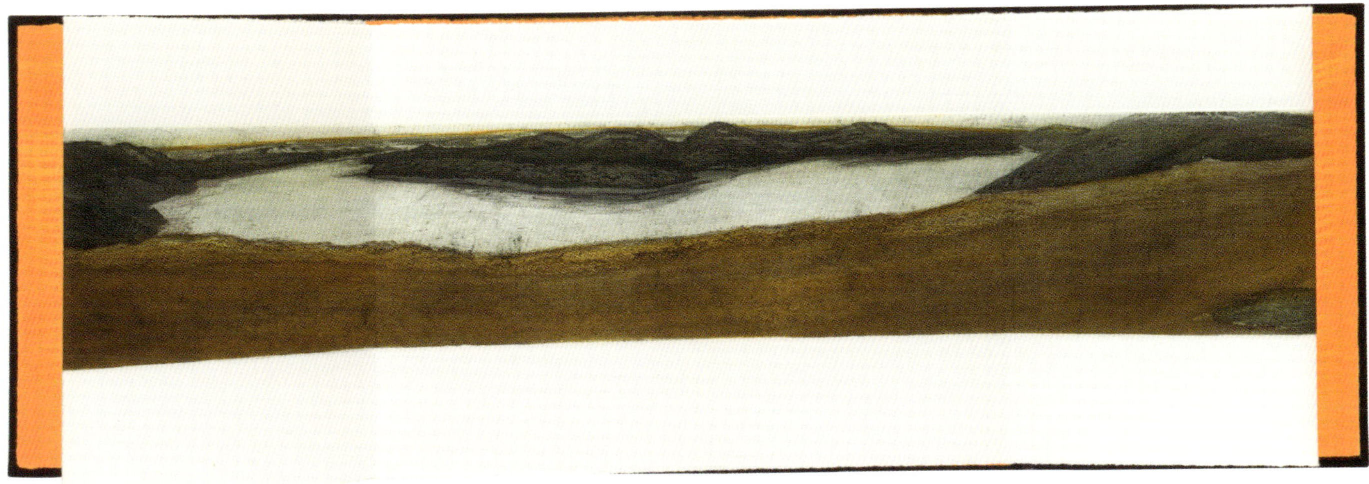

This presents problems in a museum context, where viewers are forbidden to touch works in the interests of conservation. Artists books placed under glass demonstrate that they exist, and although in some cases they can be spread out as a display, generally both sequence and tangibility are lost to the museum visitor. While useful for identification, standard captions give no indication of hidden pages, unlike a painting or sculpture, which is self-evident beside its caption.

The best descriptions of artists books seem to be a report of the performance of looking through one, like reports of a trip to another place. The performance of the reader is therefore another narrative laid over whatever narrative the artists book may contain.

Following the four essays on works by Jacks, Maddock, Burn and Parr, sixteen striking and individual books by other artists are described in this manner. These shorter texts are written as one reader's confrontation with each book, to show how an artists book is an involving and complex experience. Taken as a group, the sixteen books have also been chosen to show the wide range of approaches that currently exist in this ever-expanding field.

Alex Selenitsch

Ruth JOHNSTONE
Untitled (panoramic boxed set) 1991

FOUR APPROACHES TO ARTISTS BOOKS

Ian Burn: the noise of the machine

Robert Jacks: the artist's touch

Bea Maddock: the daily self

Mike Parr: hundreds of pages

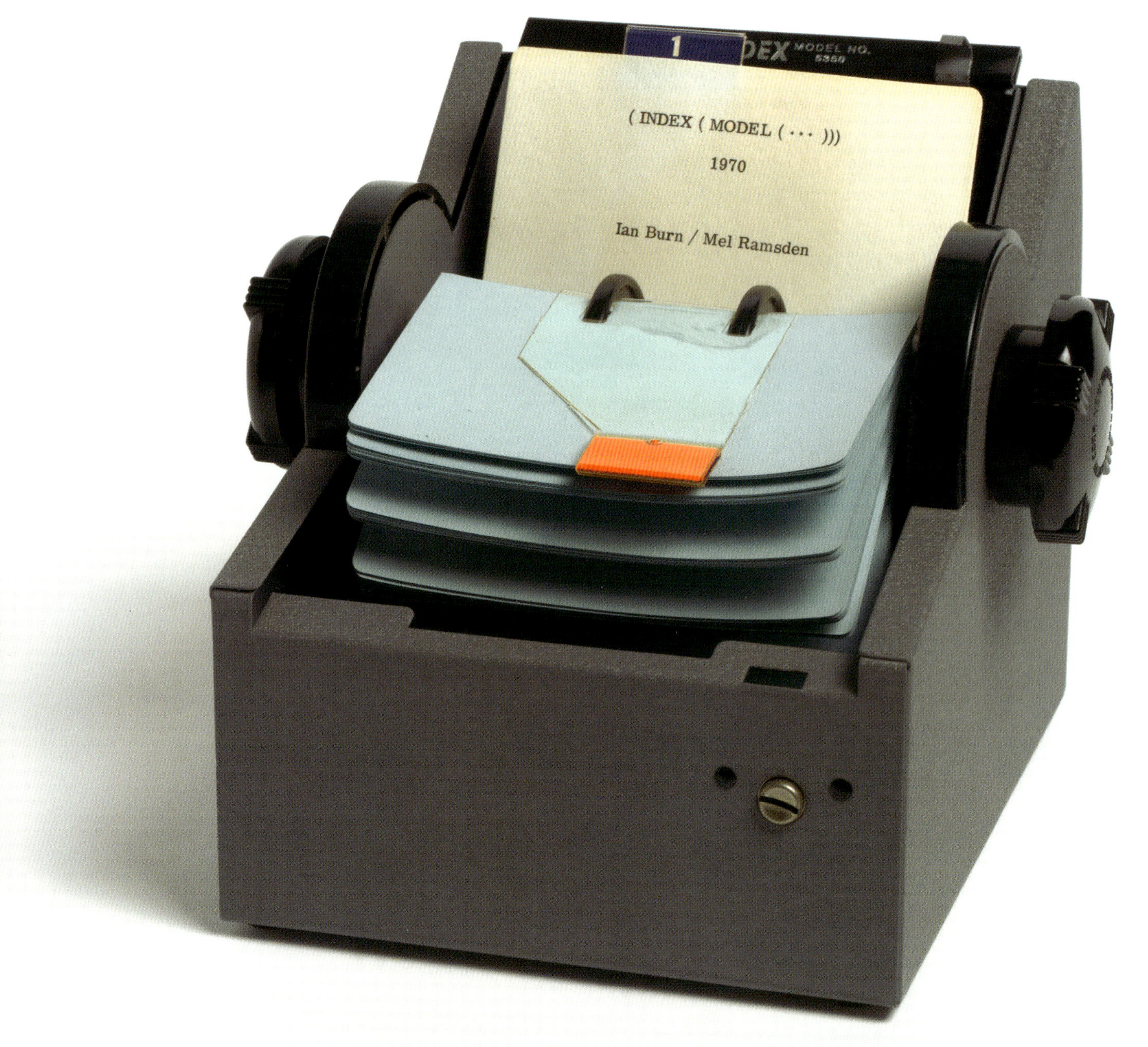
1
DEX MODEL NO.
5350
(INDEX (MODEL (···)))
1970
Ian Burn / Mel Ramsden

Ian Burn: the noise of the machine

With Ian Burn's books, you sense that they are not separate works in a defined genre, but explorations of a broader range of ideas, some of which occasionally fall into book form. *Xerox book #1* 1968 is obviously a book, *Abstracts of perception #2* 1968–69 is a report, but *Six negatives* 1968–69 is a set of pages with a text that only in storage could be thought of as a book. *Mirror piece* 1967 is a painting, sculpture and/or a book, depending on the context. *(Index (model (…)))* 1970 is similar: a found storage system and office object, used by Burn as a classification system, but in the context of artists books, a rare example of a cyclical book.

Xerox book #1 is a stapled and taped landscape-format book, bound as a pile of paper between black card covers. The title page is in Letraset (transfer adhesive lettering, a new graphic device in the 1960s); a blank sheet of tracing paper follows (a similar sheet also finishes off the book); then a page with the colophon typed on it. Ninety-eight pages follow. These demonstrate the book's method of production, which is described on the colophon page:

1. A blank sheet of paper was copied on a xerox machine.
2. This copy was used to make a second copy.
3. The second to make a third, and so on …

One hundred such copies are specified, which means that the title page and colophon page are part of the sequence, even though they have added material such as Letraset and typewriter marks. Burn's apparently rational and mechanical recipe has produced a startling book. Because of the inability of a photocopier to select what to copy and its tendency to enlarge shadows and skew the image through lateral scans, any grime, dust, marks in the paper or on the copying glass are progressively processed, enlarged or moved across the paper. The first two pages of *Xerox book #1* are somewhat grey and photo-like, but at page four the grey becomes grimy and separated, at page five more granulated, at page six a shadow appears at the bottom of the paper and a flare at the top of the page. By page nine, the grime becomes dot-like and after this the dots get finer and finer. In the middle of the book, more and more horizontal lines appear, and slowly the dots become short lines and dashes.

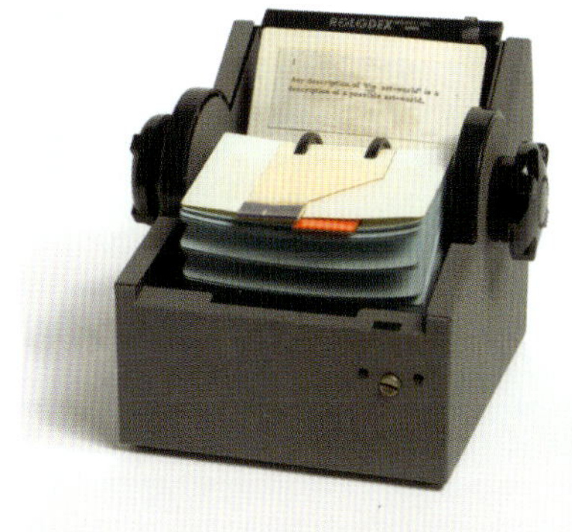

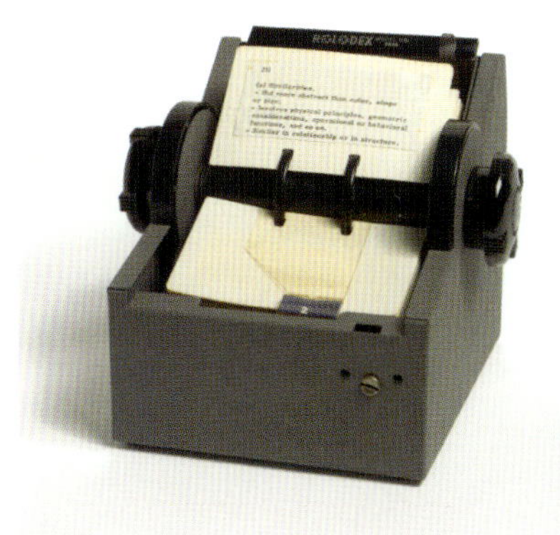

Ian **BURN** and Mel **RAMSDEN**
(Index (model (…))) 1970

15

Ian **BURN** *Xerox book #1* 1968

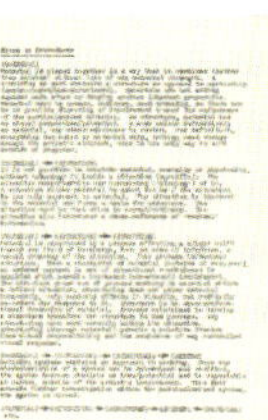

All of this has been generated from a blank page, from nothing but the machine itself. Conventionally, the machine is ignored in photocopying, even where its effects are visible, as it is meant to be a transparent vehicle for processing data. In *Xerox book #1*, the data is the noise of the machine, in the sense that noise is unintended data in a communication system created by the transmission of a message.

The formula for *Xerox book #1* has been repeated by others, for example by American artists Kinsley Parker (*Black holes* 1979) and George Gessert (*Dust and light* 1987). Significantly, their versions have poetic titles, shifting attention away from the machine itself to the semantic potential of its effects. By contrast, the machine is the central point of Burn's version: his book demonstrates the power and effects of what we normally ignore. By implication, the book points to any other apparently transparent system or convention. It would be difficult to produce Burn's book now, using contemporary photocopiers. Rather than cancelling out Burn's proposition, it makes it more pertinent. As technology becomes more developed and more intrusive, it also becomes more and more invisible, with the copy indistinguishable from the original.

While *Xerox book #1* gives a recipe and presents its product, *Mirror piece* is all specifications. The book is an instruction manual for a simple object: a mirror in a frame. The manual treats this object as something to be made and does this through a certification of the idea and

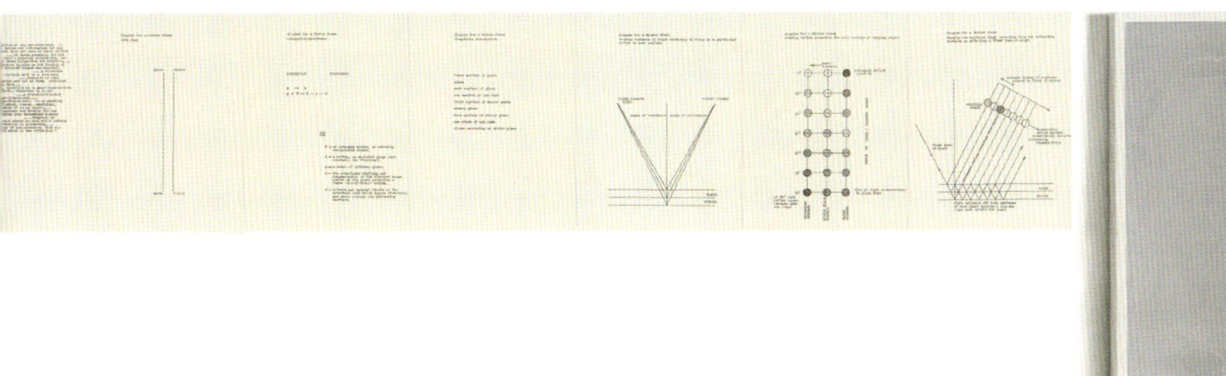

a signed manufacturer's compliance sheet (signed by the artist), a description, a specification of materials, notes on making procedures, and various notes on philosophical issues of manufacture, description and perception. Notably, there are no speculations on what the object might represent or mean, as if that were obvious. In the same spirit of objectivity, the material descriptions and philosophical notes are presented as part of the same continuum of information, without hierarchy.

Each separate idea in *Mirror piece* is allocated a separate page or section of pages, and the data is carried only on one side of the sheet. The artist notes that the work can be displayed with the mirror object on the wall 'as if they were the artwork too'. To this end, *Mirror piece* is bound with a plastic channel binder that enables it to be taken apart and put back together. In this case, displaying the book on the wall is a variation on opening it as a fan: the sequence must still be kept on the wall, and the pages returned to their bound format for storage.

In *Abstracts of perception #2*, Burn takes his examination of context and framing into photography. The book is a set of photographs with associated text typed on sheets of paper, all presented in a standard office folder of bound, clear plastic sleeves. Three photographs are subjected to five different analyses. The photographs are black and white, square format, but against this formality, two are of Avril Burn and one is of Ian Burn and Mel Ramsden: the

Ian BURN *Mirror piece* 1967

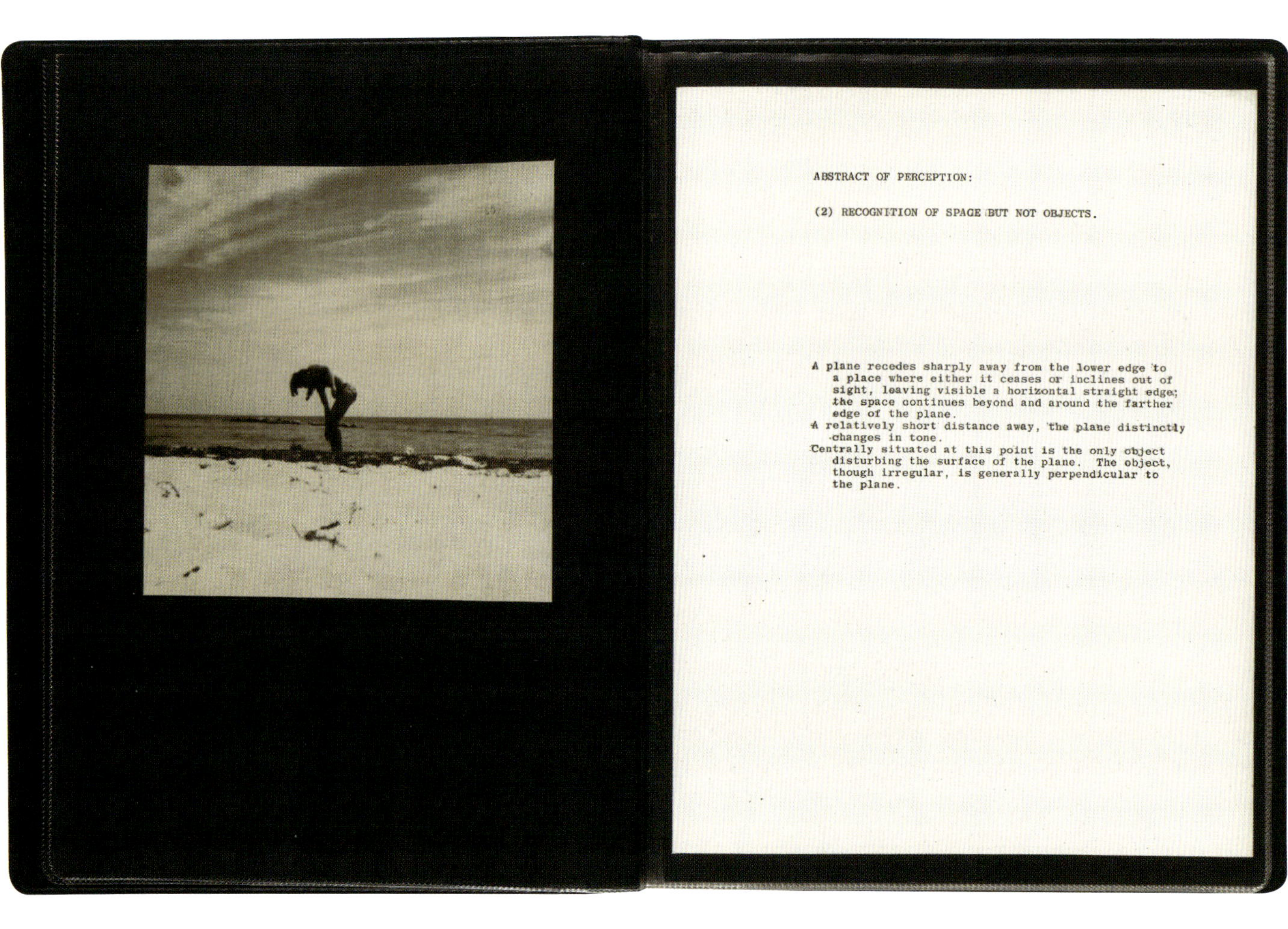

ABSTRACT OF PERCEPTION:

(2) RECOGNITION OF SPACE BUT NOT OBJECTS.

A plane recedes sharply away from the lower edge to
a place where either it ceases or inclines out of
sight, leaving visible a horizontal straight edge;
the space continues beyond and around the farther
edge of the plane.
A relatively short distance away, the plane distinctly
changes in tone.
Centrally situated at this point is the only object
disturbing the surface of the plane. The object,
though irregular, is generally perpendicular to
the plane.

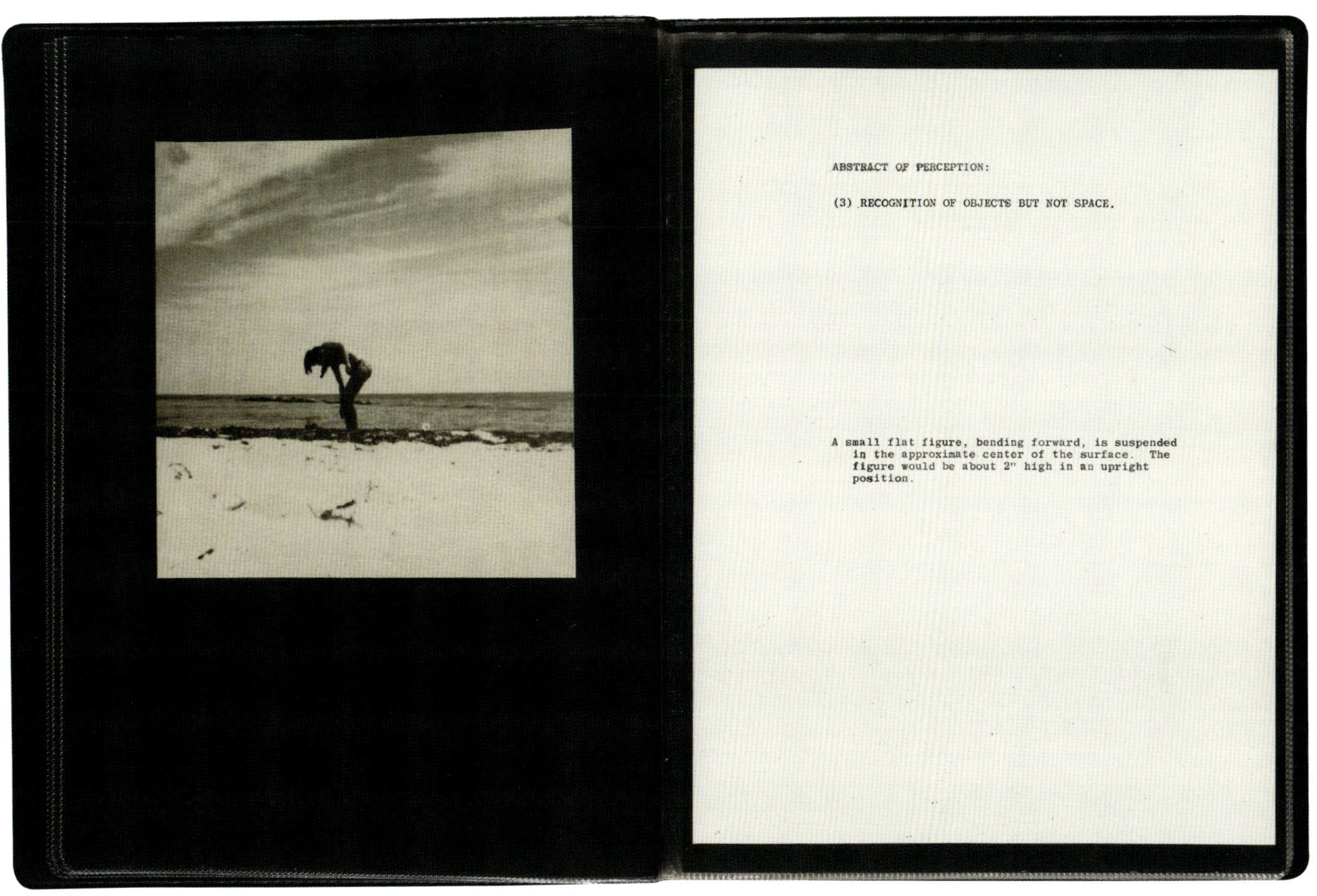

Ian BURN
Abstracts of perception #2 1968–69

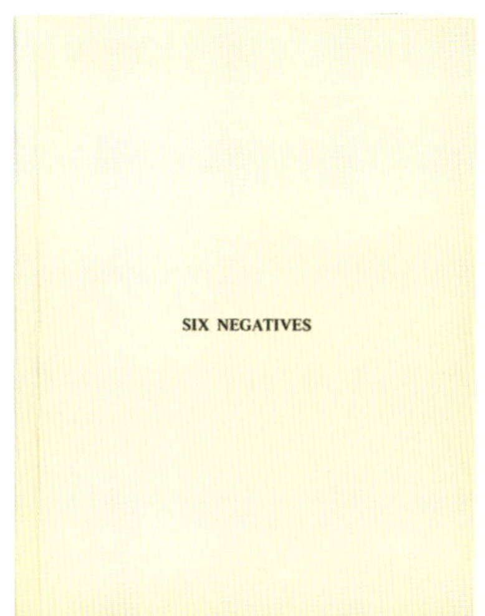

artist's wife and the artist's friend and collaborator. All photographs are taken at a beach, and are summer photographs of the sort that end up in personal albums. The analyses range – in logical order, of course – from 'no recognition' (the description of the photo as a pure object), through various kinds of recognition, to finally the 'recognition of an event' (in which case there is a statistical list of what the photograph represents). In this work Burn points out a common property of photographs, unnoticed by most commentators: our responses to photographs lie somewhere between the two extremes of analysis Burn puts forward, that is, somewhere between pure materiality and recognition of the event. This latter response only happens when we have a personal record or memory of the experience shown in the photograph. For most photographs we cannot do this, and this is why unidentified, ordinary photographs can seem so enigmatic and ultimately meaningless.

Six negatives is another collaboration by Ian Burn and Mel Ramsden. Despite its contemporary, conceptual look, it treats collaboration in a traditional way – one artist does the visual images, the other does the writing. Ramsden's contribution consists of double-page spreads from Roget's *Thesaurus*. These have been printed in negative after the evenly numbered categories have been struck out. Conveniently, in the *Thesaurus*'s original typography, odd and even numbered categories are positioned in two parallel columns per page, and are read down the page. Ramsden's graphic is a double column also, but one is of original text and one has thick furry lines where the words would be. Positive and negative there-and-not-there, line by line, vie with the negative reprint of the pages, with the original black of the obliterations appearing as thick white lines.

Burn's accompanying text is entitled 'Holding system for 6 negatives' and discusses the problems of readymades (Marcel Duchamp's label for the found object), and of the *Thesaurus* as an epistemological example. Burn's essay functions as a self-contained text if you simply read it, but it also connects to Ramsden's images, when the text is thought of as a negative of the first set of pages (which are white on black), and as continuous prose with a non-numeric structure. The revealed duality of Roget's system is given an image when the two parts of this collaboration are considered together. In *Six negatives*, the noise of the machine becomes the noise of thought, or rather, its printed representation.

Ian BURN and Mel RAMSDEN
Six negatives 1968–69

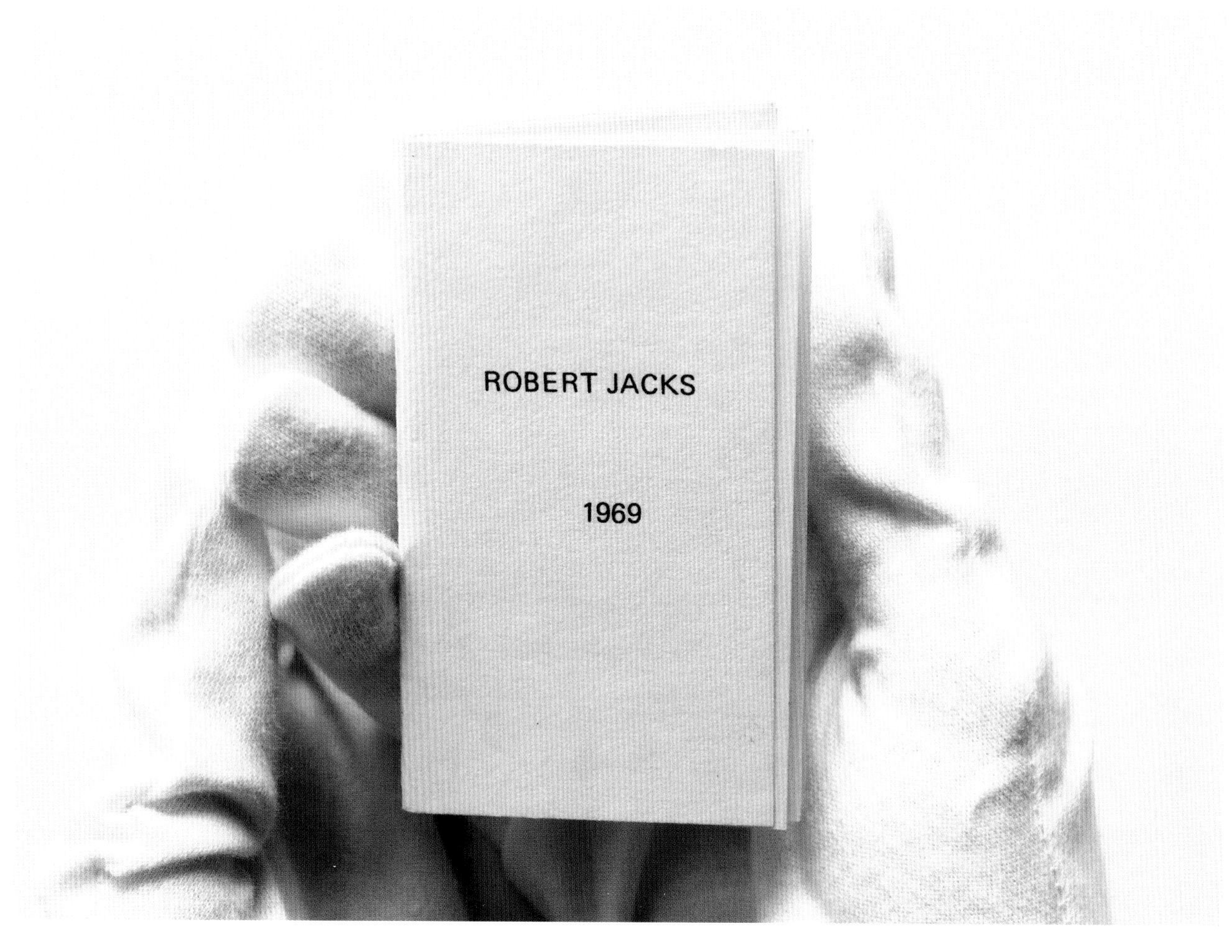
ROBERT JACKS
1969

Robert Jacks: the artist's touch

Robert Jacks's paintings, drawings and prints share a formal consistency, and he produces many works as groups. Not surprisingly, his books are no exception to this, as the repeated page easily parallels the repeated rhythms of serial works. Yet the charm of Jacks's books is achieved not through the uniformity that printed matter encourages, but through an exploitation of the artist's touch – of the acceptance of chance and individual nuances made possible through hand, rather than machine, action. These nuances are further inflected by the particular materiality of the medium Jacks uses in a particular work.

Although Jacks's earliest book, *1–12* 1969, has no handmade touches, it sets some of the rules for his subsequent books. This first book is tiny, printed offset and bound by a single staple. Inside there is a simple sequence, beginning with a single vertical line in the centre of the page. Each following page has one more vertical line, until twelve such lines form a horizontal band across the full width of the page. The sequence is limited by the page size, drawing attention to the book itself – in other words, the book shows a simple systematic sequence, which, at completion, points to its context or setting.

Jacks's interest in the way materiality alters or inflects an idea finds expression in *Twelve drawings* 1970. This is an A4 report. It consists of twelve sheets of drawings and a title page with an acetate cover, and is held together in a blue plastic binder. The twelve drawings share a 3 x 5 grid of points, giving a 2 x 4 grid of squares set vertically on the page. This grid then also manifests through cut paper and cut cloth as numbers, letters and pen drawings of crosses or discs, and finally ends up as a simple line drawing joining up all the grid points. The paper and cloth versions are shown as photographs, but at the same size as the other graphics. The sequence represents a slow, page-by-page removal of materiality, going down to a diagram. When the book is laid flat on a table, this sequence is easy to imagine as also going the other way: as a stack of increasingly materialised versions of the simple grid located at the bottom of the pile.

An unfinished work 1966–71 is also a report, but more complex and self-conscious than *Twelve drawings*. *An unfinished work* exists in two versions. The simpler one is bound like an office document, and it consists of three main sections of three parts each. Through diagrams

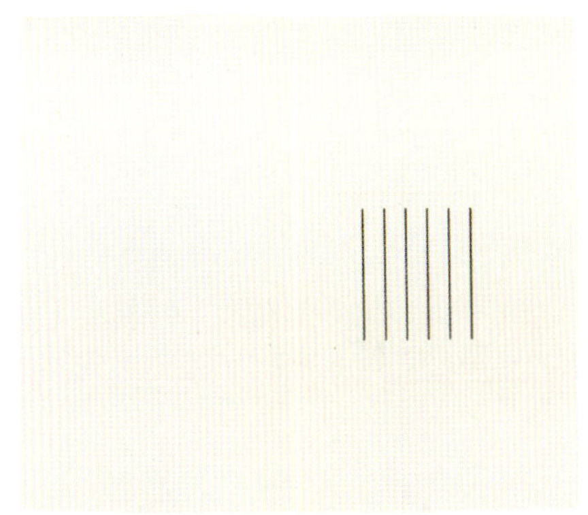

Robert JACKS *1–12* 1969

A   B   C

D   E   F

G   H   I

J   K   L

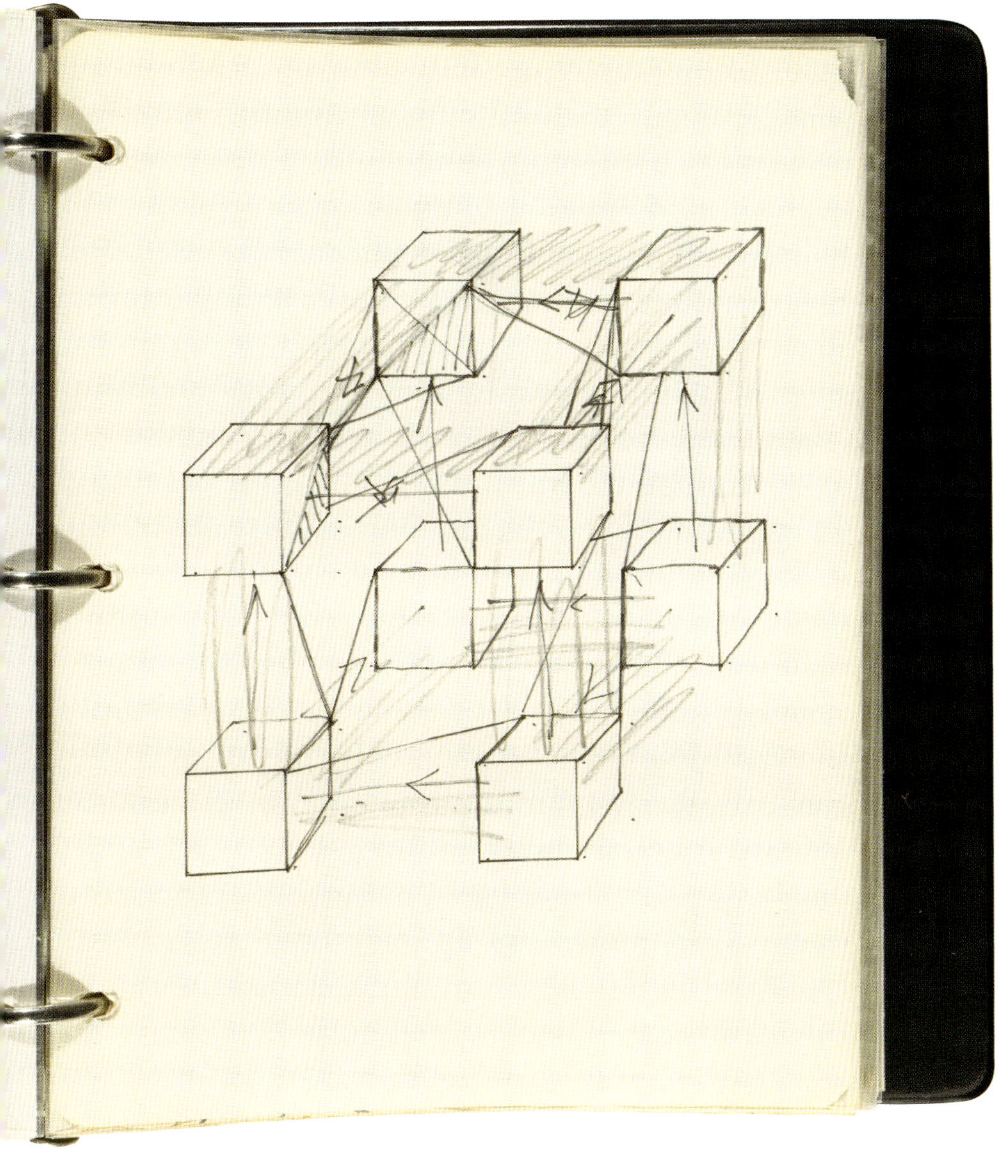

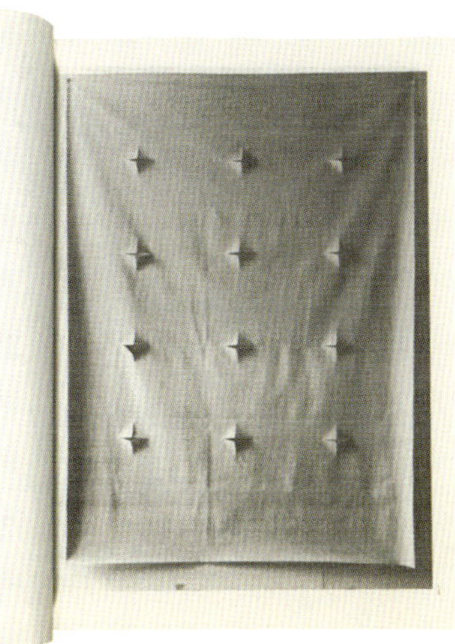

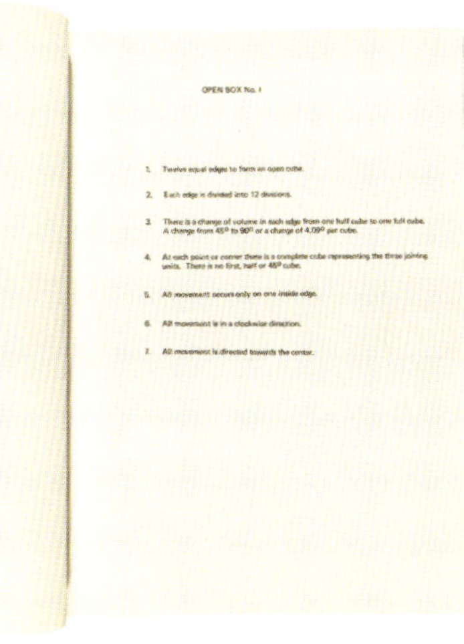

(opposite page and top)
Robert JACKS *Twelve drawings* 1970

(left and above)
Robert JACKS *An unfinished work Volume I* 1966–71

and statistics, each successive part describes the character of a cube as an open box, as four edges and as one edge respectively. Within each main section, the material becomes more and more abstract and diagrammatic. The second version, using the same title, consists of two volumes, both bound in a double-arch file with stiff black covers. These volumes assemble an exhaustive analysis of proposals for sculptures, as diagrams and sets of instructions, along with photographs of related exhibition installations by Jacks. The whole work presents an intricate and systematic analysis of the cube. For many artists working at that time, the cube was a primary form, with either weak or no representational emphasis at all. Using the cube as an arbitrary starting point, this work directs the viewer's attention to the aesthetic potential of analytic processes.

Twelve is the number of edges in a wire model of a cube, and is the structuring number for the three bookworks discussed above, explicitly in the first two and implicitly through the figure of the cube in *An unfinished work*. It is also evident in the structure of Jacks's books of hand-stamped images (made from 1973 to 1980), a series of small, square-format books, stapled and edged with coloured tape to accent the spine. The hand-stamped works' cover papers are machine-printed, and give the artist's name, the specific nature of that set of images, the fact that they are hand stamped, and the date and place of making. The places are an itinerary of Jacks's career: New York; Austin and Houston, Texas; Melbourne and Sydney, Australia. One book in the series, *Color book* 1975, has fifteen images; all others have twelve.

Each page in these little books is marked with a single small rectangle, printed off a rubber stamp. Each stamp is a grid of lines or dots, with most stamps being about the size of a medium-sized postage stamp. Where the stamped image is larger, its area is four times the area of the standard smaller one. Some books are stamped in a single colour, others feature overlaid stamps of different colours. The bindings differ in colour for each edition, until the last two in this set repeat the first two. Jacks has also produced envelopes of stamped works, using similar imagery to the little books. In these, viewers are free to find their own sequence for the images, and also to spread them out so that they are all visible in a single glance. The envelopes are in editions of 100. Jacks has also published a loose folio of stamped cards using single and double colours: *40 stamped prints* 1976, in an edition of thirty. *Stamp post cards* 1980, which contains fifteen stamped postcards by fifteen Australian artists – Suzanne Archer,

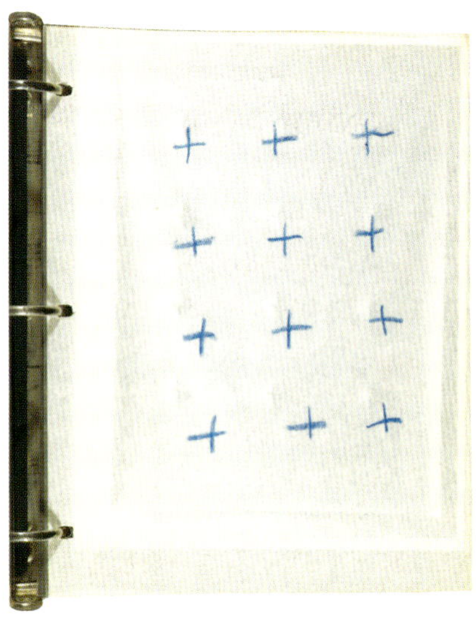

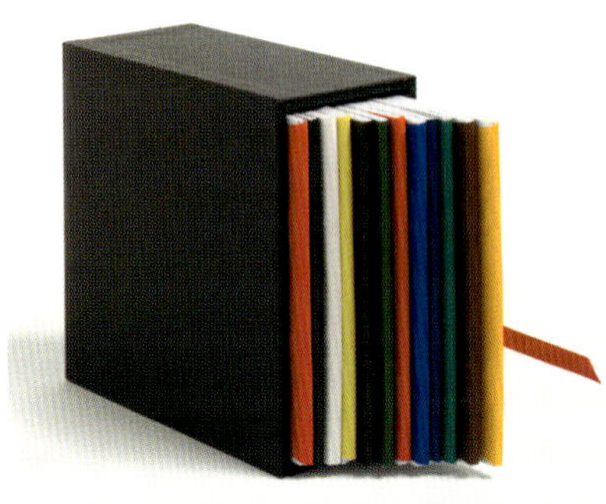

(top)
Robert JACKS *An unfinished work Volume II* 1966–71

(bottom and right)
Robert JACKS Selection of hand-stamped artists books 1973–80

ROBERT JACKS
TWELVE RED GRIDS
HAND STAMPED
NEW YORK 1973

ROBERT JACKS
COLOR BOOK
HAND STAMPED
NEW YORK 1975

ROBERT JACKS
1975 — 1976
HAND STAMPED
NEW YORK

ROBERT JACKS
LINES DOTS
HAND STAMPED
AUSTIN TEXAS
1976

ROBERT JACKS
LINES DOTS
NUMBER TWO
HAND STAMPED
HOUSTON TEXAS
1977

ROBERT JACKS
VERTICAL & HORIZONTAL
HAND STAMPED
MELBOURNE
1978

ROBERT JACKS
DOTS
HAND STAMPED
NEW YORK 1978

ROBERT JACKS
RED DOTS
HAND STAMPED
SYDNEY
1979

ROBERT JACKS
BLACK LINES
HAND STAMPED
SYDNEY
1980

Tom Arthur, Tony Coleing, John Firth-Smith, Arthur Leyden, Jennifer Marshall, Michael C McMillen, Robert Owen, Peter Powditch, Gary Shead, Tim Storrier, Ann Thomson, David van Nunen, Guy Warren and Robert Jacks – was organised by Jacks, and belongs to his stamped series of works due to its technique.

It is probable – if not certain – that not one of the stamped images is repeated. The technical difficulty of applying a stamp with the same inking, same pressure and angle, and in the same position each time has been exploited by Jacks to produce a set of works that:

- denote repetition but are actually unique due to the action of the hand

- produce optical effects through overlay 'misalignments', and

- produce kinetic effects when the bound books are flicked through, because of slight dislocations of the stamped image on the page.

Further, the stamps are the same size as postage stamps and traditional franking stamps. Each stamped page or card is thus simultaneously labelled and cancelled by the artist; perhaps they may even be 'signed', if one could read the stamping gesture as such.

Jacks also exploits optical effects in *Red diagonals* 1976. In this book, which is machine-printed, sixteen pages each present a hatched horizontal band that is divided into adjacent rectangles through changes in the direction of the diagonal hatching. There is a sequence of such divisions: the band on the first page is divided once; on subsequent pages the hatched band is divided twice; then three, four and finally five times. There are four pages of one, two and five subdivisions, but three pages of three subdivisions and one page of four subdivisions. Five dividing lines to the band produces a band of six squares; again the six faces of a cube find a voice, and remind the viewer of the way the sequence is closed in the earlier small book, *1–12* 1969.

The hatched patterns in *Red diagonals* pick out symmetrical and left-to-right sequences. This creates a narrative variety against the repeated single band and the apparently systematic increase in numbers of subdivisions as the pages progress. The book is floppy and seems fragile when handled, and its red ink is softened by the colour and texture of the background paper. The delicacy of the hand-marks in the stamped publications continues in *Red diagonals*, in both its graphics and the physicality of its paper.

Robert JACKS *Hand stamped New York* 1975–76 (actual size)

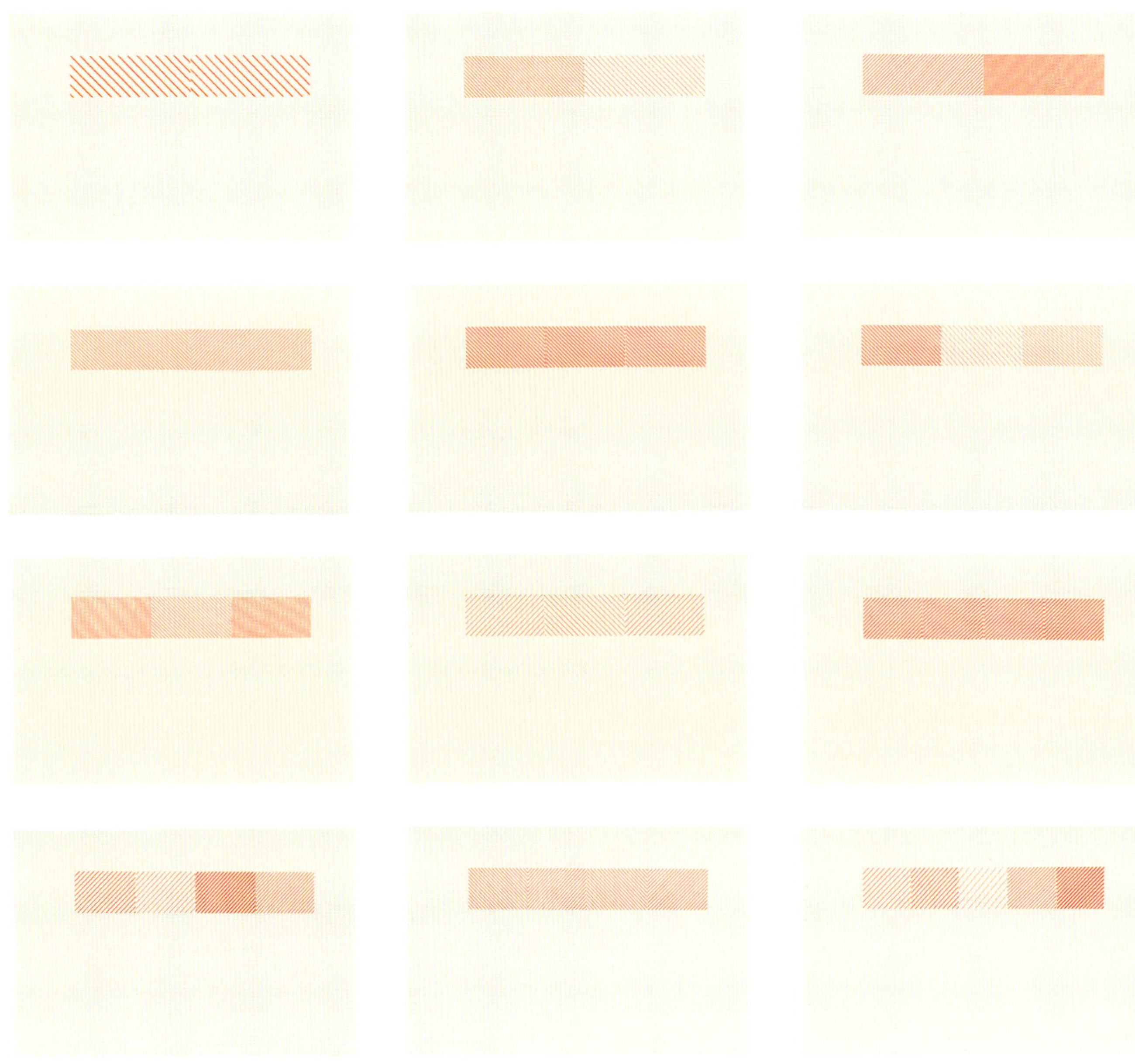

Somewhere between the individual hand-stamped books and the identicality of *Red diagonals*, there is Jacks's *Texas sketch book* 1978. This is a book of fifty etchings in an edition of three, with one artist's proof (making a total of four, the number of a square). Each book of etchings is covered by black-leather-covered boards and bound with brass Chicago screws. The book feels like a stamp or photo album. All of the etchings are small, and are of the same proportion of image-to-page as are the images in Jacks's hand-stamped series of artists books.

The images in *Texas sketch book* are made up of thick, freehand lines, and are somewhat diagrammatic. As a book, they deliver a narrative of landscape perception. Beginning with a single drawing of the horizon, then three of the sky, the etchings then explore labyrinths, squiggles, dazzle and explosion patterns, until the final set shows a radiant rectangle, at first represented inside the drawing as an object in the landscape, then as the whole etched image itself. Here, too, the sequence is closed through the square, when the radiant rectangle in the landscape becomes a radiant square on its own: the whole narrative of the book thus shifting from landscape to geometry.

Robert JACKS *Red diagonals* 1976

Texas Sketch Book
50 Etchings
by
Robert Jacks
Number 3
From an Edition of 3
with one artist proof
printed Melbourne
1978

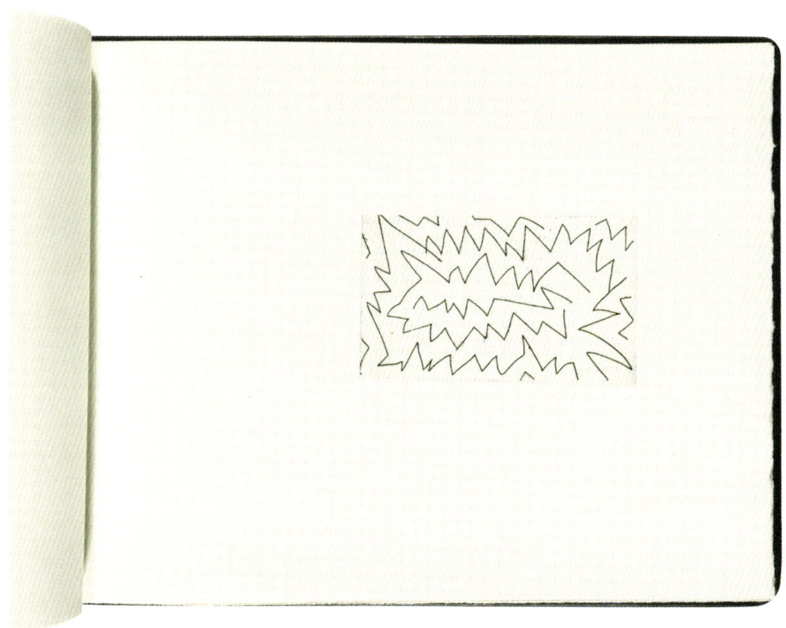

Robert **JACKS** *Texas sketch book* 1978

Bea Maddock: the daily self

In Bea Maddock's bookworks, diaristic tendencies come to the fore. Her books are all diaries in one sense or another, and although there is a personal voice, the condition they describe resonates for many of us. This is because autobiography is always weighed against a larger force, and played out through Maddock's individual response to a found narrative or literary structure such as a pre-existing text, an actual book, a month's run of newspapers or a collection of objects.

While there is always a clear presentation of a narrative sequence, Maddock handles or materialises it in such a way that the overall work appears to be motionless, or timeless. Maddock's books are unmistakably single objects or concepts, seemingly made of one material.

Five books made by the artist over eleven years (1979–90) show this diaristic aspect. In these works, there appears to be no chronological development of idea or technique. Each of the five books is individual, and each book is as developed as any other.

Nevertheless, the first book in this group, *Colour* 1979, is unusual for its non-representational content. Maddock's later books all refer to some aspect of experience outside of the structure of books and the craft of print, but *Colour* is almost entirely a bookish image of printing. It is a book of etchings, bound in raw canvas-covered boards with oriental binding, and set in a white, paper-covered slip-case. The etched pages are folded so that the open edges are buried in the binding and the fold exhibited at the outside edge. The right-hand-side image in the book and its reverse side, which were initially printed as one page, are thus bound into the book as image and label, back to back, with the label now referring to the image on the previous page, and not to the one immediately following on the right-hand side.

The etchings in *Colour* are all vertical columns of three near-squares of colour, with top and bottom colours being mixed for the middle square. Three sets of etchings are presented using the same colour sequence, but showing its effects through hatched texture, flat colour, then stipple. Generally, the rule is that the bottom colour of one page becomes the top colour of the next; this is violated between moves three to four and four to five in each of the three sections. The three sections of ten original etchings (which becomes sixty pages) complete the colour and texture sequences. As you shut the book, there is a tangible sense that the whole spectrum has been captured, especially when you slide the book back into its white (all-colours-mixed) slip-case.

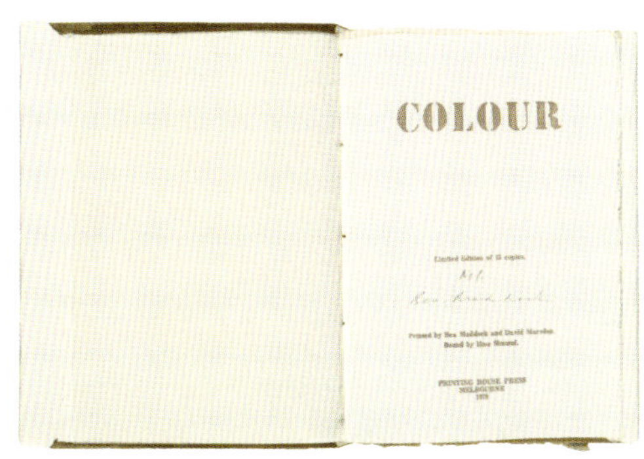

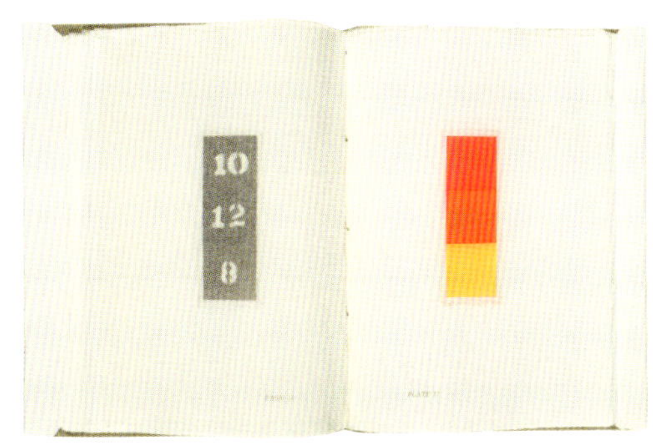

Bea MADDOCK *Colour* 1979

Being and nothingness by Jean-Paul Sartre 1982 is a box containing twenty-five sheets of handmade paper, that is, fifty pages, on which the artist has handwritten excerpts from Jean-Paul Sartre's text *Being and Nothingness*, and then impregnated the sheets with wax. Two more sheets, a title page and a preface share this treatment. While Sartre's text retains its identity, Maddock's rewriting and subsequent treatment of the paper create both a commentary on the text and a separate work altogether. On the preface sheet, Maddock quotes Edward Johnston on writing, illuminating and lettering: 'the key here is the multiple meanings of illuminating'. By rewriting a text, the artist preserves it, physically and in memory: the wax makes this tangible, presenting a record of Maddock's reading and transcription.

Covering something with wax preserves it. In this case, the wax has made the paper semi-transparent, so that not only are both sides of the paper visible as recto and verso (for both sides), but non-transparent flecks and fragments in the handmade paper have also become evident as floating solids. Wax tablets come to mind; also, detritus. As you handle the slightly tacky sheets, which slowly flex under their own weight, you get the impression that something atavistic or archeological is present.

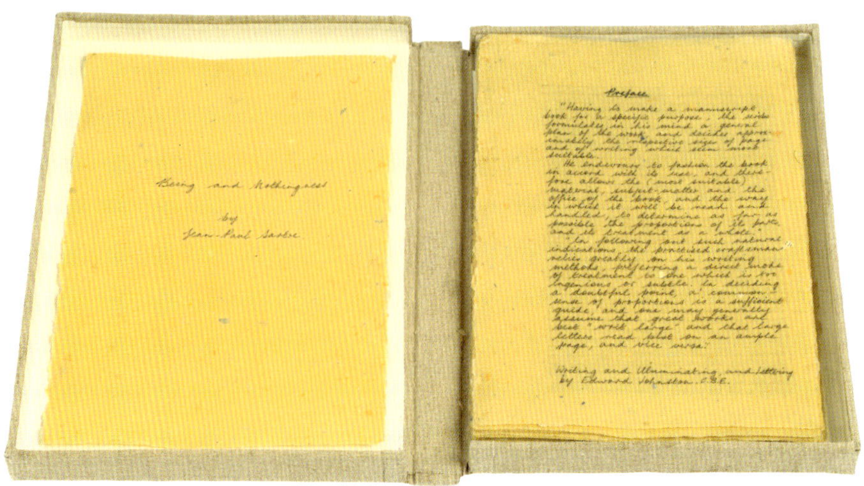

Bea MADDOCK
Being and nothingness
by Jean-Paul Sartre 1982

ed on itself. Quite the contrary, it is the non-reflective consciousness which renders the reflection possible; there is a pre-reflective cogito which is the condition of the Cartesian cogito. At the same time it is the non-thetic consciousness of counting which is the very condition of my act of adding. If it were otherwise, how would the addition be the unifying theme of my consciousnesses? In order that this theme should preside over a whole series of syntheses of unifications and recognitions, it must be present to itself, not as a thing but as an operative intention which can exist only as the revealing-revealed (révélante-révélée), to use an expression of Heidegger's. Thus in order to count it is necessary to be conscious of counting.

Of course, someone may say, but this makes a circle. For is it not necessary that I count in fact in order to be conscious of counting? That is true. However there is no circle, or if you like, it is the very nature of consciousness to exist "in a circle." The idea can be expressed in these terms: Every conscious existence exists as consciousness of existing. We understand now why the first consciousness of consciousness is not positional; it is because it is one with the consciousness of which it is consciousness. At one stroke it determines

itself as consciousness of perception and as perception. The necessity of syntax has compelled us hitherto to speak of the "non-positional consciousness of self." But we can no longer use this expression in which the "of self" still awakens the idea of knowledge. (Henceforth we shall put the "of" inside parentheses to show that it merely satisfies a grammatical requirement.)

This self-consciousness we ought to consider not as a new consciousness, but as the only mode of existence which is possible for a consciousness of something. Just as an extended object is compelled to exist according to three dimensions, so an intention, a pleasure, a grief can exist only as immediate self-consciousness. If the intention is not a thing in consciousness, then the being of the intention can be only consciousness. It is not necessary to understand by this that on the one hand some external cause (an organic trouble, an unconscious impulse, another Erlebnis) could determine that a psychic event — a pleasure, for example — produce itself, and that on the other hand this event so determined into material structure should be compelled to produce itself as self-consciousness. This would be to make the non-thetic consciousness a quality of the positional consciousness (the

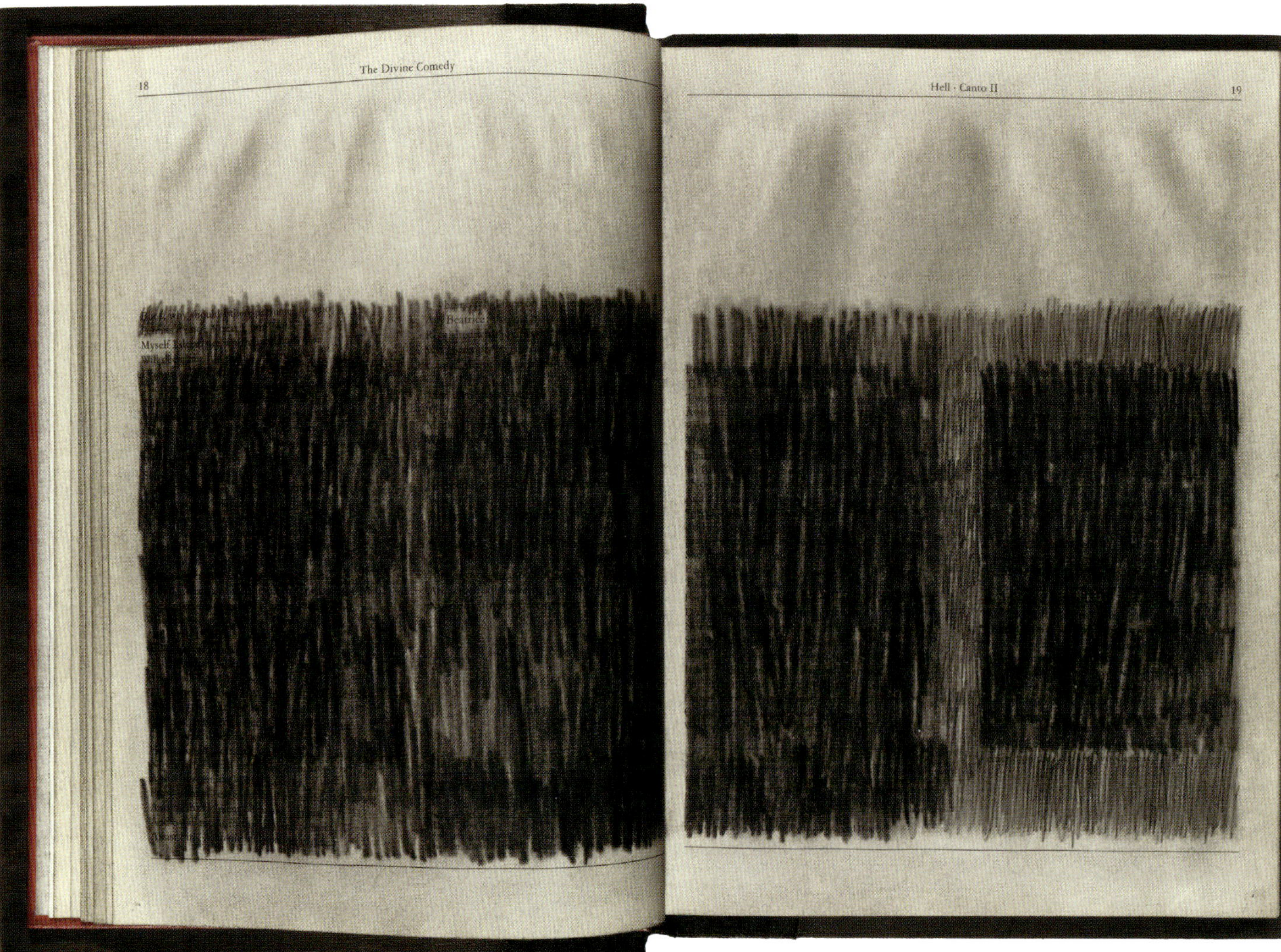
Myself
Beatrice

In *The Divine Comedy* 1984–88, Maddock uses a found book and text to structure her working procedures and, at the same time, to deal with other issues. In this work, the artist has taken a large reprint of Dante's *The Divine Comedy* and overdrawn the pages of the first six 'Cantos' with graphite and conté crayon, leaving some words visible here and there. The rest of the 'Cantos' are inaccessible, as all of the following pages have been tied together with five black vertical bands. The book has black-stained plywood glued to its existing covers and spine, giving it a funerary mood.

There is a simple narrative in the overdrawing, which moves from a full page of black to a revelation of the two-column structure of the book's typography. The visible or leftover words, which begin with the fortuitous 'myself Beatrice' on page 18, appear every few pages, and form an extracted poem of the type explored by such English artist–poets as dsh (dom sylvester houedard) and Tom Phillips in the 1960s. The sentiment of Maddock's text is typical: the last five fragments from pages 92 to 96 are 'so far removed/teach me/silence/the nature of the place/deep within me'.

The text Maddock covers in black is Dante's vision of hell: a place of eternal punishment, and associated in the popular imagination with fire. The book is one of Maddock's responses to a specific bushfire and, in this context, the final object resembles a smoked, charred thing, with the wrinkled, blackened pages demonstrating what happens when a fire goes through. Some things survive a fire – these are the words left visible by the artist as the graphite sweeps through the book, page by page. When handling charred remains, carbon comes off on the hands – the same happens with Maddock's book. It reverses the usual problem of the care required by museums when handling books – with this book you have to wash your hands/ gloves *after* handling it.

Impressions of forty working days 1985 takes the normally private working routine of an artist and makes it explicit. Each page/sheet of this work consists of the front page of a daily newspaper mulched and made into a thick, A4-size sheet, with the date and hours worked on that day blind-printed onto it. Maddock did this for forty consecutive days. The stack of sheets is held loose in a plywood box with tan leather hinges, visible steel nails, an inset engraved metal title strip on the top, and leather thongs at the right-hand side to tie it shut.

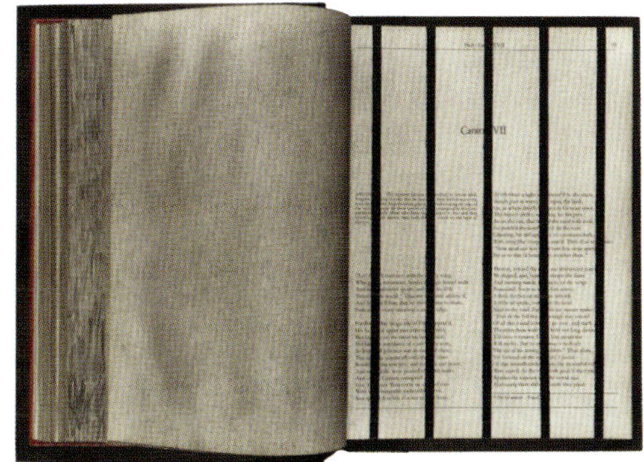

Bea MADDOCK *The Divine Comedy* 1984–88

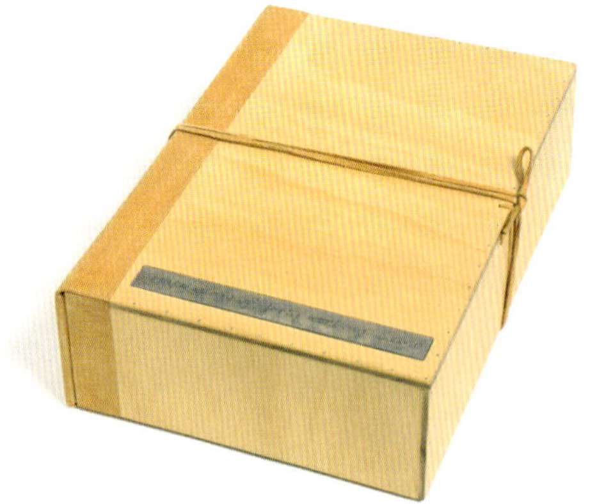

In this book, each day's transient events as recorded by the newspaper have been made permanent. The forty days have become a slightly spongy pile of thick sheets, with only slight variations in colour for each mulched sheet/day. In this monotony, the different dates and times become crucially interesting, but even these are reticent: the sheets need to be held up and moved about in the light to be read. And there are also other orders in which the sheets can be examined. Being loose, you are tempted to jump here and there and, at the end of examining the stack, you face the decision of whether to re-establish the chronological order or to just put them back in any order.

Forty is the number that traditionally means 'many' in the Middle East. In the biblical story of Noah's ark, it rained for forty days and nights. This trial by water is hinted at in Maddock's book. Making paper is a craft that uses lots of water: immersion, soaking and the final emergence of a new material from the water are integral to its birth. Just as the plywood covers in *The Divine Comedy* hold in imagined and represented fire, the plywood box of *Impressions of forty working days* holds in the memory of real water.

Artefacts from Tromemanner 1990 is a spin-off from Maddock's multi-panel painting called *Tromemanner – forgive us our trespass, panels I–IV* 1988–89. Maddock placed stones in a row of niches at the bottom of these paintings and, for *Artefacts from Tromemanner*, she has traced the stones directly onto etching plates. She then printed two such tracings on a single sheet, which was folded like the pages in *Colour*. Forty-eight sheets were bound into a sequence of coloured etchings, with an engraved perimeter description around each tracing, following the edge of the page. For each stone, the text describes its shape, edge type and name, going around the edge of the stone in the same way that you might examine the actual stone by turning it in your hands. It is tempting to do this with the book while viewing, too.

Bea MADDOCK
Impressions of forty working days 1985

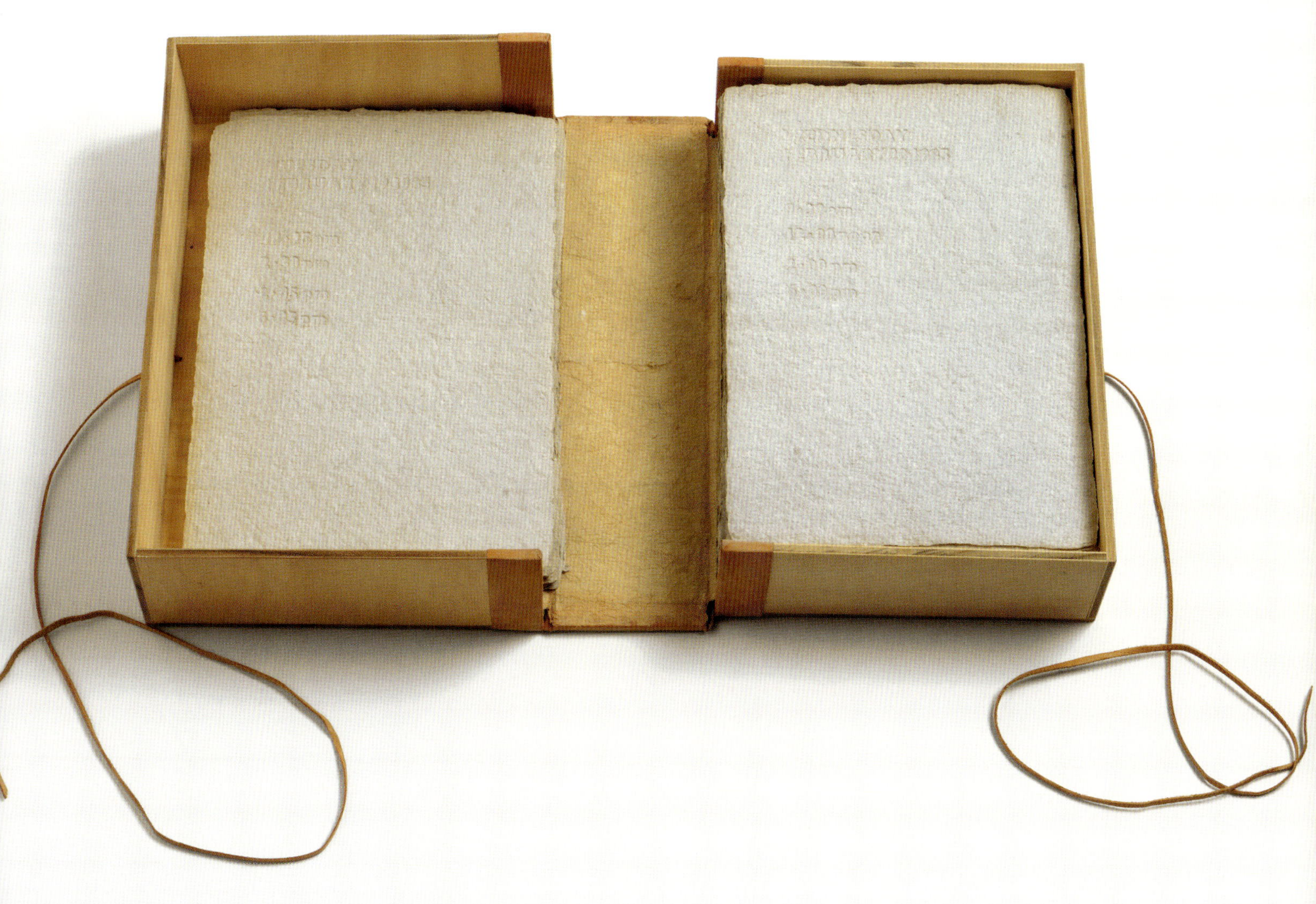

parrawem-
menne
meemurrer
peoora
mienteina

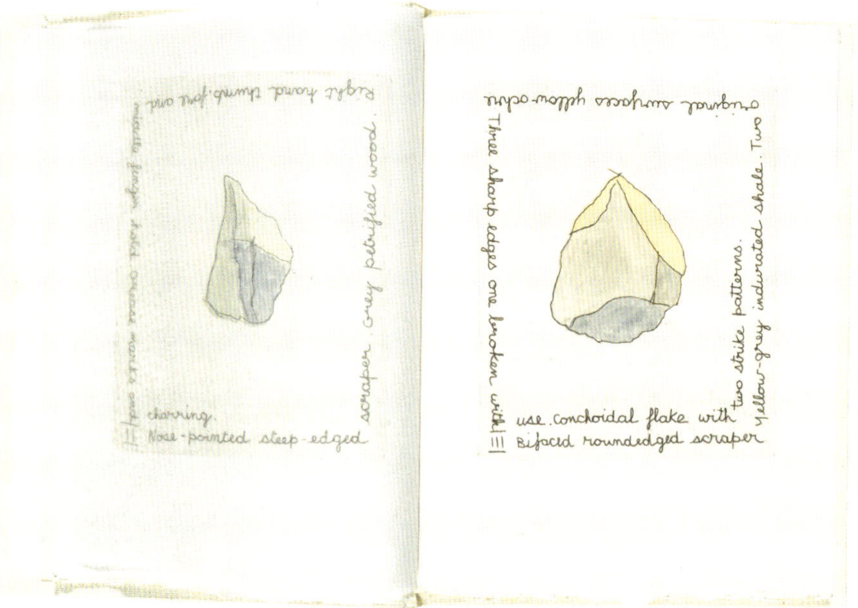

(above)
Bea MADDOCK *Artefacts from Tromemanner* 1990

(opposite page)
Bea MADDOCK *Melbourne series* 1964–81

(following two pages)
Bea MADDOCK *This time* 1967–69

Artefacts from Tromemanner is similar to *Colour* in structure, but with no specific narrative. It is a collection of images unified by a repetitive rhythm. Just as it comes out of Maddock's painting, it also points to an even larger work by the artist: *Terra Spiritus ... with a darker shade of pale* 1993–98, in which Maddock has drawn the landward profile of the entire coast of Tasmania on fifty-two consecutive sheets. Properly installed, this work forms a loop, and involves a walk around a representation of the island as if it were a large stone or rock.

Two early books by Maddock are also worth noting, for their attempts at structuring a narrative without recourse to a pre-existing format, process or system. *Melbourne series* 1964–81 is a box of eighteen dry point prints. Each print is the same size, and the images include figures and portraits, with one image hinting at a bird. *Melbourne series* reveals its images one by one, and each image is equivalent to one unit of time (as Maddock later presented more specifically in *Impressions of forty working days*). But in *Melbourne series*, the images seem so connected that their actual order is arbitrary: you need only to see them one after the other. *This time* 1967–69 is an illustrated book with linocut images and linocut text, its thick sheets held together by string ties through punched holes. In *This time*, Maddock's text carries a symmetrical narrative of going out into the world and then coming back, which is at counterpoint to the alternating portraits and figures clustered between the pages of text.

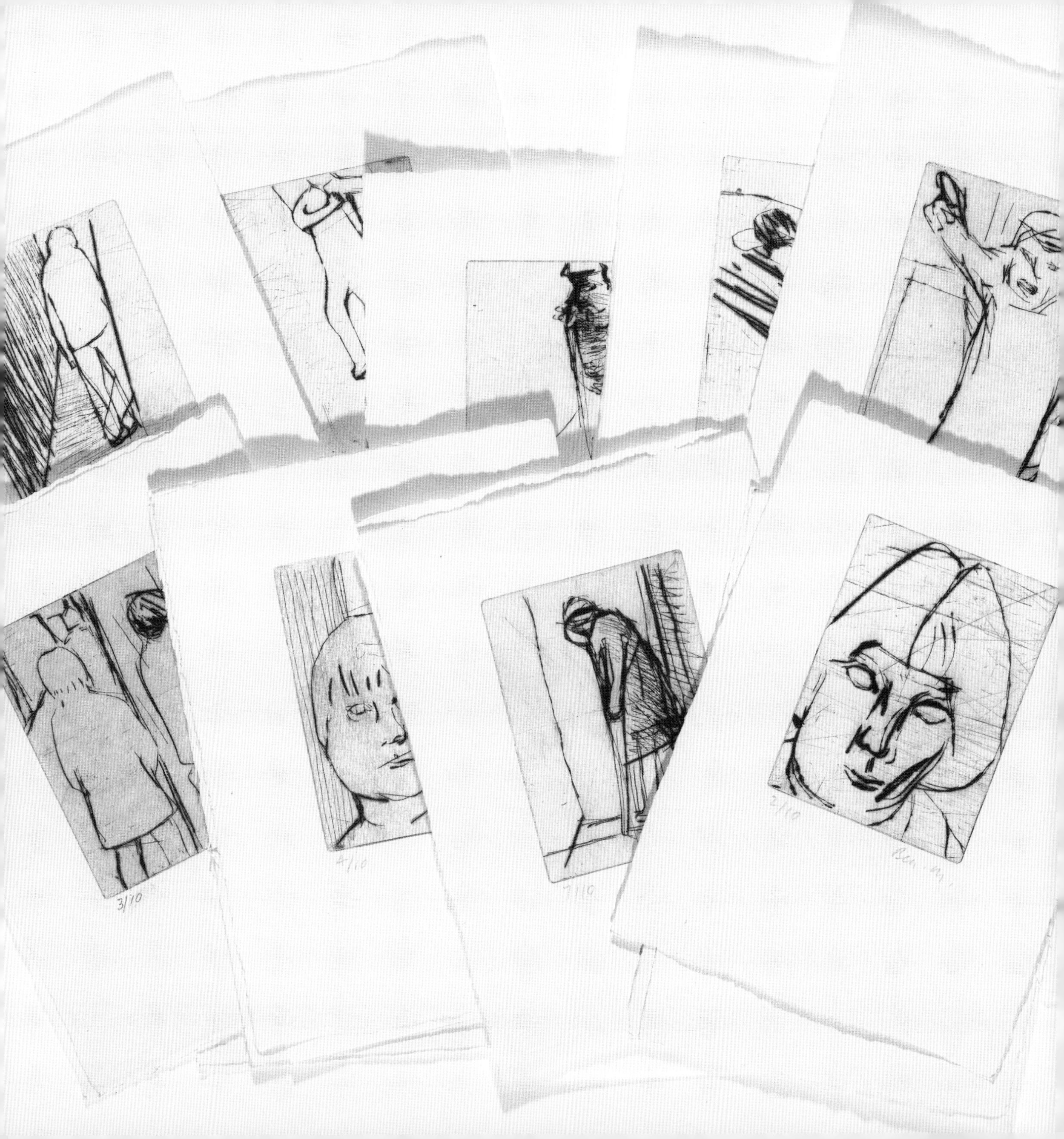

THIS TIME

Limited edition of 25 copies.

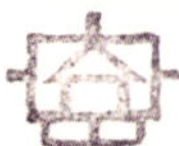 No. 13.

Bea. Maddock. '69.

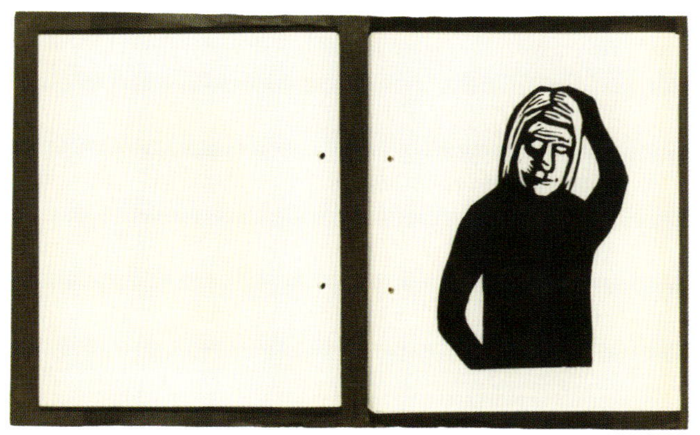

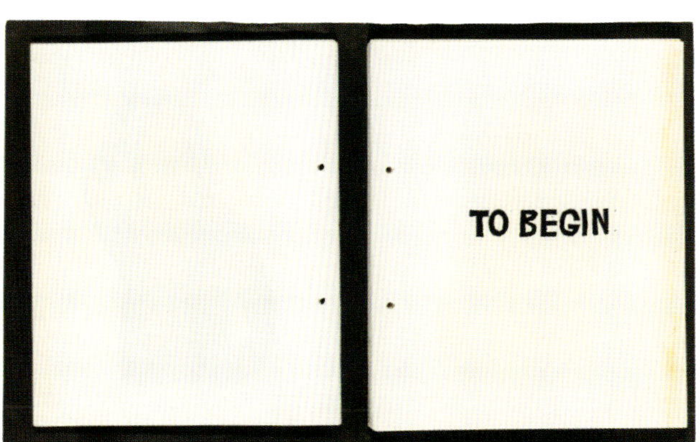
TO BEGIN

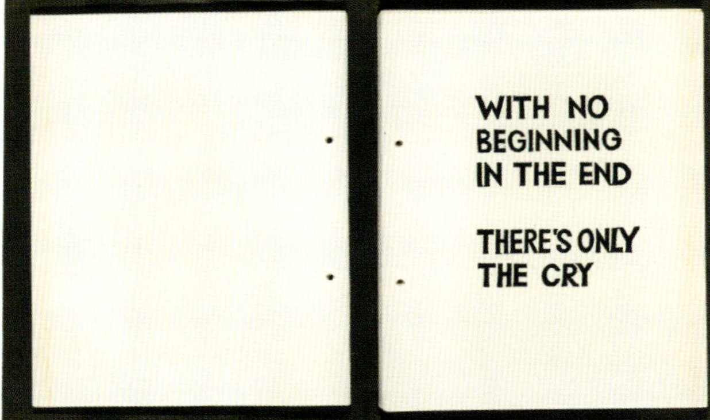
WITH NO
BEGINNING
IN THE END

THERE'S ONLY
THE CRY

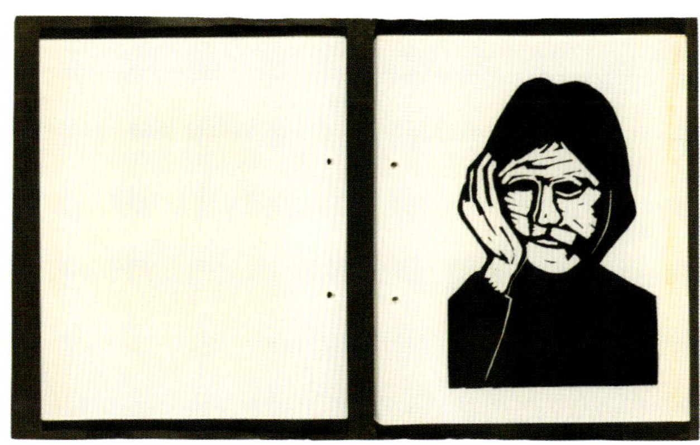

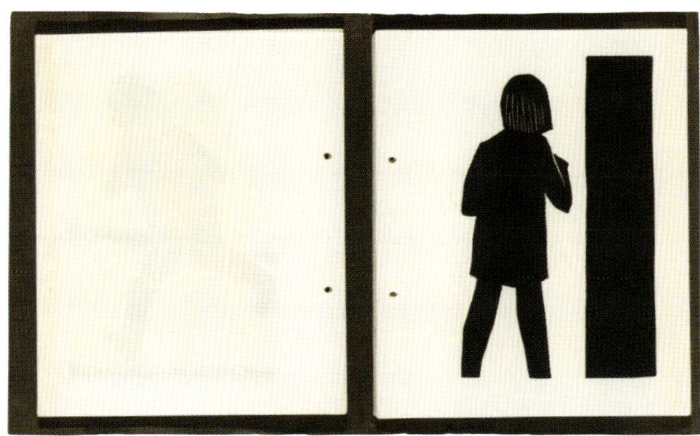

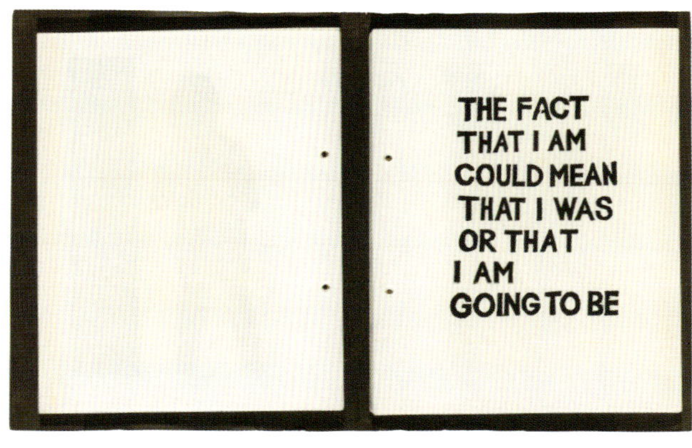
THE FACT
THAT I AM
COULD MEAN
THAT I WAS
OR THAT
I AM
GOING TO BE

ONE HUNDRED PAGE BOOK

MIKE PARR   1971

Mike Parr: hundreds of pages

A number of Mike Parr's preoccupations and working methods find a natural expression in books or book formats. Parr challenges conventional structures and assumptions through techniques of literal interpretation and exaggeration. He connects his objects to psychological states, and uses art as a record of a performance or action. All of these strategies have their parallel in books. Parr's books and book-like works take up the spatial and temporal properties of books – both the still page and the turning page are ritualised in his works. Nearly all of Parr's bookworks have been presented publicly in galleries and, through this technique of display, his books also straddle the spectrum of individual readership and public spectacle.

Of all of the artist's books, *One hundred page book* 1971 is the most like a conventional book. Quarto in size, with hinged, stiff card covers, the book is trimmed to feel like a wad or stack of paper. The title is a photocopy print glued to the cover; inside, the text begins immediately with the word 'ONE' in capitals placed centrally on the first page. The words 'ONE' to 'ONE HUNDRED' follow, number by consecutive number, right-hand page after right-hand page, for the whole book.

This work is a literal manifestation of a common way of defining a book, that is, through the number of pages it contains. The text presents this definition by example. It is an idea made tangible, but also works as an experience or a performance. As you turn the pages, reading the numbers, interest grows as the novelty sinks in, then it wears off and you settle in for the long haul of the middle section when, towards the end, the sequence seems to race to a close. Because the numbers are written out as words, the tens are single words, with the 'decades' between them growing in length until they reach another decade. The book thus has a kind of internal visual rhythm.

Another surprise awaits those who venture past the book's conceptual title: the 'FIFTY-SIX' page is repeated. Is this intended and, if not (knowing that this is a book by Parr), what does such a glitch mean? Does it mean that there is a copy without a page 56? *One hundred page book* is handmade, and although there is a number '79' on a round sticker in the top right-hand corner of the cover, and the book is signed, there is no indication that it is part of an edition. Missing or doubled-up pages are a hazard in hand-collated publications; in this copy, perhaps a momentary slip of attention (or finger control, or sticking paper), leavens what is a preset, remorseless system.

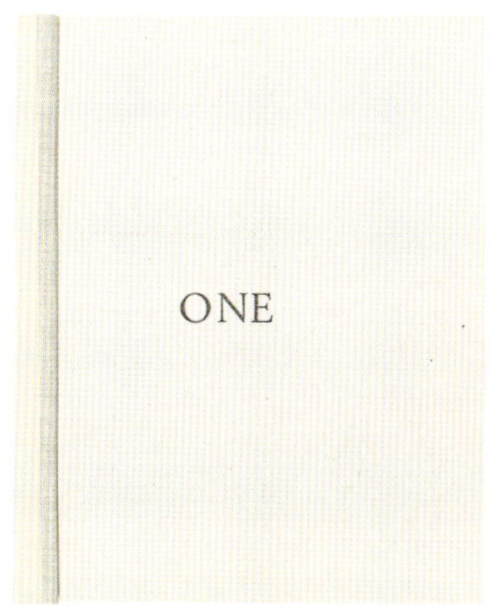

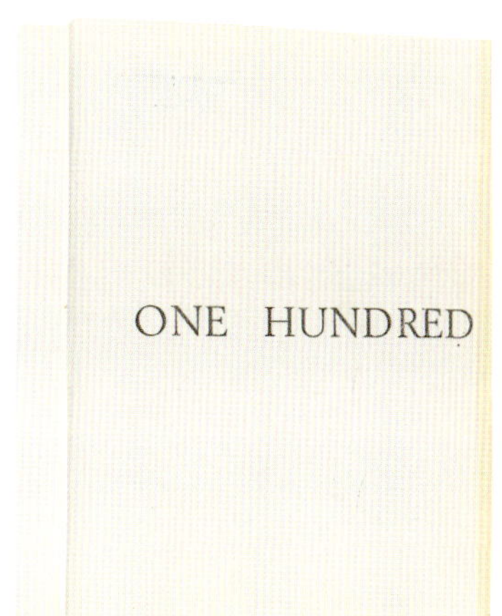

Mike PARR *One hundred page book* 1971

Two boxed books, also made around the same time as *One hundred page book*, continue Parr's exploration of definitions: *Word situations 1 & 2* 1970–71 and *Wall definition* August 1971. Of the two, *Word situations 1 & 2* is the more complex or, rather, conglomerate in structure. A glossy black box file opens up to reveal a sheet with title, contents and introduction glued to the inside of the lid, and two piles of papers in the box: Section A and Section B. Section A is a 3.5 cm-thick pile of 'Functions' (single sheets of paper with typewriter graphics on them); while Section B is made up of six folders of loose papers of 'quarto window installations'.

Parr notes in the introduction to *Word situations 1 & 2* that all the works are from exhibitions and are 'concerned with my investigations into the problem of meaning and language'. Except for 'Function 1' in Section A, where a square, rectangle and triangle are shown in pencil line and paper glued to the page, all the sheets in Section A are typed patterns. Parr uses single words such as 'square', 'red', 'black', 'strips', 'bands', 'structure', and 'series', all of which deal with spatial and visual aspects of writing and thinking, in this case, through the properties of the typewriter. Mechanical typewriters work through a grid that produces accurate horizontal and vertical lines of letters and signs, with degrees of touch giving spatial depth to typed patterns, and Parr's 'Functions' are a tour de force on the use of this instrument. The 'Functions' are suites of concrete poems in the classical manner, integrating page, typing and thinking in one gesture.

The 'quarto window installations' are archived exhibition pieces, designed to be displayed on windows or walls. Each of the five sets comes with a sheet of instructions and sometimes a diagram for installation, which helps the reader to visualise the effect of the pages in situ. For instance, 'Horizontal vertical' has this instruction:

> HORIZONTAL … the 20 sheets marked with the word 'horizontal' should be stretched out end to end, scrupulously on the horizontal, and at eye-level on a clear white wall. The level should be taken from a piece of string stretched taut across the face of the sheets, in line with the printed word. The string should be left in place for the duration of the work, so that the propositional status of the work is affected by the string's sag with the passage of time. The sag of the string is recorded as a shadow on the face of the work.

> The actual length of the work should not be restricted to the 20 sheets, but it should correspond with the length of the wall used. It is a good idea that the sheets should effectively fill the whole wall.

Mike Parr, January 1971

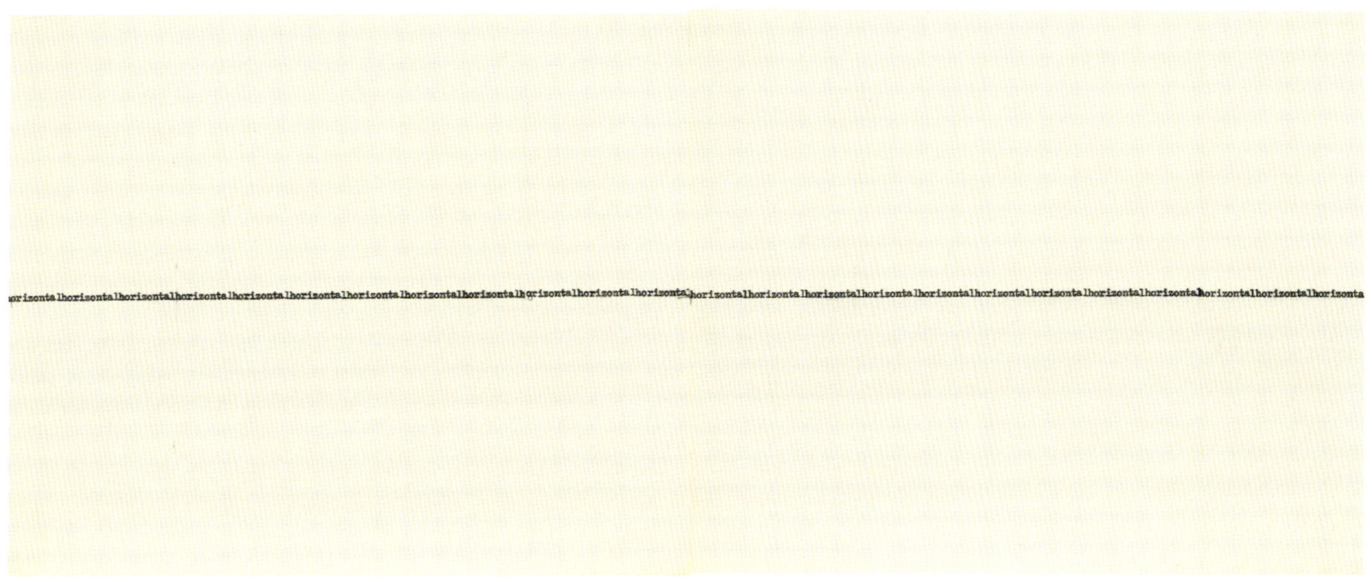

You can imagine the concept of 'horizontal' being given physicality through the words typed on paper and through their set-out via the string, with the effect of gravity on the string producing the 'vertical' suggested in the title.

Like *One hundred page book*, *Wall definition* is a single text and single concept. Presented in a box file painted glossy white (so that it makes an obvious pair with *Word situations 1 & 2*), *Wall definition* contains 254 sheets of continuous typing on quarto paper. The text takes a dictionary definition of the word 'wall', gives it in full, and then proceeds to list the dictionary definition of every word in that first definition, in the same order, complete with repeats. As with *One hundred page book*, a reading (that is, a performance) of the whole text reveals more than the concept suggests.

(above and following two pages)
Mike PARR *Word situations 1 & 2* 1970–71

Wall Plan for 32 situations. . . the 32 sheets in the pack should be organized
on the wall in accordance with the diagram below. . . the area bounded by line
a.) is in this case merely a description of the content of the whole work. . . this
line may be letralined straight onto the wall. . in an approximation to line a.)
in the diagram. .

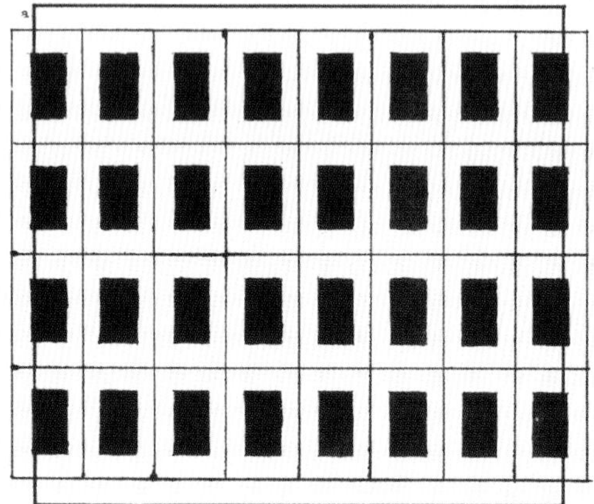

. . the whole work is derived from the following statement. . "The potential
for a situation is contained in all or any of the possibilities."

structurestructurestructurestructurestructurestructurestructures
structurestructurestructurestructurestructurestructures
structurestructurestructurestructurestructurestructures
structurestructurestructurestructurestructures
structurestructurestructurestructurestructurestructures
structurestructurestructurestructurestructurestructurestructures
structurestructurestructurestructurestructurestructurestructures
structurestructurestructurestructurestructurestructurestructures
structurestructurestructurestructurestructurestructures
structurestructurestructurestructurestructures
structurestructurestructurestructurestructurestructurestructurestructures
structurestructurestructurestructurestructurestructurestructures
structurestructurestructurestructurestructurestructures
structurestructurestructurestructurestructurestr
structurestructurestructurestructurestructurestructurestructure
structurestructurestructurestructurestructurestructurestructures
structurestructurestructurestructurestructurestructures
structurestructurestructurestructures
structurestructurestructurestructurestructurestruc
structurestructurestructurestructurestructures
structurestructurestructurestructurestructures
structurestructurestructurestructures
structurestructurestructurestructurestructurestructures

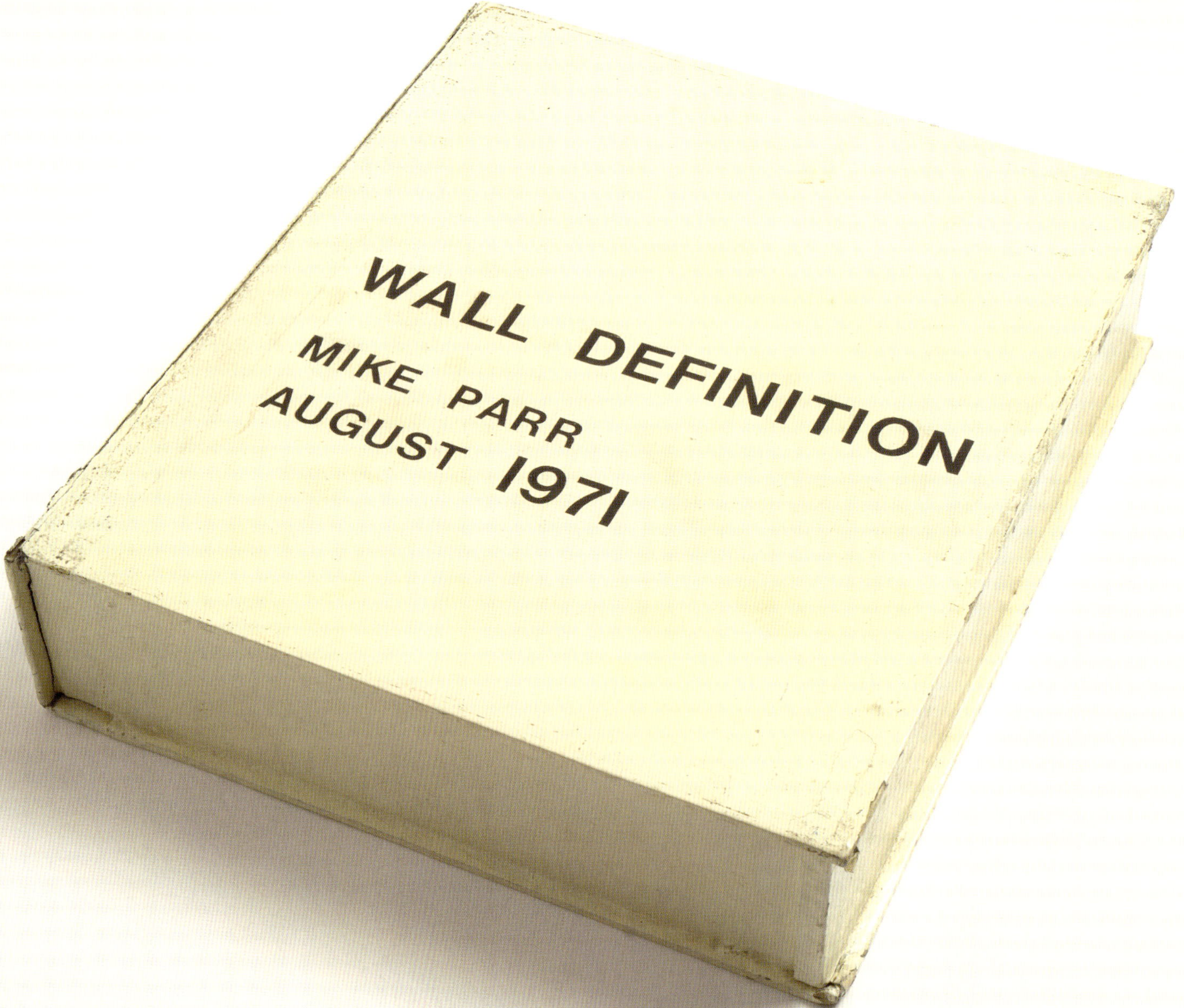

WALL DEFINITION

MIKE PARR

AUGUST 1971

The text has a conceptually precise and predictive structure, but with so many pages of typing and no story or apparent narrative, it is a daunting thing to read. But once you start, some marvellous things happen. If you read with the first page, that is, with the primary 'definition' set aside as a reference, you tend to read like a proofreader. This level of reading reveals a number of details in the text. Numbers that separate the original sub-definitions are not given their own definitions in the follow-on text; underlining of defined words is sometimes missing; plurals are altered to singulars. There are a few omissions of main words – these seem to occur with words that fall between repeats, for example where the original definition has 'with a wall often with', the follow-on text omits the words between the two 'with's, probably through a slip of attention. Elsewhere, typing errors are left in and simply crossed out. The most intriguing 'mistake' occurs when the primary definition gives the word 'House' and the follow-on definition takes it as 'Home'. There is a touch of Schadenfreude in such a reading, which is balanced by a growing admiration for the persistence of the typist. Did Parr do anything else except type in 1971, given that *Word situations 1 & 2* was also being produced in that year? Did someone else help? Was there a team of typists?

There are many repeats throughout the text. Because of the dictionary prose of the original text, the most common are 'a', 'of', 'the' and 'or'. The first of these is defined thus: 'Aa any of several rivers of Europe especially in Latvia, both emptying into the Gulf of Riga'. In the context of this text, the repetition of 'Latvia' is a surprise and ensures that the word is remembered both for its

Mike PARR *Wall definition* 1971

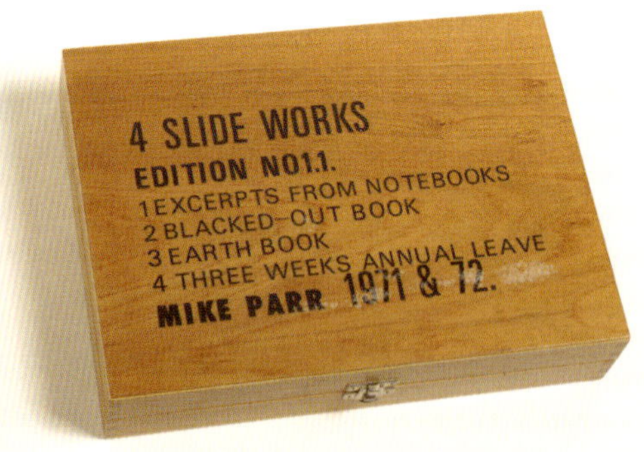

strange irrelevance and its frequency. But the biggest impact occurs when the text begins to quote itself. At page 64 in the follow-on text, 'wall' reappears as a complete definition. This occurs again at pages 73, 79 and 106, and continues with increasing frequency to the end of the text. Looking back at the primary definition, you can see that after setting out a generic explanation, the definition begins to categorise different sorts of walls and begins to use the word unselfconsciously in short definitions. In the follow-on, this reoccurrence of the definition itself has the effect of self-reference or modelling, like the observation that every leaf is a model of the tree it grows on. For a moment, you imagine that each of the definitions in the follow-on pages could be given the same treatment as the primary definition, so that the resulting text could be very, very long, maybe never ending.

As with *Word situations 1 & 2*, Parr exhibited *Wall definition* in 1971. The entire text was taped to a wall, where it formed a horizontal rectangle of paper. In such an installation, the *'Wall'* is defined by the text and demonstrated through consecutive walks/reads along its length. Parr's spatialisation of text in this way is made possible through a conceptual crack that reveals his origins as a visual artist. Strictly, in any book, a page is the surface of a flat sheet of paper, with each sheet holding two pages, the first on one side, the second on the other. Printmakers, painters and graphic artists habitually use only one side and find it logical to see a sheet of paper as a page. This allows any work of many sheets to be presented as a pile of pages, read incrementally as a book, or to be pinned up on a wall and viewed as a whole as a painting or a drawing. Looking at Parr's *One hundred page book* from this point of view means that the book is actually 200 pages long, within which a 100-page book is represented through a series of drawings.

Parr's *4 slide works* 1971 and 1972 extends the conceptual challenge of the 'page'. This work is a standard timber slide-box containing four sets of slides, which are placed in running order inside the box. The four sets are given their full titles in the beginning slide of each sequence and these are:

1. *Excerpts from notebooks* 1971 and 1972

2. *Earth book* 1972

3. *Blacked-out book* 1972

4. *Three weeks annual leave* 1971 and 1972

Mike PARR *4 slide works* 1971 and 1972

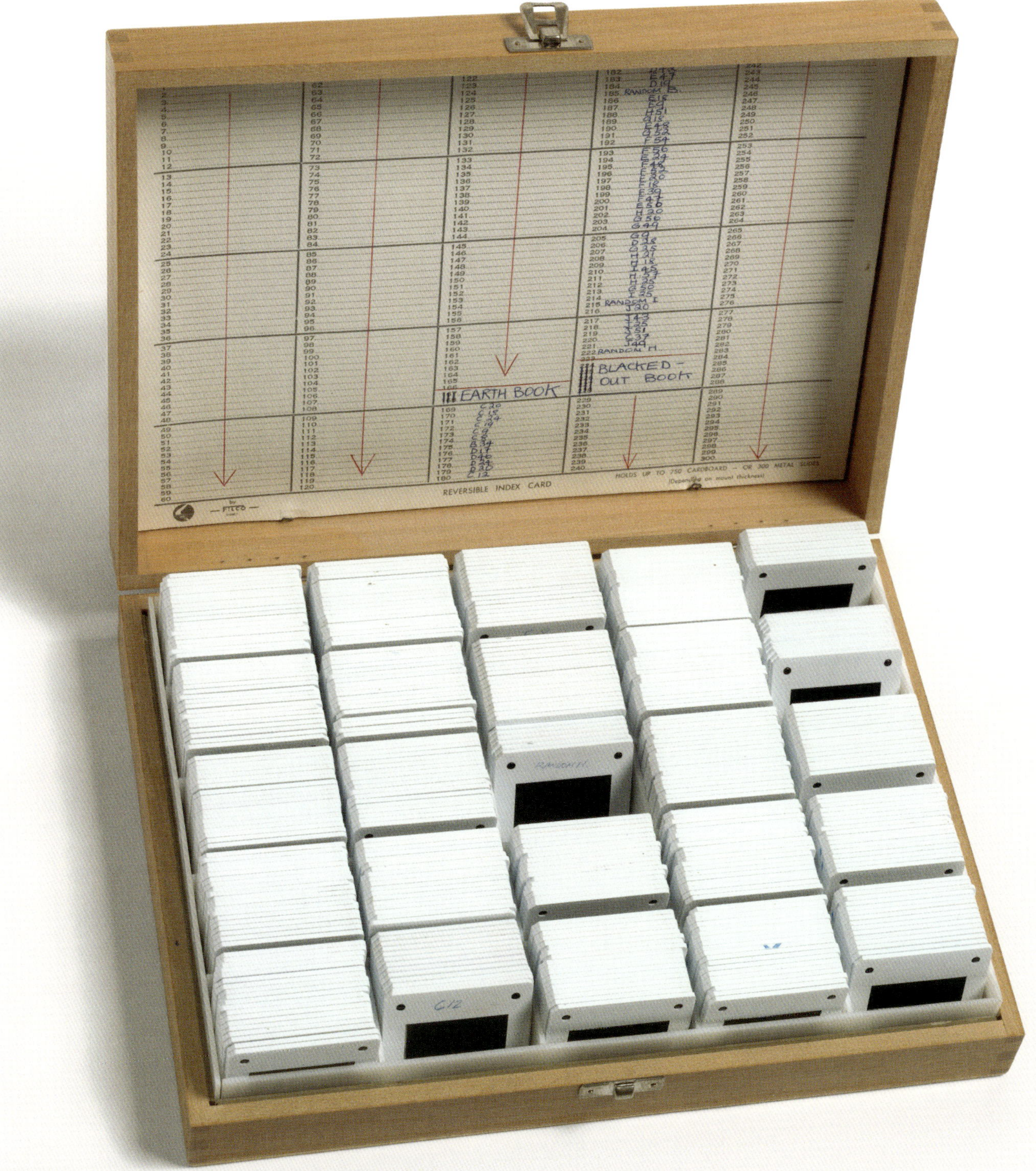
EARTH BOOK
BLACKED-
OUT BOOK
REVERSIBLE INDEX CARD
HOLDS UP TO 750 CARDBOARD — OR 300 METAL SLIDES
(Depending on mount thickness)

(above)
Mike PARR *Excerpts from notebooks*
1971 and 1972

(opposite page)
Mike PARR *Earth book* 1972

(following pages left)
Mike PARR *Blacked-out book* 1972

(following pages right)
Mike PARR *Three weeks annual leave*
1971 and 1972

The first sequence, *Excerpts from notebooks*, consists of a slide show of mostly typed phrases in black and white, with, every fifteen slides or so, a detailed colour slide of something being done to the surface of a human body. Many of the texts are concerned with images of the body and self and making art. In the present context, two stand out. Slide 66 states that 'first i make a book then i work on its contents' and slide 82 states 'the size of the page is part of the content of the book'. In this presentation, Parr is giving us a low-tech performing exposition of his work. A similar kind of survey might now exist as a videotape, CD-ROM or DVD, but the slide format keeps the page format alive in that, when projected, one image follows another, with a darkened phase between each image, similar to the lapsed time when a page is turned in a book.

Earth book and *Blacked-out book* both also use the slide format to record the treatment given to a found book. In *Earth book*, the slides show the progressive deterioration of a book object, from a soiled, slightly tattered book at slide 2 to something like a blackened cabbage at slide 54. *Earth book* has a rich set of integrated narratives of decay, transformation, return, and digging/ recording/burial as the book is re-buried after each photograph. *Blacked-out book* relies on the book format to keep a narrative in place. In this work, which uses a found book, all the text is blacked out but the maps are left untouched. The result is a succession of images of double-page spreads of black rectangles, with only the page numbers establishing the order. Through its presentation as successive slides, which are like successive slices, the closed book can be imagined as a block of black ink.

The first forty-seven slides of *Three weeks annual leave* are black and white. After these, colour slides and black-and-white slides alternate in an irregular way. All of the slides are amateur-like views and details, and some are indistinct and uncomposed. In sequence, they record a journey from inner Sydney to a camping holiday destination, from a brick house in the city to a campfire in an Austral Eden. The colour slides begin to appear as the city is left behind. In this work, Parr points to one of the most widespread and generally unnoticed narrative genres in Australia: there must be thousands of slides stored in Australian houses, all records of the annual ritual of getting back to nature, back to some kind of de-conditioned paradise.

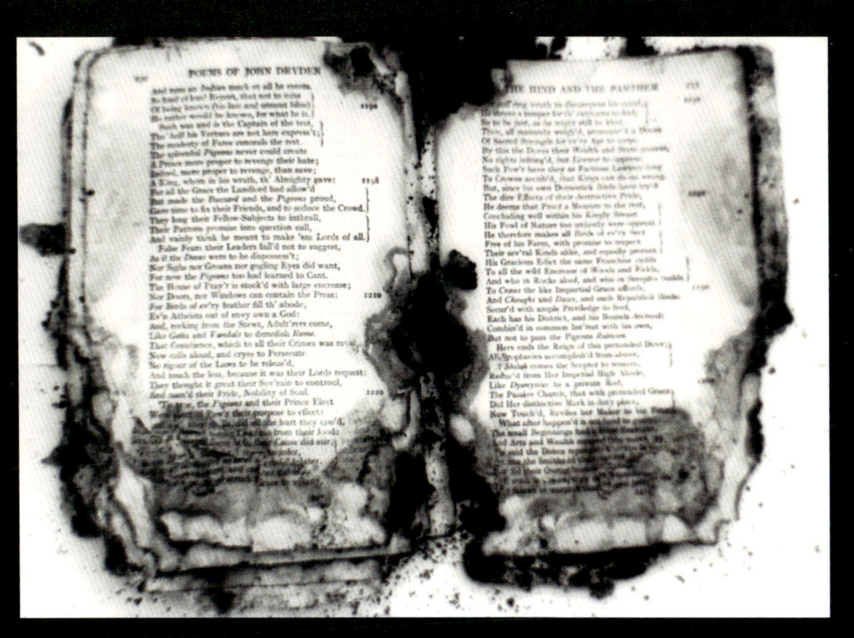

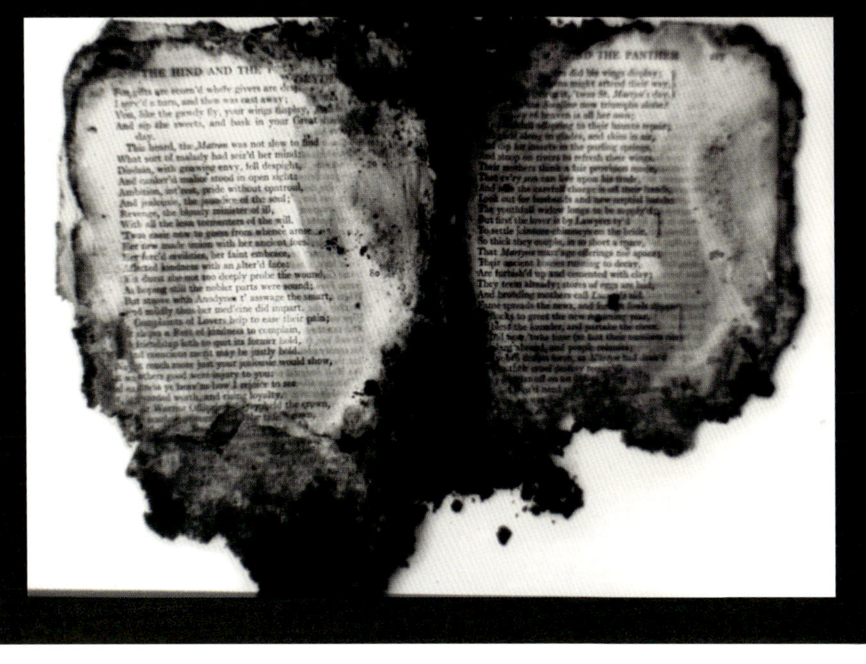

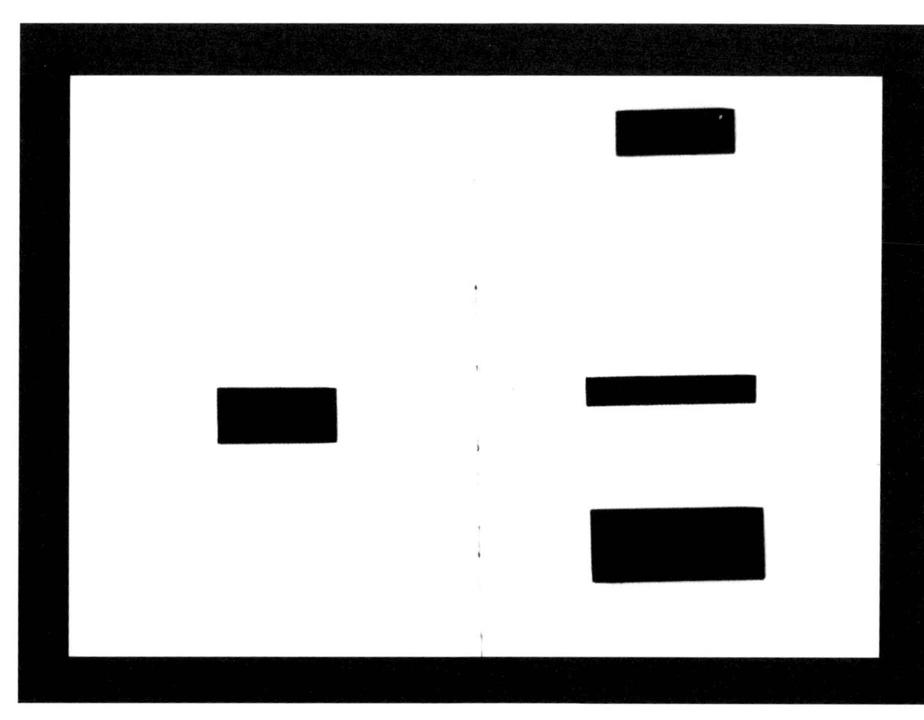

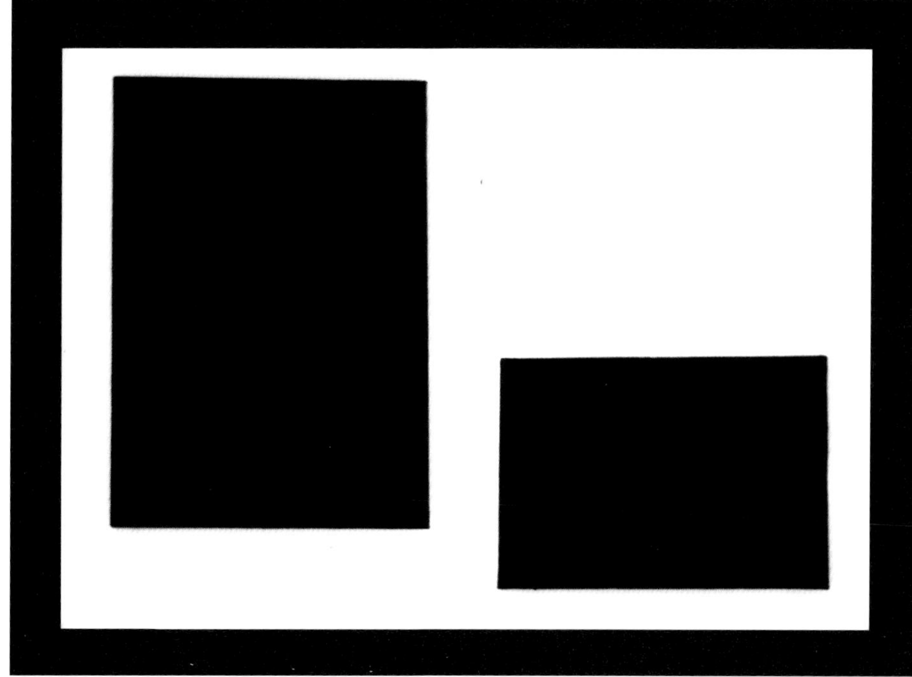

3WEEKS ANNUAL LEAVE

mike parr   1971 & 1972

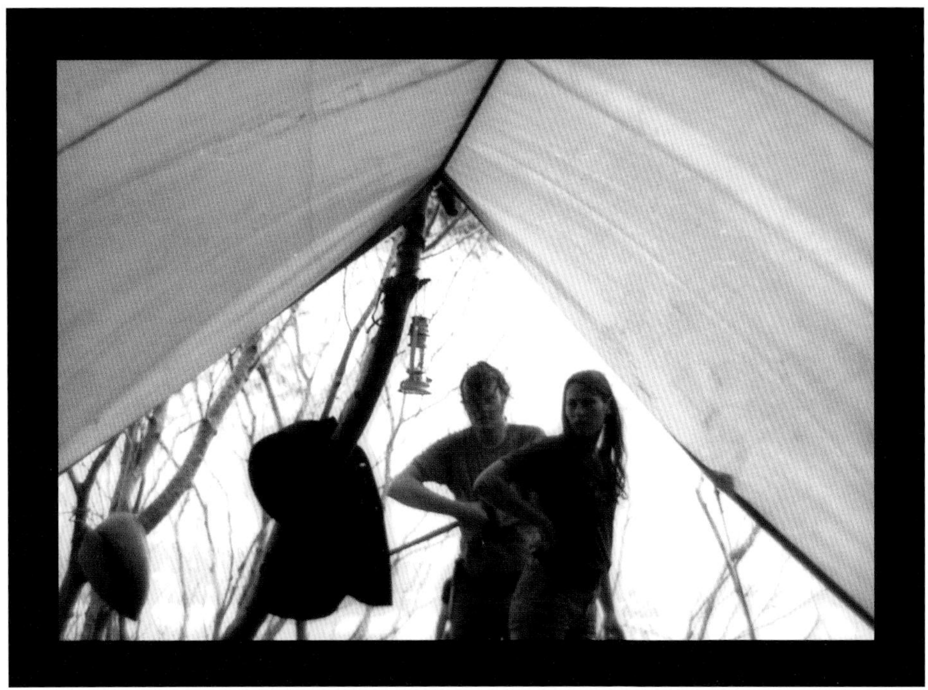

SELECTED ARTISTS BOOKS

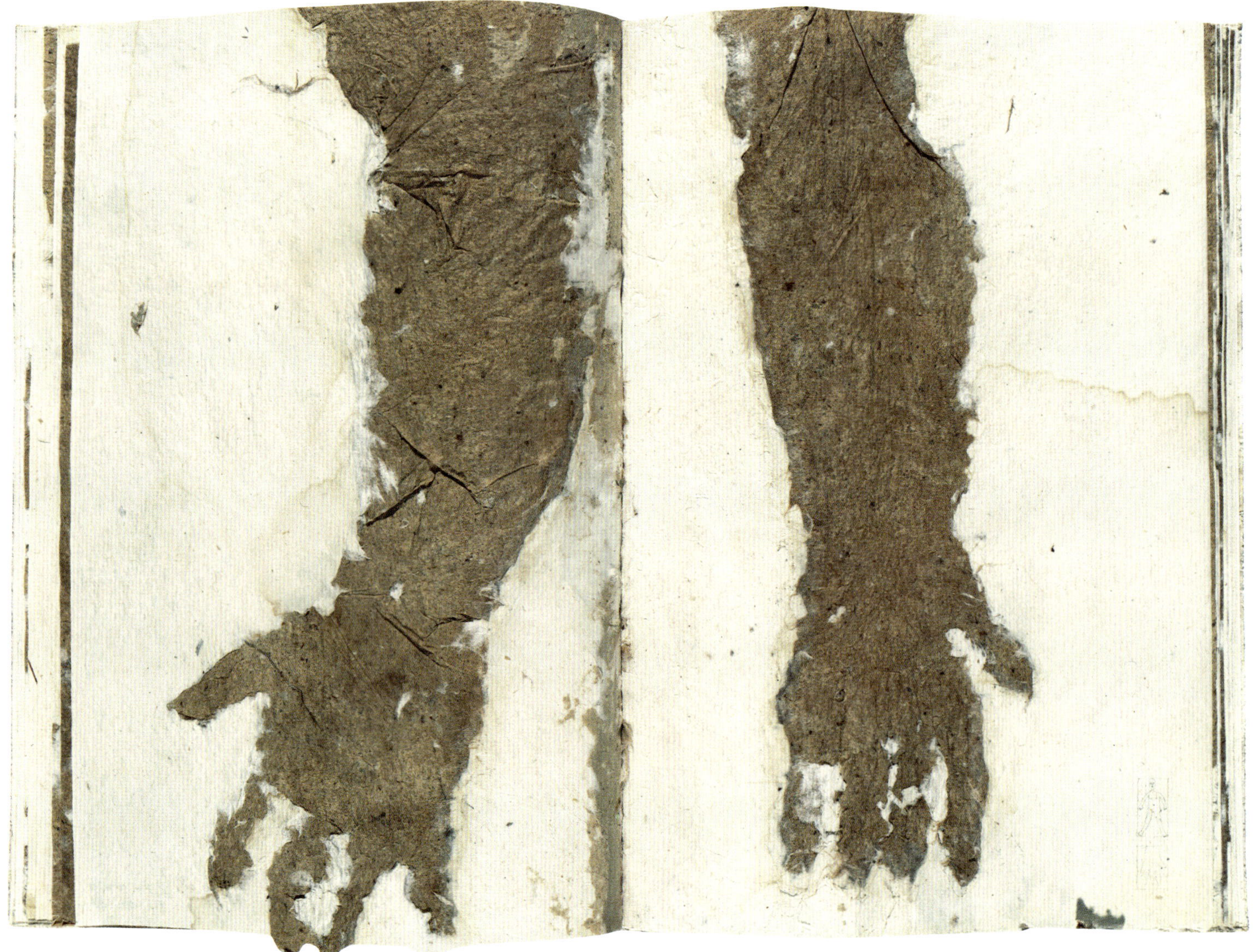

Gaynor Cardew
Requiem to an epidermis 1984

This appears to be a standard art book, largish, heavy, with stiff board covers. Too heavy to lift easily and too large to hold in the air, it belongs on a table or on one's lap. The front and back covers are made of a combination of two types of flattened-out paper – one, off-white, the other, brown wrinkled paper. A head in profile appears on the front cover, a pair of feet on the back. The title is blind-printed on the first page – to touch as much as to see – and following this there are sixteen pages of two-tone wrinkled paper, with images of body parts emerging from the patterns of colour. There is no text through the book.

At the bottom of the final right-hand page, there are three small pencil line drawings – diagrams – of three bodies: a baby, a youth and an adult. Leafing back through the pages, you can see that each double-page spread also has two small drawings on the right-hand page. One is of a full body, the other is an enlargement of the particular anatomical detail that is sculpted in the paper of that page. The left-hand page also shows an image, but it is the reverse of the previous page's body detail which has been sculpted in the paper. Is the left-hand page, then, the underside of the 'skin'?

The book allocates three double-page spreads for baby skins, six for youth and seven for adult skins. The details move from the feet, upwards to the head. As the book moves through its narrative of ageing, the brown paper gets darker and darker, the wrinkles and tears more apparent. Sometimes the double-page spread suggests a whole flayed skin. Sometimes your attention wanders to the real hands handling the book, and you note their paper-like surface …

When the back cover is folded over, the image of the feet combine with the memory of the head on the front cover to suggest that the whole book is a body, with the pages in it a flattening of the body's surface into a rising and ageing narrative. *Requiem to an epidermis* plays with the expectation that a book should have flat, white pages, and hints at a further question: what kind of body does a book of flat white pages represent? The book also plays with representation. The images are real paper and consume the thickness of the page. The real, paper-like skin represents human skin. Real wrinkles represent real wrinkles: one kind of skin for another.

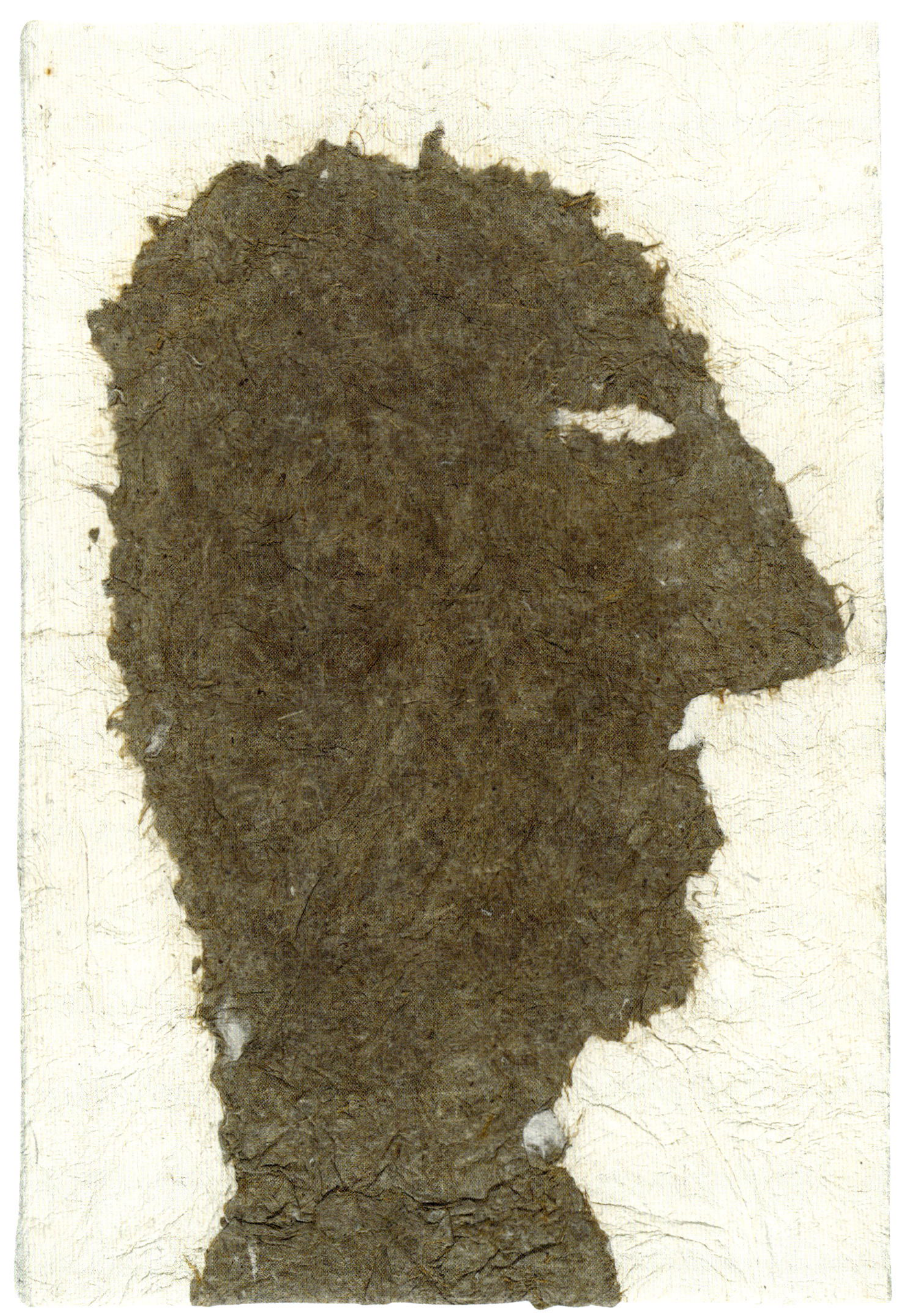

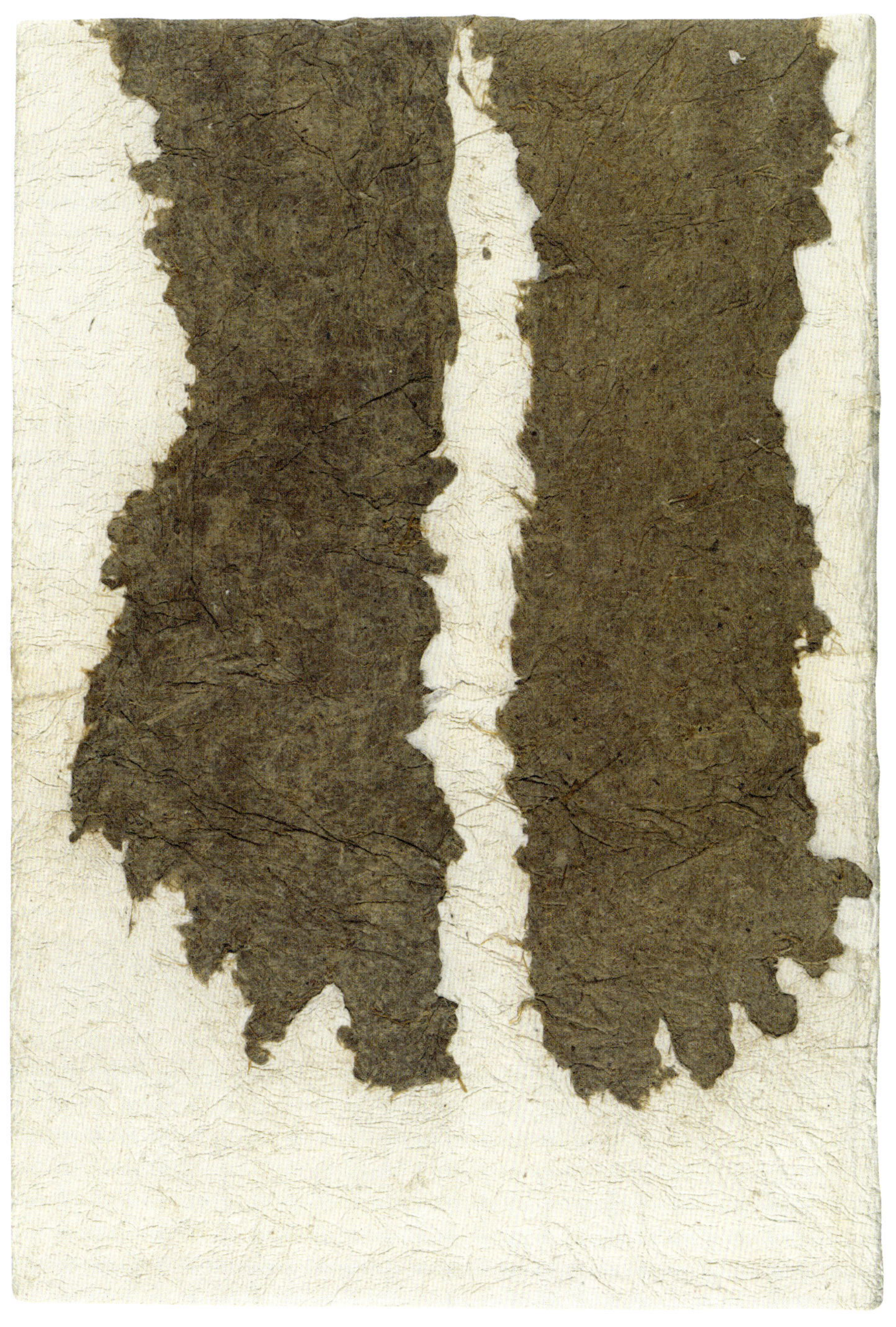

Christopher Croft
Sketch-of-book 1983

Confronted by a large box, you discover that the edge with the title (in gold, as in standard library binding) is one that you can grasp, and from which you can also pull out a slip-case. Because of the bulk of the box, removing the slip-case feels like removing a book from a library shelf. Inside the slip-case there is a wooden frame, which, when lifted out, can be placed vertically or horizontally on a table. The frame consists of two, book-like forms, hinged at the back so that they open out. Between them, they hold a paper insert of seven accordion folds. The folded paper is a long sheet of handmade paper, printed with etchings: line drawings of piping, conduits, collections of various kinds, storage objects and other miscellanea.

The whole book is a cascade of sketches of a 'book', from the box, which is a diagram of a large book; the slip-case, which is a sketch of library retrieval; the wooden frame, which is a working sculpture of the binding hinge of books; to the folded paper. All of these sketches are held inside the other, but are distinct: like worlds within worlds, from library to book to text. The sequence of actions required to open the book parallel this cascade: different actions, one after another, until at the end the book is a stationary sculpture.

The finish of the large box, the fine joinery of the wooden frame and the paper, the materials and colour combine to evoke the stereotypical nineteenth-century library book. The etchings could be field book entries, analytic diagrams or a specific collection, reminding you of the use of books as compendia of disparate information. As you click shut the timber frame, lower it into the slip case and slide the ensemble into its box, you can get a strong sense of another sketch: the book as a cage or prison.

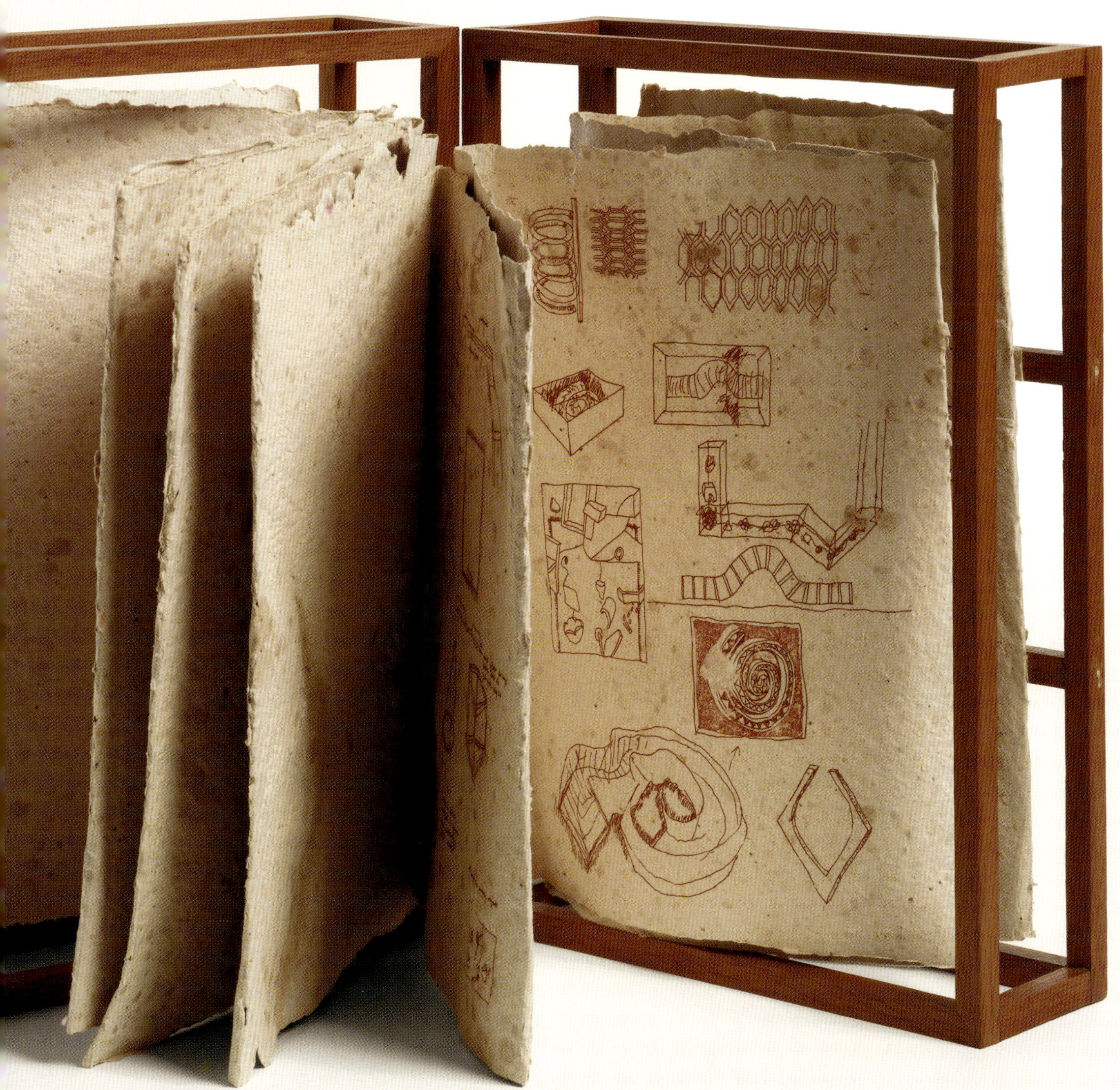

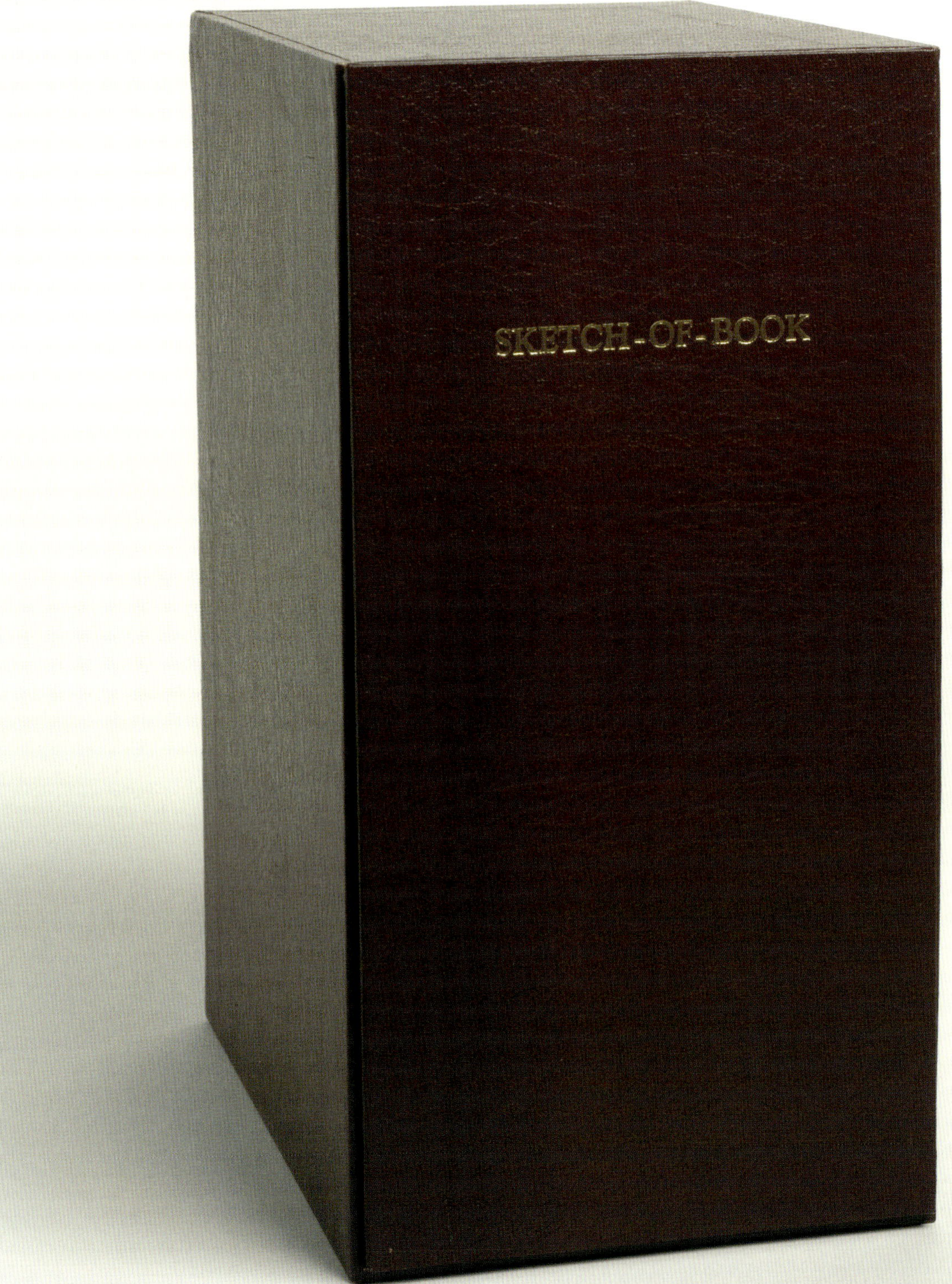
SKETCH-OF-BOOK

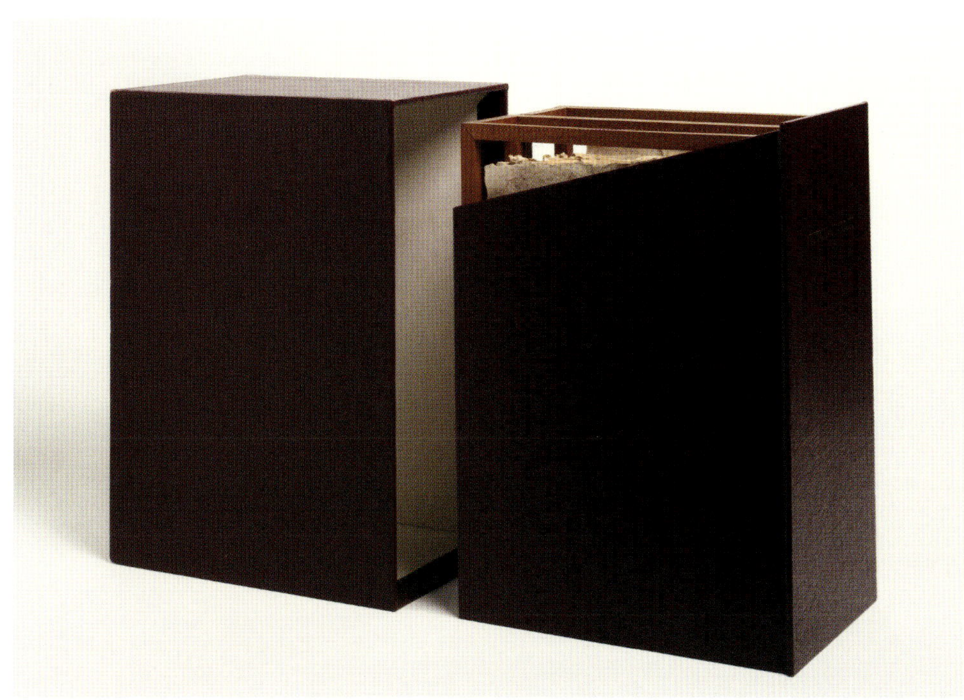

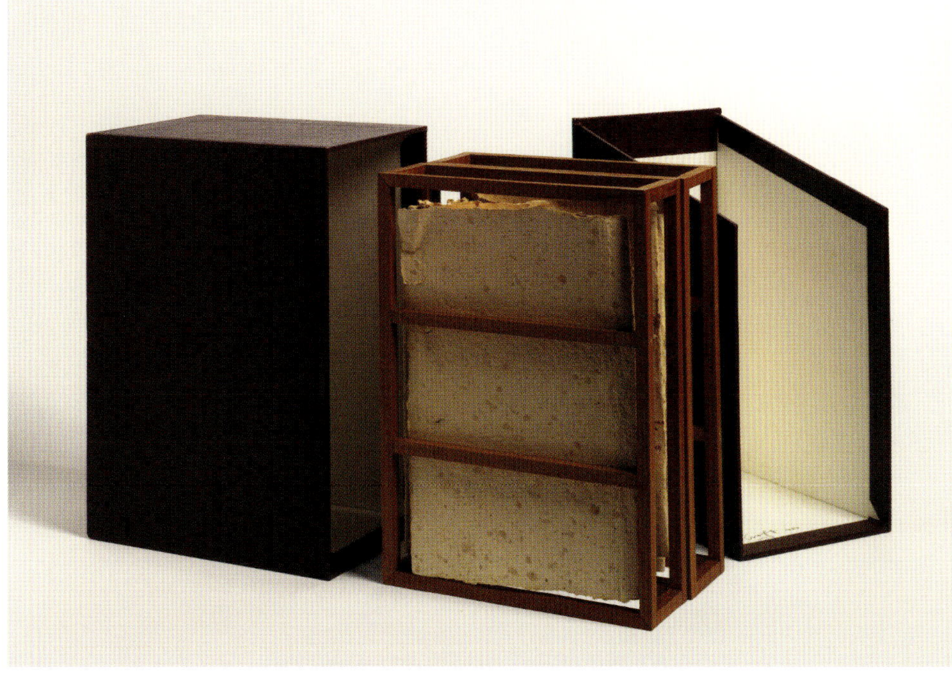

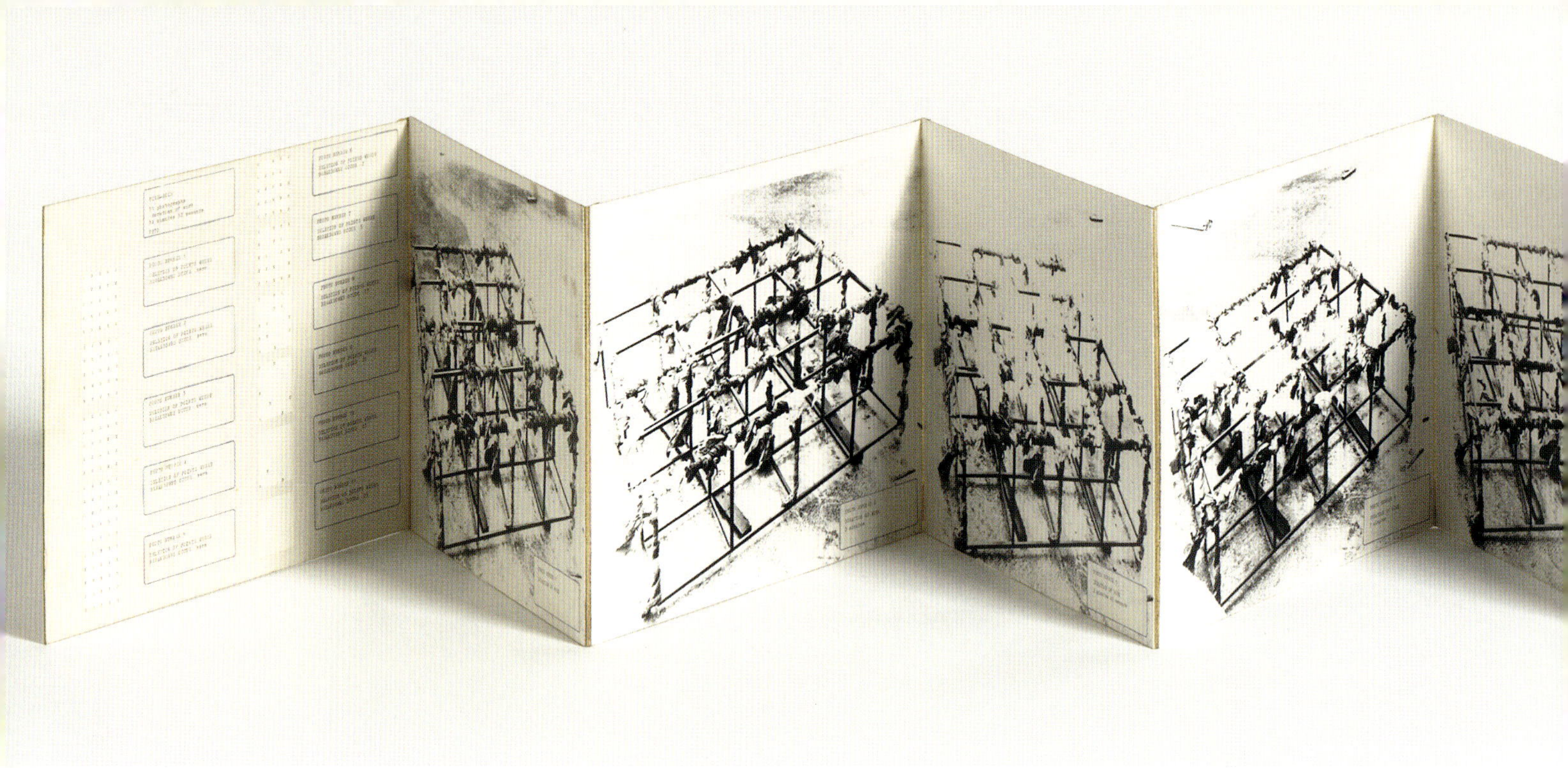

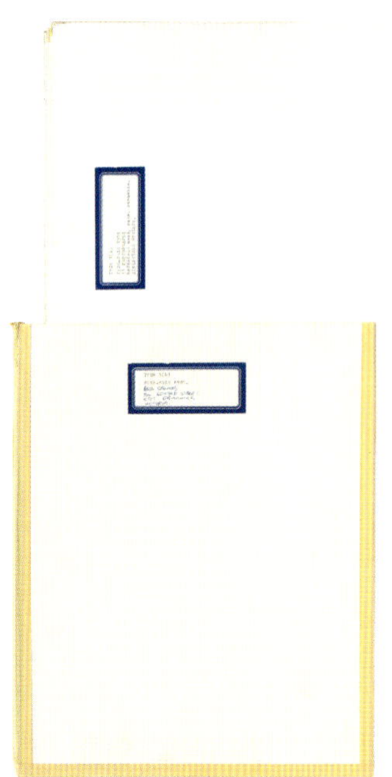

Ross Grounds
Fire-grid 1970

Fire-grid presents itself as a large, white card slip-case, with masking tape over its edges. There is a blue-bordered office label with the work's title typed on it, stuck on the front of the slip-case. Out of this office-like package, you pull a stack of white cardboard, similar to the slip-case, also with masking tape on some of the edges and another blue-edged label stuck on the top sheet. This set of cards opens out as a book of thick accordion-folded pages. The first page has a summary, giving typewriter diagrams and descriptions of 'breakdowns' which are then demonstrated on following pages by eleven photographs, all taken of the same object from the same camera position. The photographs document a progressive deterioration.

The photographed object is the centre of attention in this book. It is, or rather *was*, a horizontal grid of cubes made from wooden sticks – 4 x 4 cubes giving a top layer of 5 x 5 intersections. The artist bound the intersections of the sticks in kerosene-soaked rags, set them alight and photographed them at intervals until the structure flattened out into an array of burned bits.

The photographs, their preceding diagrams and summary records of the breakdowns thus record an event set up by the artist. The event is formalised through fundamental and elemental means,

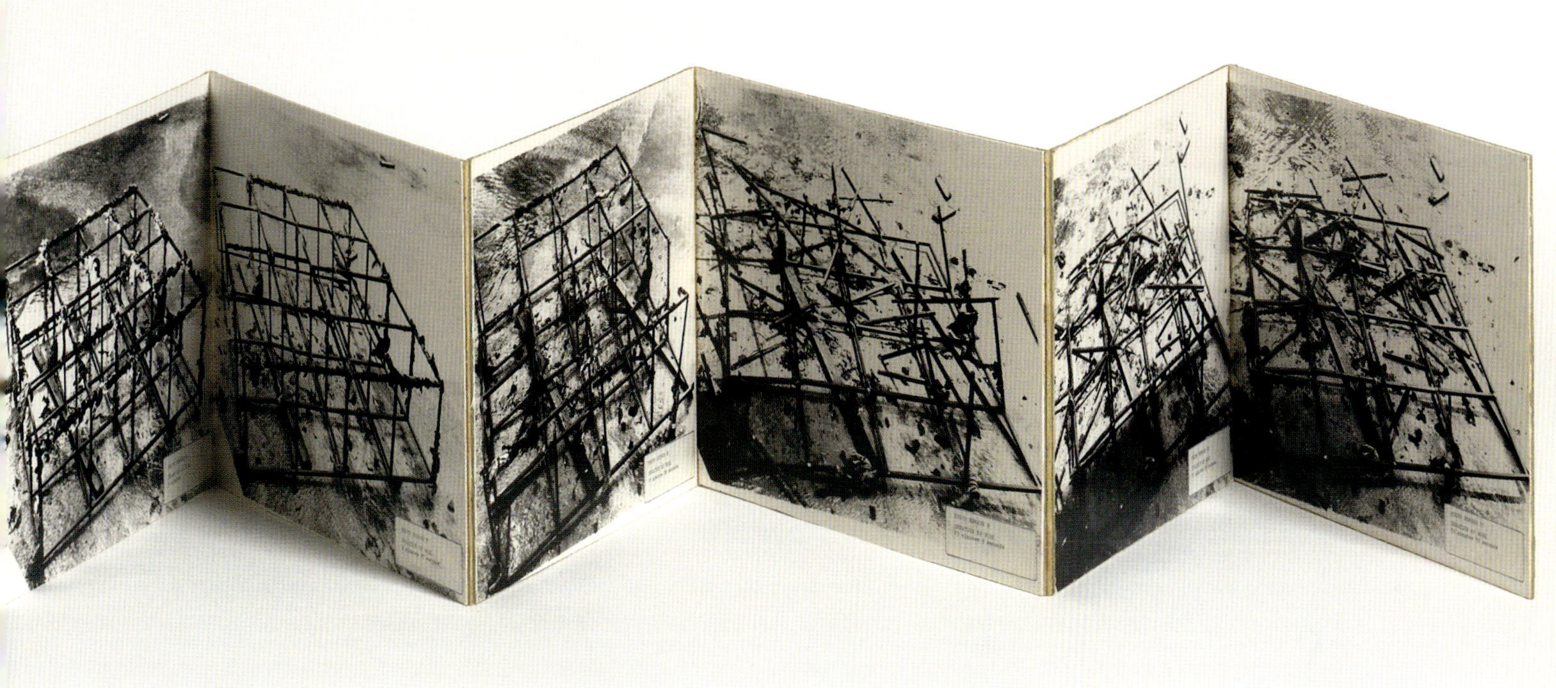

i.e. the cube, the grid and fire (and maybe water and earth also, as the grid is judiciously set somewhere over sand, at the edge of water). The quasi-scientific reporting suggests that the subject is entropy, but the handmade quality of the whole package and the grainy photographs suggest that the breakdown may signify a wider human or experiential metaphor.

Despite the book's homespun technique, it supports a sophisticated narrative structure. The statistics and photographs give a documentary record of seemingly artless realism, and the accordion folds break the flow of the real event into an edited sequence of repeats. This is more apparent when the book is unfolded, and either spread out or stood up in a zigzag format. Further, the times at which the photographs were taken is given: the intervals between them increase and then decrease, with the longest wait between photographs six and seven. This arch-like shape of durations, which must be calculated and held in the head, is a counterpoint to the serial images of the pages and photographs. The book thus puts forward a number of related narratives, real and represented, which its physical structure initiates and then stabilises.

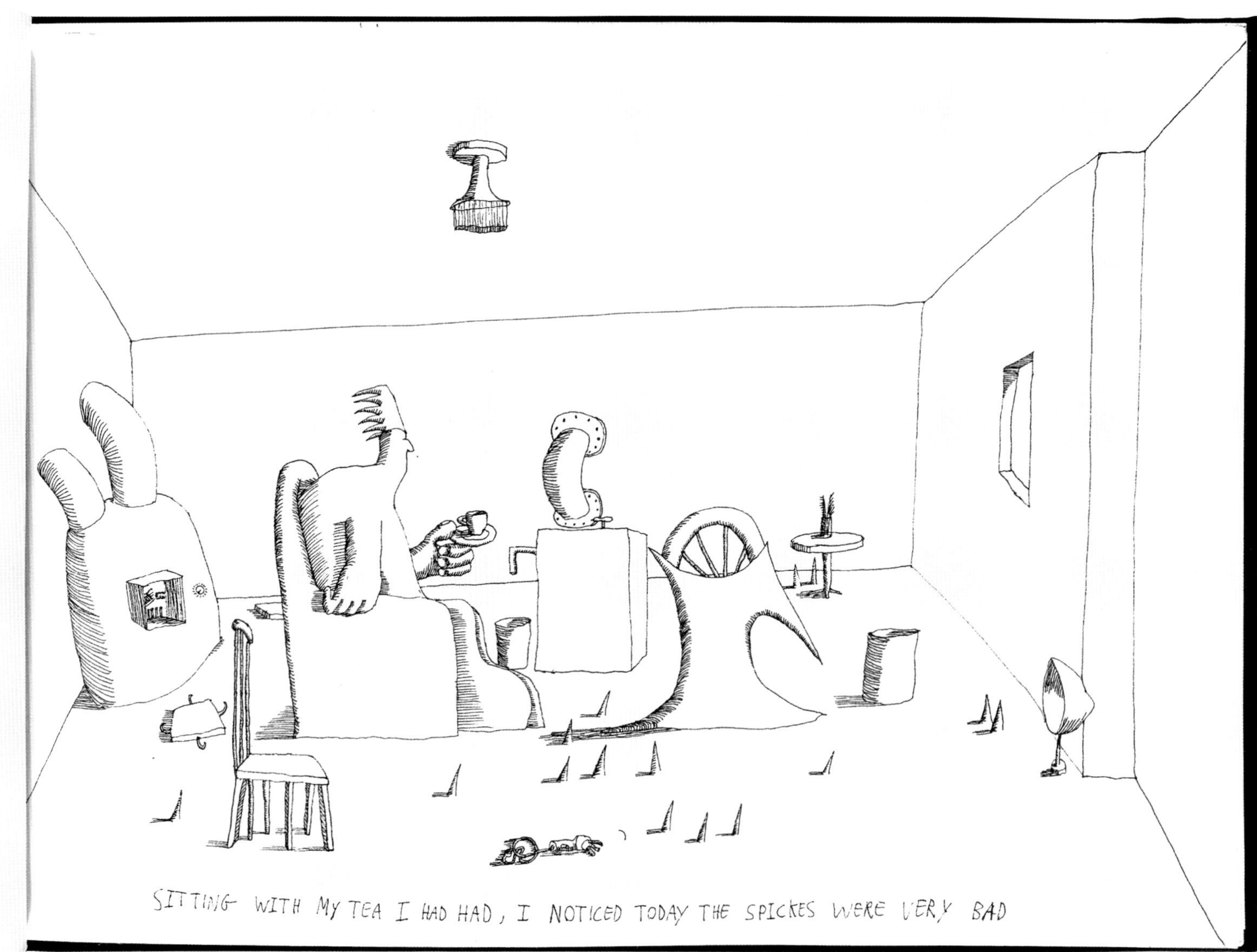

SITTING WITH MY TEA I HAD HAD, I NOTICED TODAY THE SPICKES WERE VERY BAD

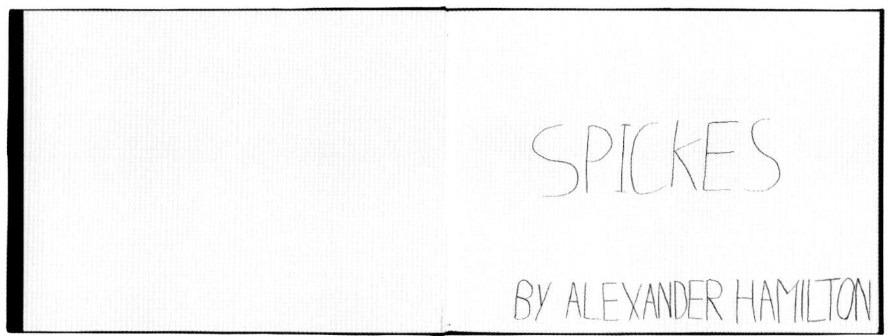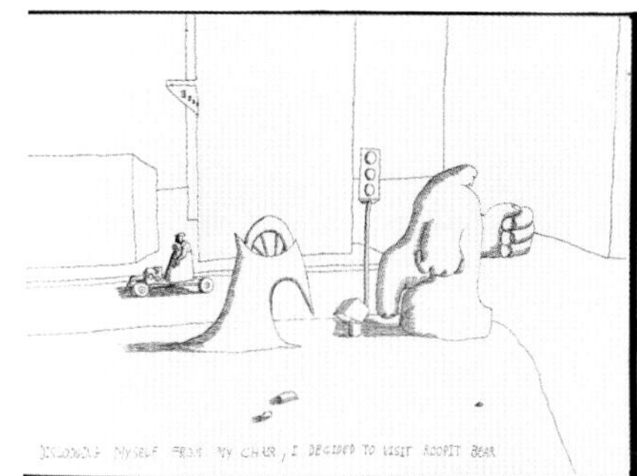

Alexander Hamilton
Spickes c.1986

This is the simplest kind of illustrated book – drawings with captions – but with a twist. Made in large landscape format, *Spickes*'s black cloth covers open out to reveal a hand-drawn title and author's name, followed by ten full-page pen drawings on the right-hand page, with hand-drawn text along the bottom edge under each drawing. All is in thin black lines, on thick white paper. The tenth, final page has an emphatic 'THE END', and under it, the artist's signature and edition number.

In nine phrases, one per page, the text tells of a catastrophic event involving the mysterious 'spickes'. With occasional spelling mistakes and alterations, the texts make intricate and suggestive titles for the drawings above them. Except for the last one, they are all set in Euclidean, three-dimensional space, like the cuboid rooms and streets with which we are all so familiar. But, as in many of Hamilton's drawings, these places are occupied by strange beings and objects, which are cartoonish and possibly menacing – an adults' version of the illustrations that appear in classic children's books, although more Sendak than Bruna. The spickes erupt in drawing after drawing as thorn-like growths. The artist himself (I think) appears on page 8, 'spicked' (if that's the right word).

Page nine has no text and is a field of incidents, objects and scenes. It is the everything 'that has been miraculously trancformed [*sic*]' after progressive increases in 'spickes' have caused a 'huge explosion'.

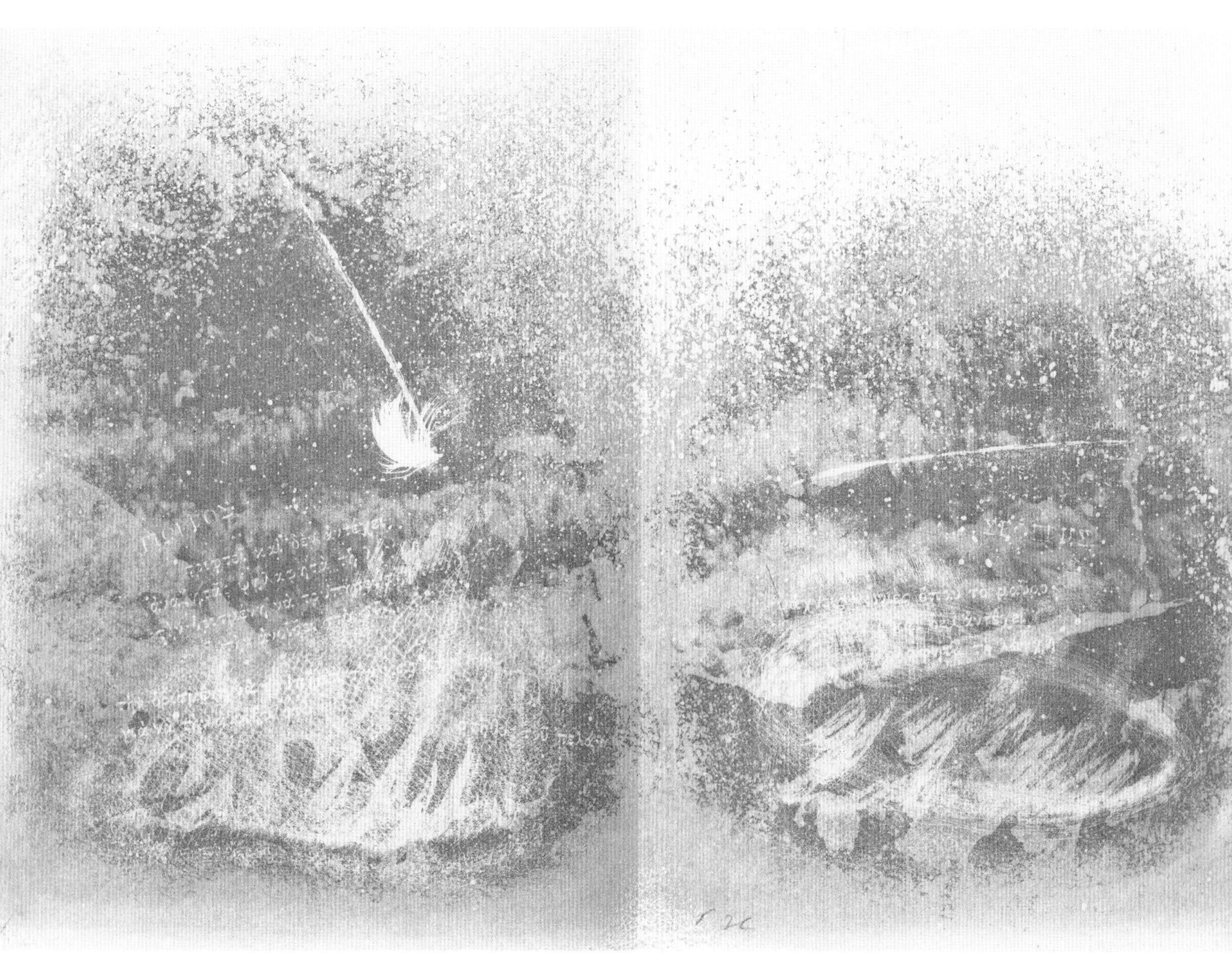

Petr Herel
On a ray of winter sun 1988

Held in the hands, then placed on a table, this publication presents itself as a small wad of white paper wrapped in a blue map. The map is of Australian desert country, near the Great Australian Bight, with marbling added by the artist, giving an effect of shadows. The title is on the cover in Greek, hinting already at a game of linguistic and visual contrasts. When you open the book, the cover is revealed to be a folded jacket, and the white paper of the pages emerges as a stack of folios. Each folio consists of folded pages set into a folded cover sheet.

The first folio opens to a tissue-paper page with a map-like pattern of marbling and a tiny, real feather stuck on the page, covering an English title. On the next page, the name of the Greek poet, George Seferis, appears in English, and on the following page, the poet's name appears in English with a Greek text under it.

The second folio has the Greek letter delta on its cover. It then opens to show Seferis's poem on the left-hand page in Greek, with an etching of a rock (or fist-like object) in fine line over a haze on the right-hand page, then a double-page spread of marbling with a white feather embossed in the paper. This is followed by another poem/image pairing, this time with left-hand/right-hand reversed, with the poem in English and the image of the fist (or rock-like object) made diagrammatic. On the back cover, there is a Roman 'IV' (the number 4).

The third folio contains two colophons: the first on one folded sheet lists the names and signatures of the people involved in conceiving and making the book; and the second describes the production of the book itself.

The folios thus set out, in order:

- the opposition of Greek and English and the reality or illusion of image and object
- the process of translation, of Greek to English, drawing to print, drawing to object, drawing to abstraction
- the production of the book – another opposition or translation of people and processes.

Εἶπες ἐδῶ καὶ χρόνια:
« Κατὰ βάθος εἶμαι ζήτημα φωτός ».
Καὶ τώρα ἀκόμη σὰν ἀκουμπᾶς
στὶς φαρδιὲς ὠμοπλάτες τοῦ ὕπνου
ἀκόμη κι' ὅταν σὲ ποντίζουν
στὸ ναρκωμένο στῆθος τοῦ πελάγου
ψάχνεις γωνιὲς ὅπου τὸ μαῦρο
ἔχει τριφτεῖ καὶ δὲν ἀντέχει
ἀναζητᾶς ψηλαφητὰ τὴ λόγχη
τὴν ὁρισμένη νὰ τρυπήσει τὴν καρδιά σου
γιὰ νὰ τὴν ἀνοίξει στὸ φῶς.

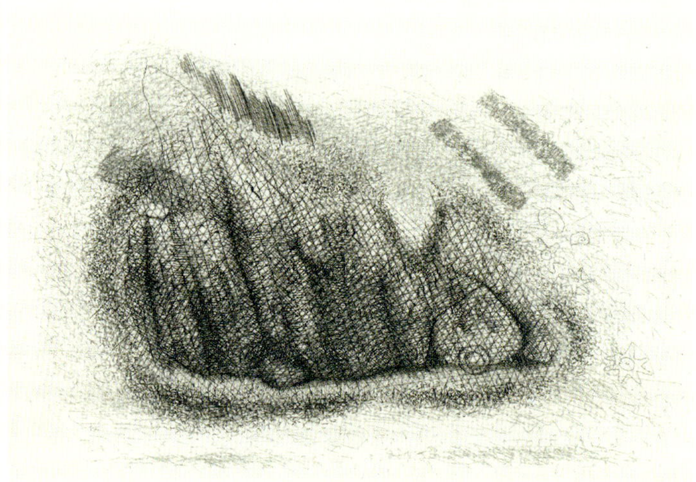

The poem at the centre of this activity is Section 4 from George Seferis's *On a ray of winter sun*. The poem's imagery presents extremes of pure light and submarine shadows, of hopelessness and hope, and ends with an image of epiphany: 'you search/for the spear destined to lance your heart/that it may open to the light'.

Herel exploits the tangible properties of print in the contrasts of the feather and its embossed reappearance, the contrast between the thick paper and the tissue, and the represented fragility of the etchings and the precision of the printing. These contrasts and their resolution right through to the finest detail constantly draw attention to the relationship of the tactile and the intangible.

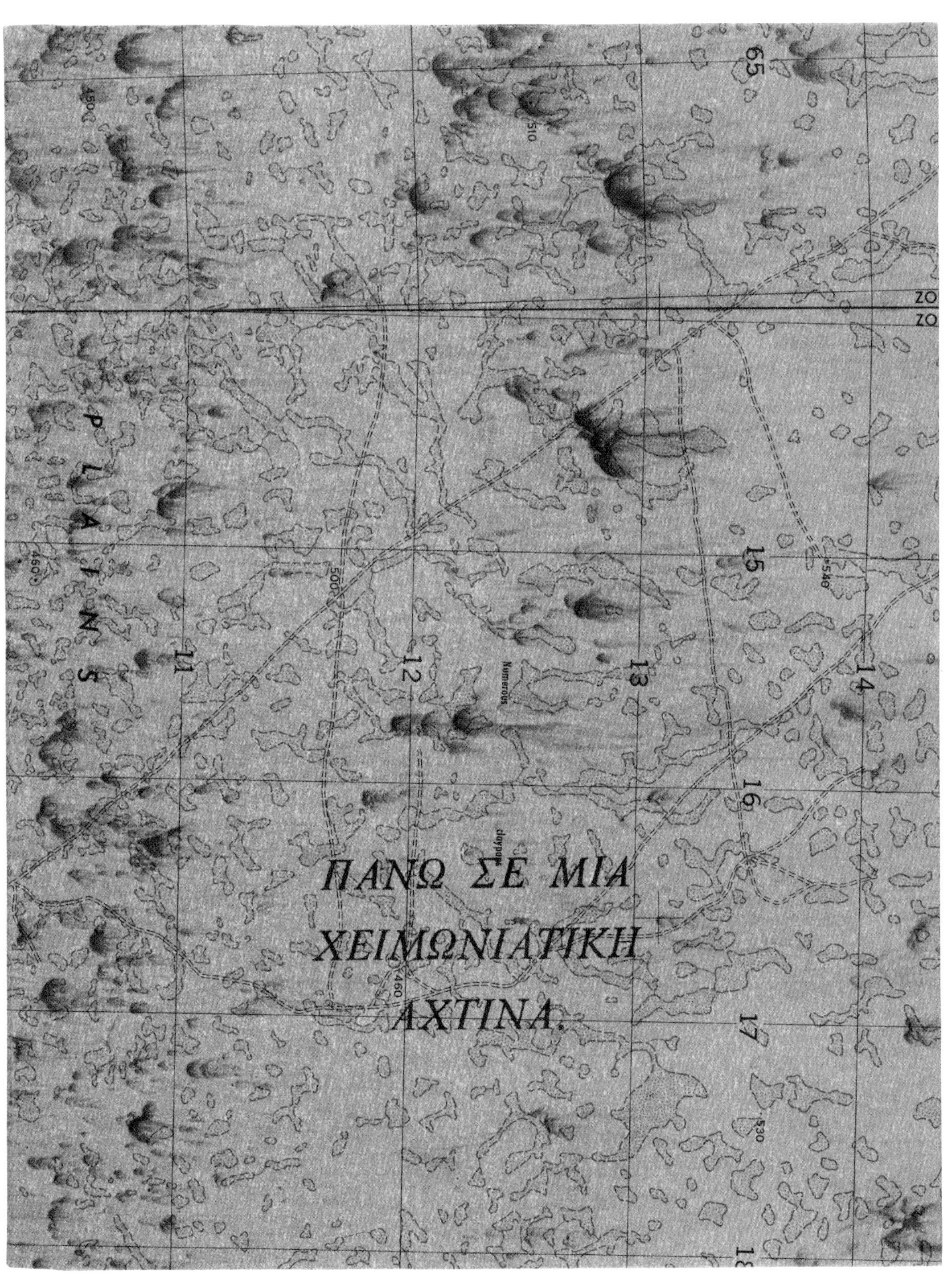

ΠΑΝΩ ΣΕ ΜΙΑ
ΧΕΙΜΩΝΙΑΤΙΚΗ
ΑΧΤΙΝΑ.

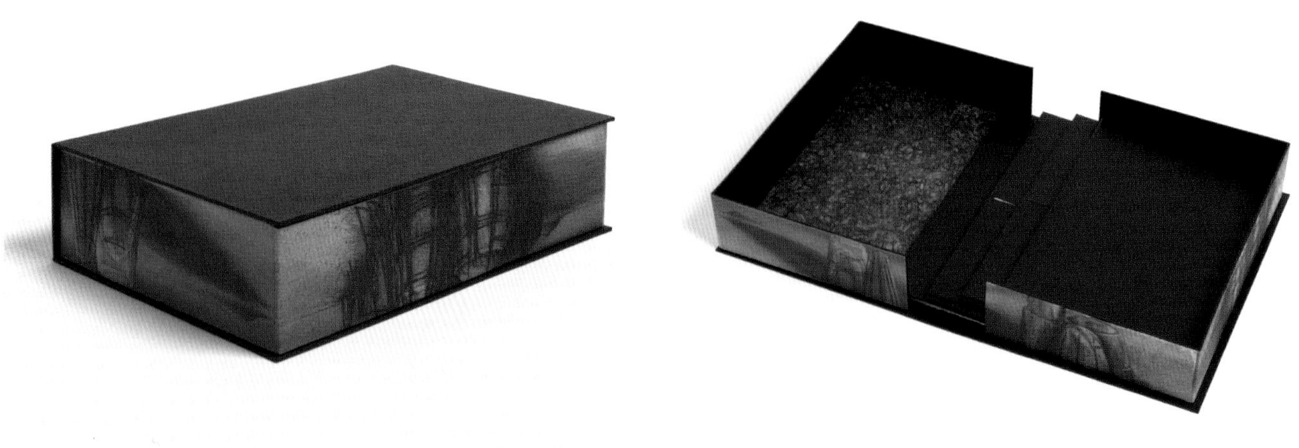

Ruth Johnstone
Untitled (panoramic boxed set) 1991

This is a big box of books. The box is substantial: black, but with a grey-toned etching over what would be the edges of the pages if it were a book. When the box is opened out flat, the left-hand side shows its interior, lined with marbled paper, and the right-hand side reveals a stack of four thin books, all the same size, all bound in black-cloth-covered boards. There are no titles either on the box or on the book covers, or in the books themselves: you have to deduce a summary from a thorough examination of the work.

The first book is an accordion fold of six etchings in a sequence of three pairs. Each pair contrasts, on the left-hand side, a cord laid out as a hexagon within a square frame, against a capital 'O' (or an oval?), on the right-hand side, printed on transparent paper fixed over a blue haze on the white paper. As the sequence reads left to right, the hexagonal cord changes from an open-ended figure, to one with a knot, to one that is whole, and the blue hazes become more sharply defined.

The second book is a symmetrical centrefold and folds out in landscape format. As the two covers fold out, they show their bright-orange inside lining and an overlay of semi-transparent paper with an image of orange parawebbing printed on it. Behind this is the hint of an image: a second fold-out reveals an image of Eugène von Guérard's painting *Tower Hill* 1855. The overlay of transparent paper spans the two fold-outs and if the book is stood up, acts as a sculptural model of the parawebbing that is used to cordon off places for safety and security.

The third book is also a symmetrical centrefold, similar to the second, except that the image of Tower Hill has been digitally enhanced. Tissue paper – which, in this book (after noting the parawebbing) now also suggests protection and security, but of fine art material – is covered in a band of grey washes.

The fourth book is an accordion fold, but the fold is gathered on the right-hand cover. Images appear on both sides of the paper fold. On the sides that you see first on opening the book, there are small landscapes, covered in tissue with torn, hairy edges. The other paper side consists of horizontal landscapes, printed across the crease of the folds, also with printed tissue over them. This tissue image is an oval with four ribbons under it; the landscape images under the tissues move progressively to the right from fold to fold.

This whole set of books has a symmetry in book format and themes, with a number of parallels around the broader idea of 'landscape':

- the frame as an implied mirror and window, and nature as a mirror and window
- the pursuit of perfection in art, and the pursuit of perfection in nature
- the role of conservation in art, and the role of conservation in nature.

A key image and ongoing event for *Untitled (panoramic boxed set)* is the reconstruction of Tower Hill in southern Victoria, where von Guérard's painting is being used as a documentary source. This ambiguous relationship of reality and fiction is built into these books through their combination of images, overlays and unfoldings.

When the books are folded up, closed and put back, you again notice the grey, panoramic edge of the big box: it shows a landscape of artificial-looking mounds and large scaffolds or machines, either in place or maybe approaching us from the distance.

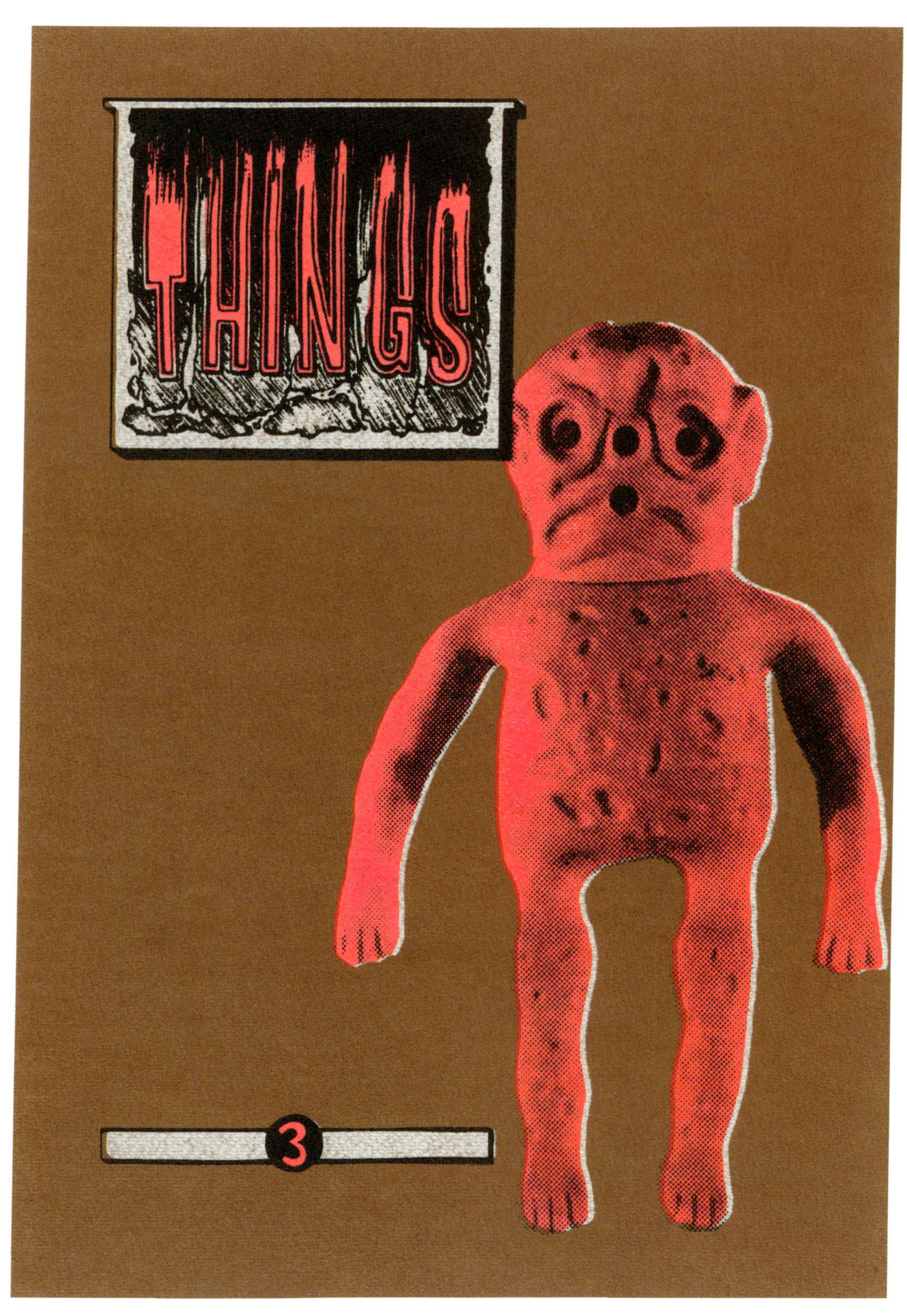

THINGS
3

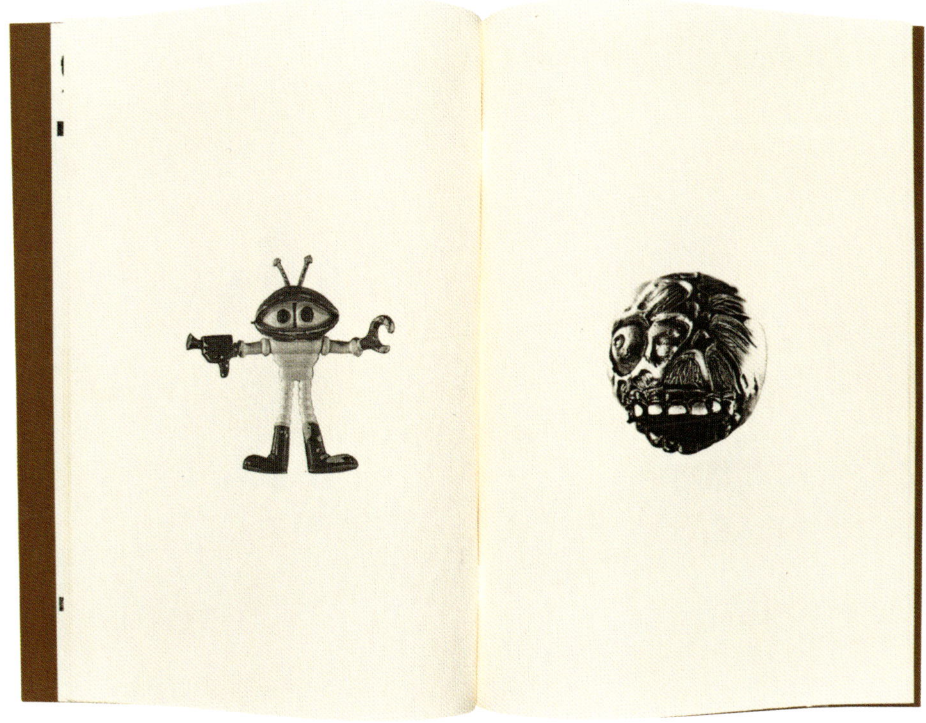

Maria Kozic
Things 1, Things 2, Things 3 1988

These are three, A4-sized books, designed to look like commercial, popular publications. About 50 pages each, stapled, with a short introduction after the title page in typewriter typeface, the publications have an ISBN number and are unsigned and unlimited in issue. Taking this further, the colophon lists Maria Kozic as 'Producer', the publisher is 'Humungous Publications' and a distributor is listed. As if they were magazines, the covers repeat the same format, with title and issue number graphics varying each time to match the contents. The covers also vary in colour, using a different, single fluorescent colour to supplement the basic black printing of each 'issue'.

When you flick through the pages of the books, you find that each is a collection of pictures, one per page. *Things 1*, subtitled 'Telephone Doodles', is a collection of such drawings done while talking on the telephone; *Things 2* is subtitled 'Dicks', and is a collection of phallic symbols; *Things 3* is subtitled 'Mutants', and is a collection of robotic/toy/monster figures. In each issue, there is no apparent narrative, except for the effect of one thing changing to a similar thing, page by page. It is possible to view the books as the artist's source imagery, set out as a demonstration or manifesto.

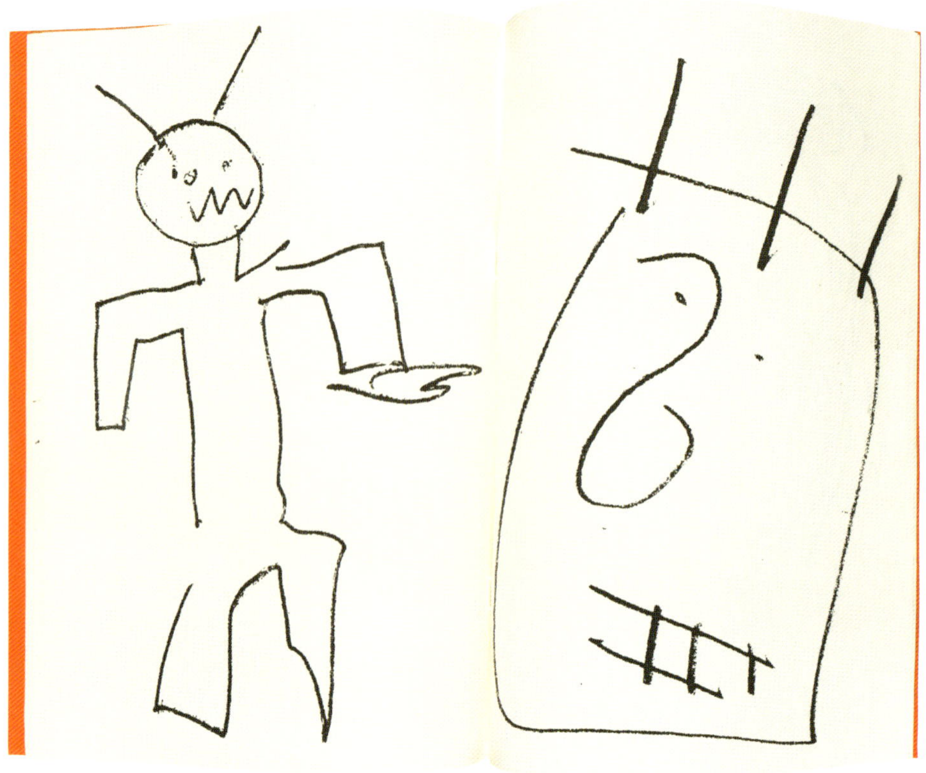

While the books present different subjects and contain pictures that mix scales and drawing techniques, there is a strong unity to the images. Each book is a typological presentation, that is, the doodle, dick or mutant is progressively understood through the comparison of different versions of the same thing. Like collectors of teapots or spoons, who display all examples together so that the idea and phenomenon of the teapot or spoon can be understood, Maria Kozic displays her collections so that each subject can be understood. Further, in putting the three books together, there is a strong sense of body image – obvious in 'Mutants', symbolically there in 'Dicks' and there by suggestion in 'Doodles'.

Typological methods are characteristic of amateur collecting, and magazines are typological by nature, giving the impression of novelty and variety through a profound sameness, issue after issue. These three books suggest that an artist's work might also strive for a similar kind of balance of variety and sameness.

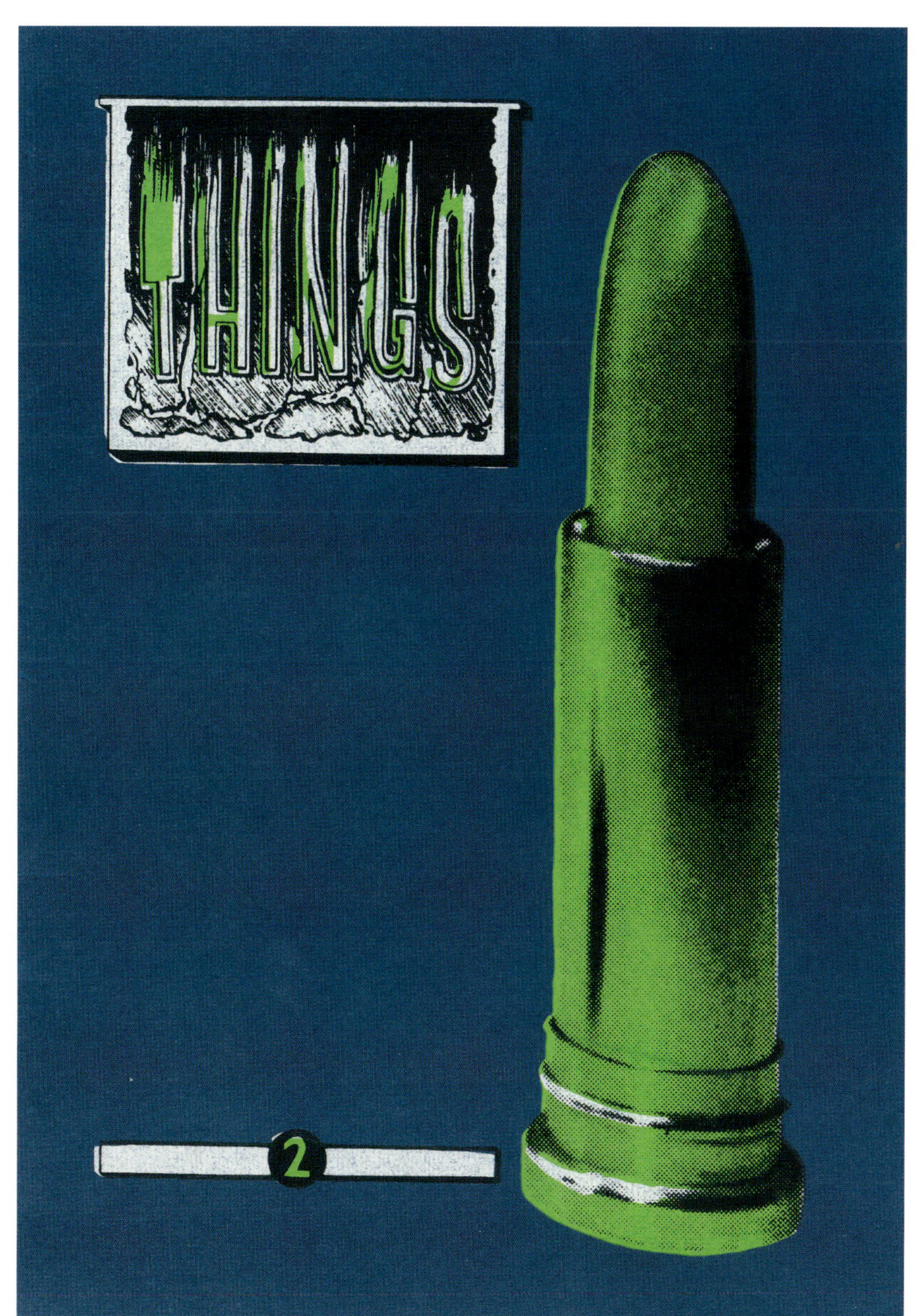
THINGS
2

TH WA WI NEVE EN

A MYT OLOG O GRT
T AEK TE ND F TIM

B UAR EWI

ONORAP ESS
99

Ruark Lewis
Th wa wi neve en 1991

You remove this booklet from its (standard, post-office-preferred) envelope to find that it contains text – just text. The book is protected by a glacime dust jacket, through which one can see a title: *Th wa wi neve en*, with a subtitle that is equally incomplete; and then, where the author's name would normally be: 'b uar ewi'. This last phrase suggests what has happened to the text above it – one letter has been removed from the ends of each word, deducible because you know that the book is bY RuarK LewiS.

Inside, the standard book format provides a blank page, then a single-line title page, followed by a standard title page (the same text as on the cover), with a paragraph-sized drawn-over text on the left-hand side where the colophon would normally be placed. Then three texts follow, over six pages, all subjected to the treatment of constantly missing letters. The first text consists of two short paragraphs; the second is a letter addressed to 'D r M k', and shaped like a free verse poem; the third text is a number of paragraphs run over two pages. Then, after a blank page, the real colophon follows and, after another blank page, you are at the back cover. The pages of *Th wa wi neve en* are uncut, and the first reaction is to put a knife through the folded edge at the top of every folded sheet to open it up.

But this slight inaccessibility can also be taken as a tangible analogue of the way the text works. As you attempt to fill in the missing letters, it becomes apparent that in many cases there are a number of options, and even where obvious or definite completions occur, these are not enough to give clues for most of the truncated words. The texts, therefore, draw you into what is apparently an easy game of corrections, only to throw you into a wider zone of new texts. But one text can be fixed: the title of the third text is 'Te ar eve nd' (another version of the book's hidden title). Combining these two versions, the corrected title can be guessed: 'The war will never end'.

D r M k
        H nd ho u re ine ing oyed thi onderf
ulome mer ak.
        Y re ro a ly gh ing fi,
                                al musc pplin
a ur mand,
        s ver th wi f iro.
ell avo!

        ere ver yth ha een ine nd ving,
                                alt ough t
ails ace,
        ough th extro eather nd inter ation
appen.
n t Sou acifi,
                ne ha almo t pe f min
t d pret uce wha ver ne's ife ires.

        ow t ost ain y s t ew Y.
                        I et tha surin
ense ost untl y y irthd n ebruar 6.
Thi i th rea
sation tha tim i ceed.
                tha tim ha beco a ignific
s th poi o n etur,
                h sa,
                        la bene thi bro f
perisnce mig b a impl arnin t slee.
        ow reifl I m itin t y t rovrd a pdat-lan
f th yea nfo.

Because this is a work by Ruark Lewis, it must also be considered as a score, that is, it must be read aloud. Doing this, you discover that that, when spoken, the text sounds like a strange language. It is like the speech of someone who drops or fades away parts of words, and also like the singsong of someone discovering or learning speech for the first time. Approaching these texts as semantic mental puzzles thus pushes them forward into multiple languages – into a Babel of mysterious invented words and phrases. Approaching them as sound texts pushes them right back to the origins of language. In both cases a kind of language potential is acted out. In this book, the 'war' is, literally, the constant struggle for correct meaning, for the correct origin, acted out by the reader.

The book's editioning takes up the theme. A loose slip of paper that comes with *Th wa wi neve en* notes that of the edition of 150 copies:

> 98 are for anonymous distribution by post. The remaining 52 have the frontispiece image disguised, that is, altered; are initialed [sic]; and are for sale by the author. These are lettered a to z and AA to ZZ.

The frontispiece drawing (the 'colophon') links the book to the kind of images usually produced by the artist: intricate textures and compressions of writing that always point to the beginnings of language and its overuse. Of course, the book must be left uncut, so that you have to peer under the pages to find the contents, which are 'disguised' and always hidden.

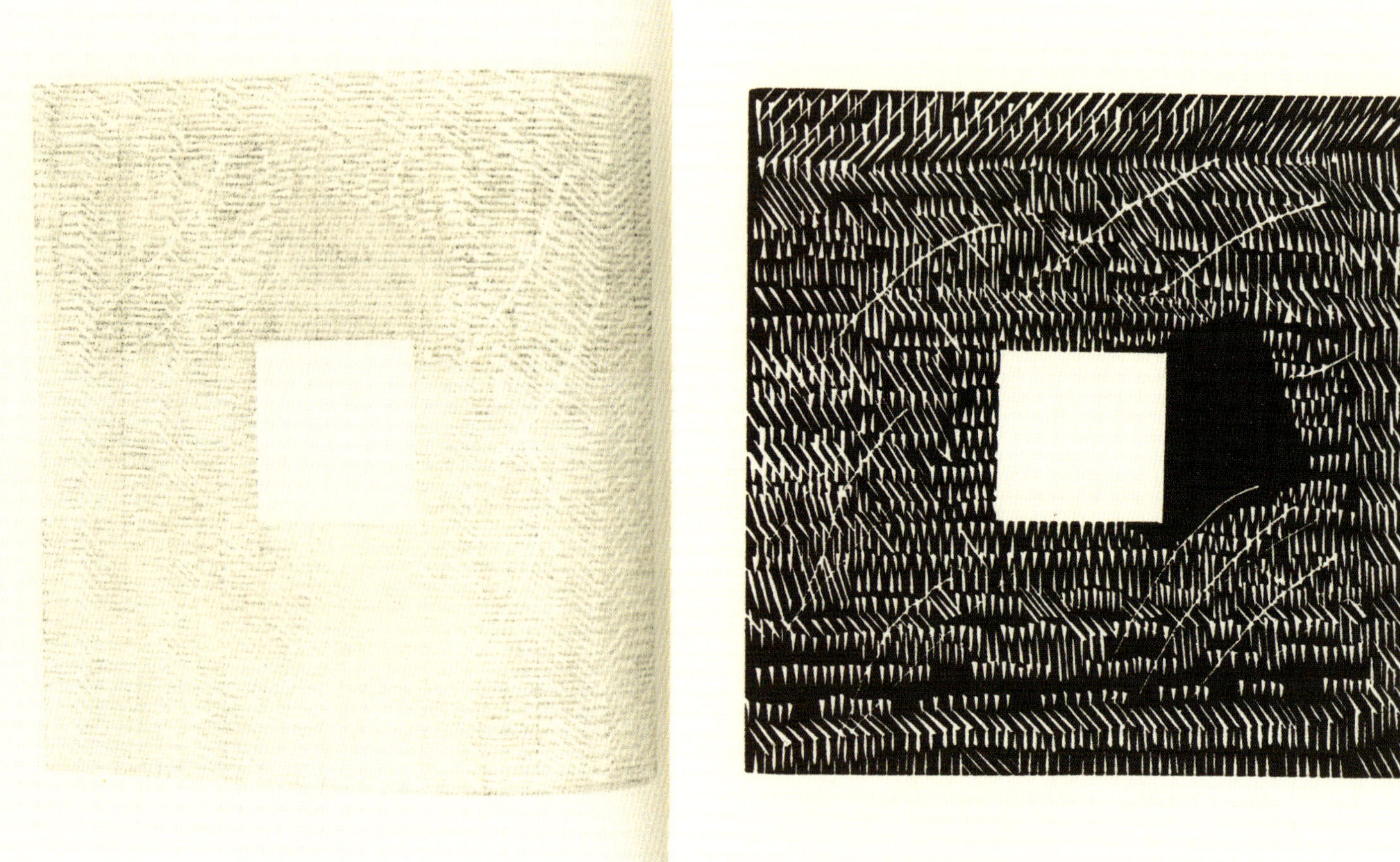

Jennifer Marshall
Flick book 1986

A square, black object, this work is a slip-case protecting what looks like a black block of papers bound with white thread. As you pull out the bound papers, you notice that its cover and the slip-case feature the same linocut print:

JMAR

SHALL

1986

The image is printed black-on-white on the slip-case, and black-on-black on the book.

The same style of lettering is repeated on the title page: black-on-black 'FLICK/BOOK' in two lines. The book then presents a long sequence of linocuts, using a white, centrally placed square (the white paper showing through) parallel to the paper edges, with hatched and black squares on opposite sides of the white square. The image can be seen as a window with shutters, or as an open cube, or as an open page of a book. This figure is rotated through 90 degrees, page by page.

The rotations are repeated through cycles of seven (the last image of one sequence becoming the first of the next, as in a musical scale), and in the last cycle the image moves into a diagonal position on the page. The marks in the woodcuts form small 'I' and 'V' strokes and, given the book format, suggest a proto-writing.

Flick book exploits an obvious but often ignored structural feature of books: one edge (the binding) is clamped together while the opposite edge fans out. The free edge can be run through the fingers and, with appropriate images on the pages, the flickering can create an illusion of movement, as in a film. In Marshall's book, the images produce a balance of stasis and movement. The black shadows of the central, white square, and its surrounding hatching, flicker around while the white square stays still. The white square, parallel to the edges of the page and thus to the book as a whole, can be seen as an image of the stability of all pages and all books, which carry a flux of data and reading while remaining stable.

When you slide the book back into its case, you notice again that the book's binding is white – the colour of stability in this work.

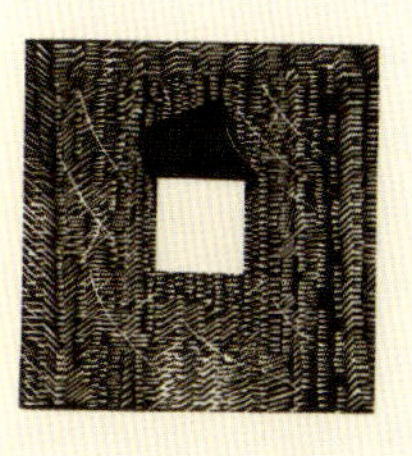

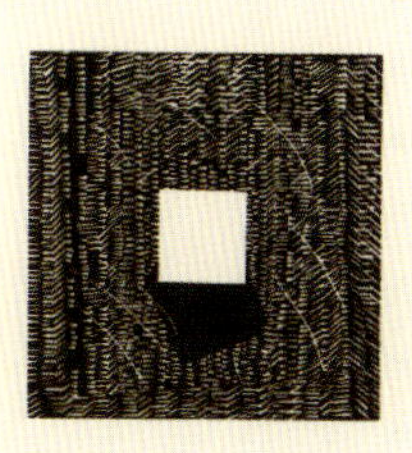

Ian Milliss
Not titled [twenty-six concepts] 1970

A large paper folder with 'IANMILLISS' in transfer letters along its bottom right-hand edge opens up to reveal a handwritten letter and a set of xerox prints of typed sheets. The letter is from the artist to curator Daniel Thomas, and concerns matters of payment. It is probably connected to the purchase of this work, and perhaps not intended as part of the original folio, but now part of its content.

The xerox sheets are all portrait format, and are double quarto untrimmed prints from foolscap originals. All have the characteristic grey bleed as a frame where the xerox process was incapable of printing solid areas of black. Except for one sheet, all pages are short, single-line typed instructions, with a title block in the lower right-hand corner giving the artist's name, the title of the work and its date. The instructions were done from 5/4/1970 to 13/4/1970, except for perhaps the 'signature page', which is undated. Each instruction varies from a single page to five pages, but all sheets use the same format.

Dating the instructions – the individual works – gives the loose set a literal chronology and a form of narrative. The xeroxed pages point to the fact that originals exist somewhere else, and that maybe more than one version of the folio may exist (although there is no indication that the folio is part of an edition). The cover, with its transfer letters, is handmade.

The instructions are for performance. Many are apparently meditative – all are aids to increased awareness, and many have unforseen results and effects if performed. For example, on one page, two typed lines, one below the other, ask you to 'close your eyes' and then 'open your eyes'. This cannot be performed if considered as two separate instructions, but can be if held in the memory. The most enigmatic instruction simply has the number '2074' typed on the page. (In the spirit of the other instructions, I took this as a clue for action, and went on a postcode hunt. From the artist's files in the Gallery's library, I found out that Milliss was living in postcode 2010 in 1970, and that 2074 is the postcode for Turramurra, New South Wales. Milliss's '2074' does not direct you to specific actions, but in my case it caused some walking, riding in lifts, looking up files and discussion – all of these actions arising out of my interpretation of the instruction's meaning.)

IANMILLISS

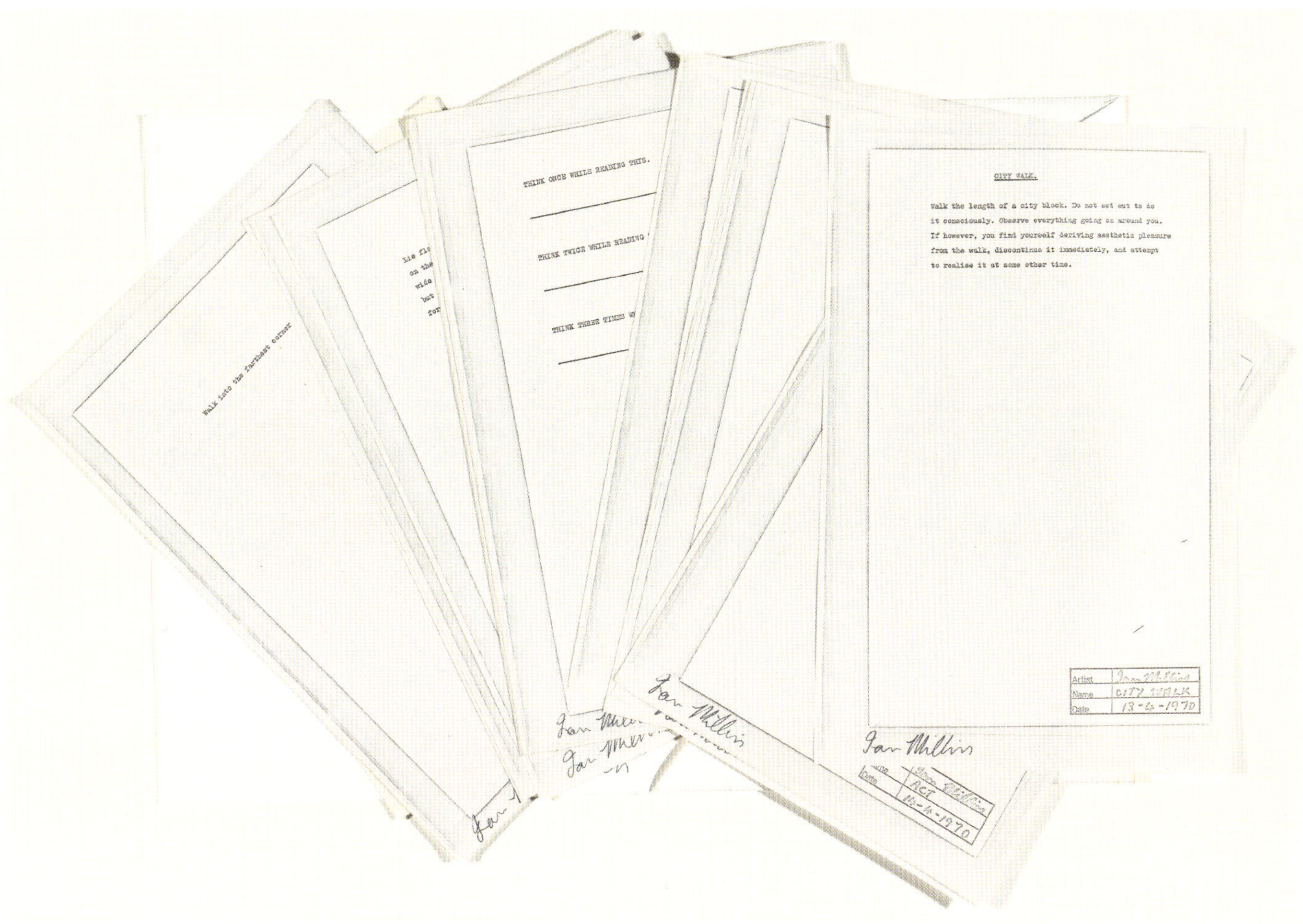

One sheet is unusual: it is an original foolscap page, with a simple horizontal line typed onto it. It is page 2 of fourteen such pages, with twelve of them (including this one) being distributed to different people in Sydney and Melbourne. Through this page, the folio is connected to a spatial network through an action performed by the artist.

The final sheet is a claim that the pages have been signed by someone else, and points to the objective non-art tone of the whole folio. The denial of the artist's touch puts this work into the realm of documents for bureaucratic production, where signatures are used to check and approve, rather than to sanctify.

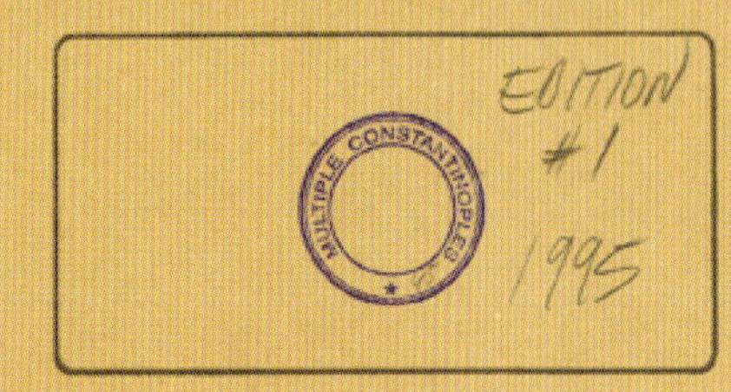

23 A4 SPIRIT-DUPLICATOR PRINTS (CARBON TRANSFER) BY:
CLAIRE BARCLAY, ANNE BRENNAN; BARBARA CAMPBELL; LINDSAY
DUNBAR; FIONA HALL; STEVEN HOLLAND; TESS HORWITZ,
STEPHANIE JONES; NIGEL LENDON; KATE LOHSE; eX de MEDICI,
GEORGE POPPERWELL, NEIL ROBERTS, PAUL SAINT, CHRISTOPHER
SNEE; CHRISTINE TARKOWSKI.

Neil Roberts (coordinator)
Multiple Constantinoples 1995

Claire Barclay, Anne Brennan, Barbara Campbell, Lindsay Dunbar, Fiona Hall,
Steven Holland, Tess Horwitz, Stephanie Jones, Nigel Lendon, Kate Lohse, eX de Medici,
George Popperwell, Neil Roberts, Paul Saint, Christopher Snee, Christine Tarkowski

This work is presented as an office file: a light-brown folder, bearing its brand name, 'slimpick wallet'. On the cover flap, the title, edition number and medium are identified through a circular rubber stamp and a handwritten note along the edge of the flap. Below this, on the body of the file, is a handwritten alphabetical list of the sixteen artists whose work is collected in this publication.

When you open the flap, you pull out a wad of A4-size pages, with a front section held between two sheets of grey cardboard (the sort that is found on the back of office pads). This front section contains a sample unused transfer sheet. Then individual contributions by each of the sixteen artists follow, all of which have used the same kind of duplicator sheet as the plate-making process. Each of the artist's works is preceded by a white A4 page with that artist's name pencilled in the bottom right-hand corner. The actual works, nearly all line drawings of various kinds, are authorised by the same circular rubber stamp that appears on the file cover, and are also individually editioned.

The transfer process, with its characteristic pink/purple fuzzy-line print soaked into matt paper, is now a superseded office copying process, but common before the introduction of photocopiers. In this publication, each of the artists uses this abandoned technique to present an image unrelated to each other thematically, but related to that artist's own work. The whole is thus a collection of individual statements, held together through format and technique, aptly summarised by the title. ('Constantinople' derives from the name of the pre-existing factory in Queanbeyan occupied by the owner of the duplicator, Neil Roberts, who also acted as the publication's commissioning editor and coordinator.) An intangible value also holds the works together – the agreement to work with a low-tech, low-status medium, which in other contexts would be considered unworthy of an artist's interest.

The sheets are too large and floppy to be easily held as a package and flipped through quickly. They are best seen one by one or spread out, and could easily be pinned up to make a standard gallery group exhibition. When putting them back, they have to be tapped into position as a neat wad and then slid back into the file – implying that the package should go back into something like a filing cabinet.

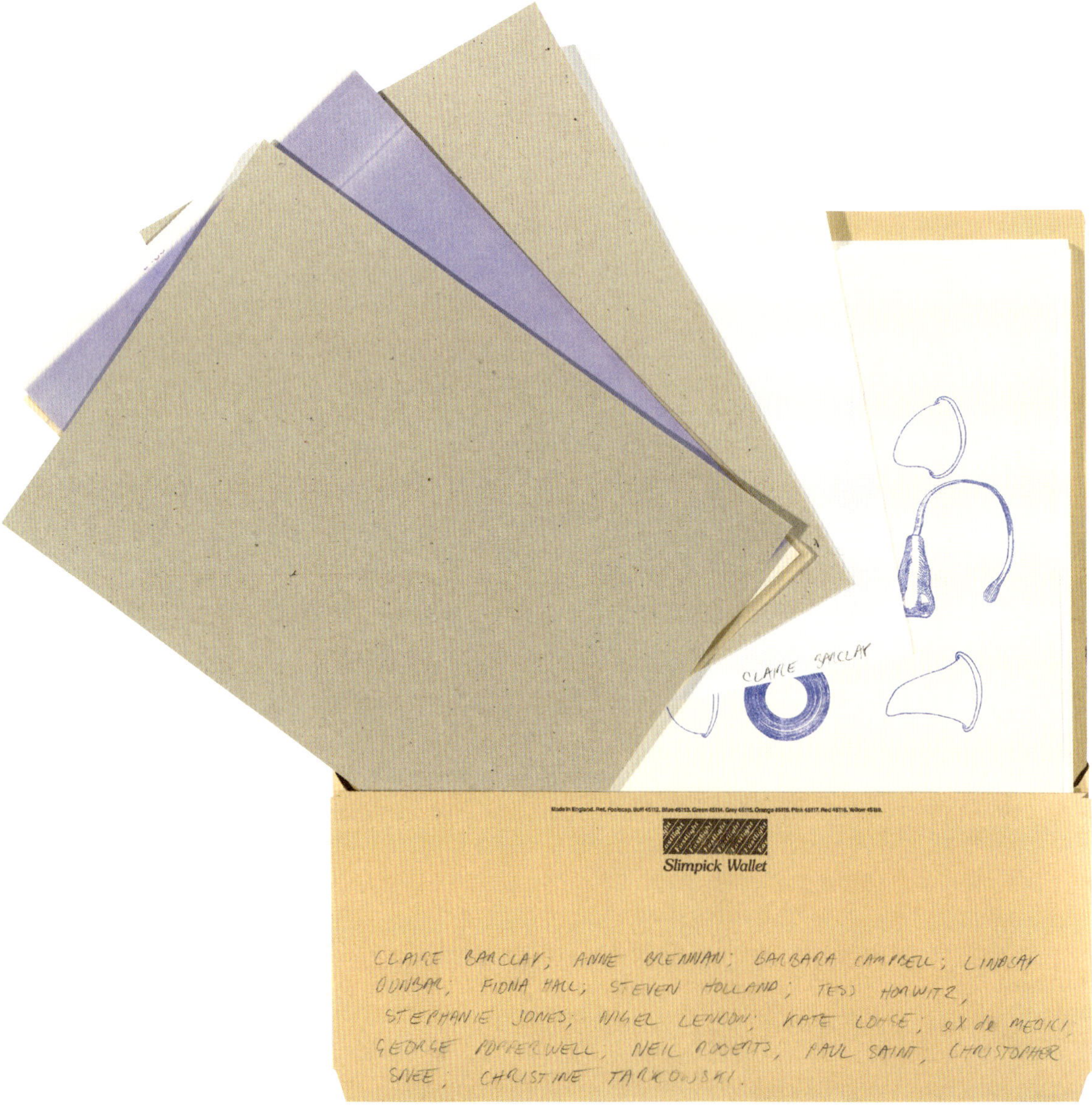

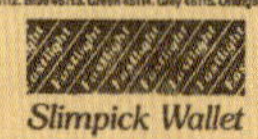

CLARE BARCLAY

CLAIRE BARCLAY; ANNE BRENNAN; BARBARA CAMPBELL; LINDSAY
DUNBAR; FIONA HALL; STEVEN HOLLAND; TESS HORWITZ,
STEPHANIE JONES; NIGEL LENDON; KATE LOHSE; eX de MEDICI,
GEORGE POPPERWELL; NEIL ROBERTS, PAUL SAINT, CHRISTOPHER
SNEE; CHRISTINE TARKOWSKI.

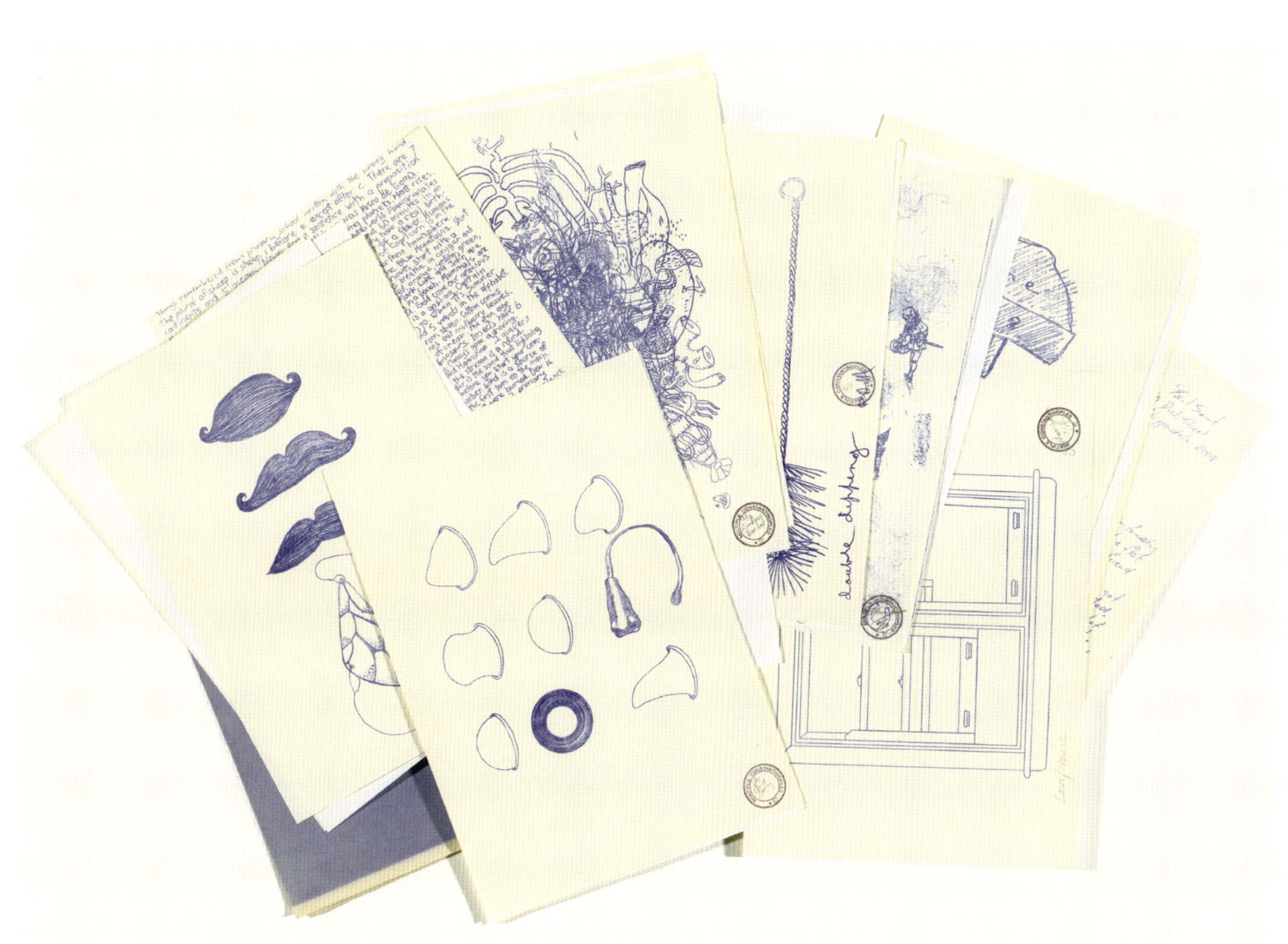

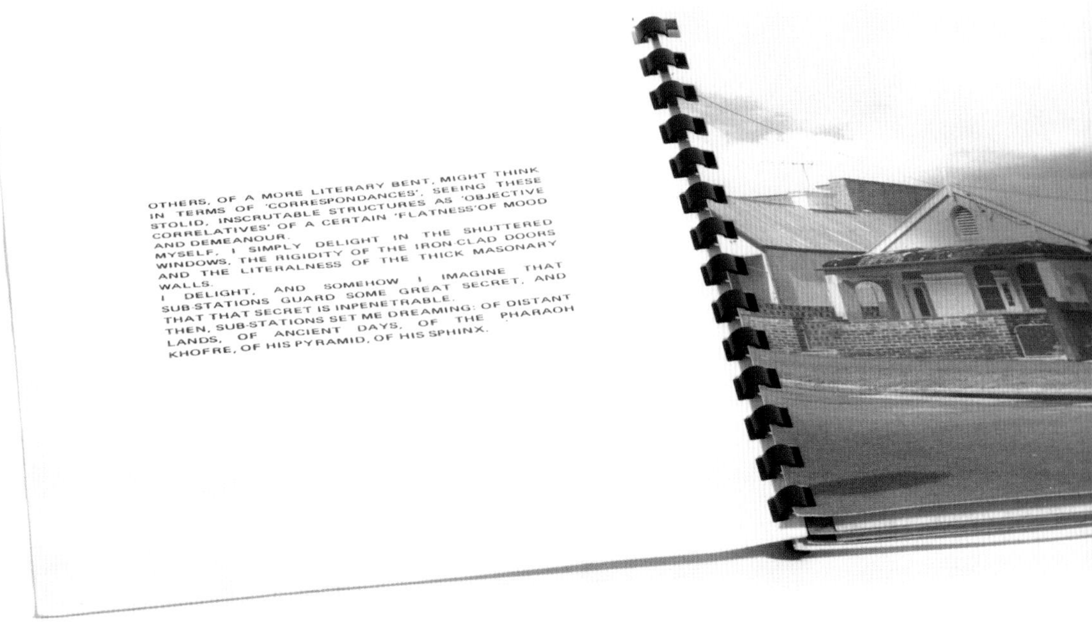

Bruce Searle
Sub-stations 1985

This is a small, A5-size portrait format booklet, with a white card cover, black plastic comb binding, and an intriguing combination of title and publisher (or series?) name on the front: 'Sub-stations/Metaphysical Sydney Pop-up Books'.

Opening the booklet, you find an introductory text on the left-hand side and a full-page flap on the right-hand side. In a few paragraphs, the text shifts your attention from the substation as a utilitarian box, to the artist's vision of them as objects that 'guard some great secret ... [which] is impenetrable', leading to an imagined connection with ancient Egypt. Opening the flap, like opening a door into a mystery, you are confronted with a photograph of an anonymous substation in a suburban context, with the substation cut out and folded to stand up from the page. Two more substation pop-ups follow, and then the back cover has the artist's initials as a signature, and what could either be an edition number or the date of making.

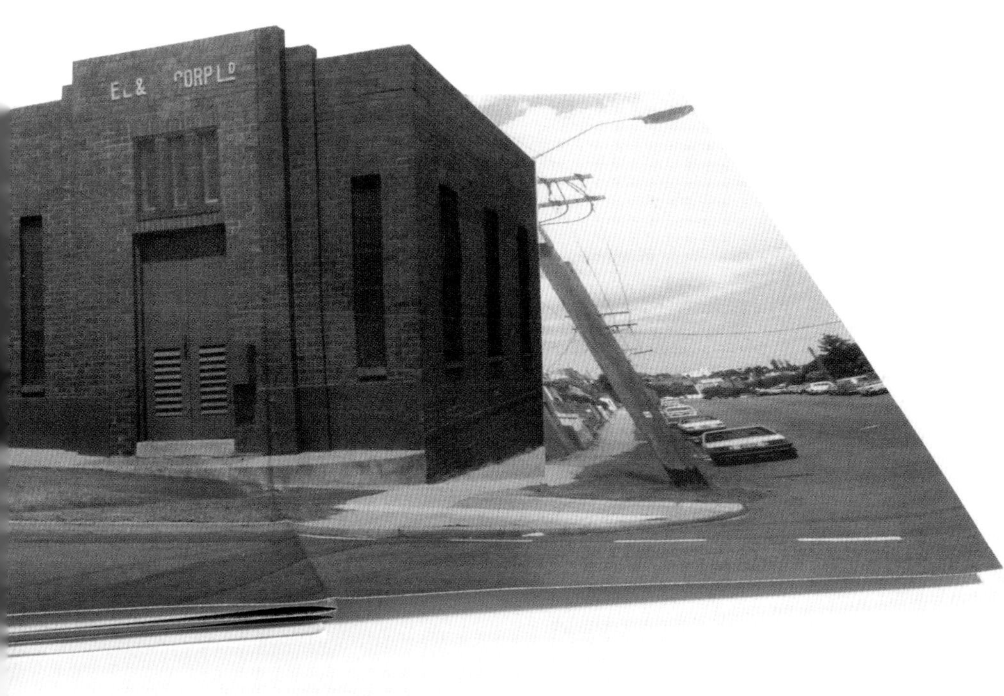

The locations of the pop-up substations are not identified, even though two have rather enigmatic company names on them, and one is marked with the date '1937'. The more you go back and forth through the three examples, the more they rise up from their black-and-white surrounding and draw attention to the fact that they are very carefully conceived buildings, rarely observed or remarked on in reality. They become more and more mysterious.

The book has no story, but is a report that literally unfolds in front of you as you open the pages. It points to all of the other substations that appear and disappear in the suburbs. After the book is closed up, the images fold back into their photographs, and into their context. As you turn the book over to its front cover, you note that the word 'Metaphysical' is an adjective describing 'Sydney', not just the booklet itself.

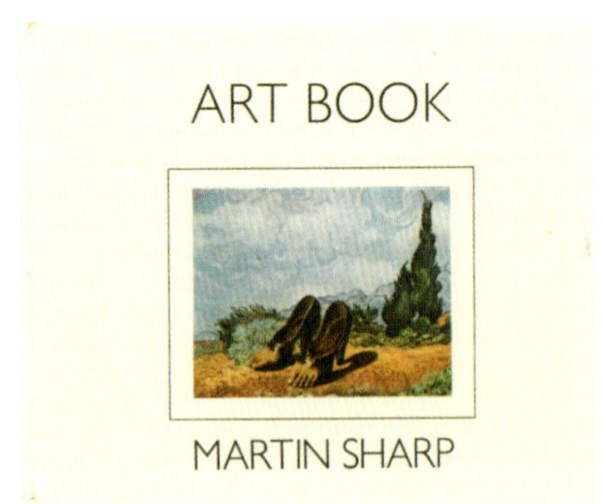

Martin Sharp
Art book 1972

The art book is a cliché among books: large, scholarly, full of images and with high production values, it is a common sign of culture and education. For Martin Sharp, satirist and journeyman through popular culture, it is a ready target.

Art book begins innocently enough, with title, author's name and one image on the cover. The book is small – much smaller than the stereotypical art book, but like a guidebook or pocket monograph. The colophon reveals that it is a commercial book. The typographer, photographer, printer, publisher and distributor are named, copyright is claimed and the usual warning against reproduction 'without permission ... except for review purposes' lends an irony to what follows.

Instead of a scholarly essay, the book begins with pictures – in fact, it is nothing but pictures, one per page. Each is a collage or merging of two well-known paintings, all highly recognisable, almost popular icons. Each image by Sharp uses a base painting by one artist, with small additions from another artist's painting. The additions are always in the same spatial schema as the host image and hence fuse into it – or maybe they do so because we are now uscd to reading multi-style images. In image after image, there is surprise and humour, not only in the unlikely pairings of artists but also in the collaged images themselves.

At the end of the book, there is a list of artists (but not the titles of the paintings, perhaps used 'without permission') 'on whose paintings Martin Sharp bases the central proposition of this book'. This is, I think, icon 1 + icon 2 = (new) double icon, or at least a new insight into icons 1 and 2. *Art book* is Sharp's reference book, both in the list of source icons and in the clear demonstration of his compositional method. At the heart of this book is the fact that all artists learn from other artists' works; and that for any practising artist, their influential precursors may well be a contradictory and strange group when brought together.

The colophon gives no indication of the print run, or that any signed or special editions might be part of the production. This is a book like any other found in a conventional book store, at one level, but an *Art book* probably like no other found in that same book store.

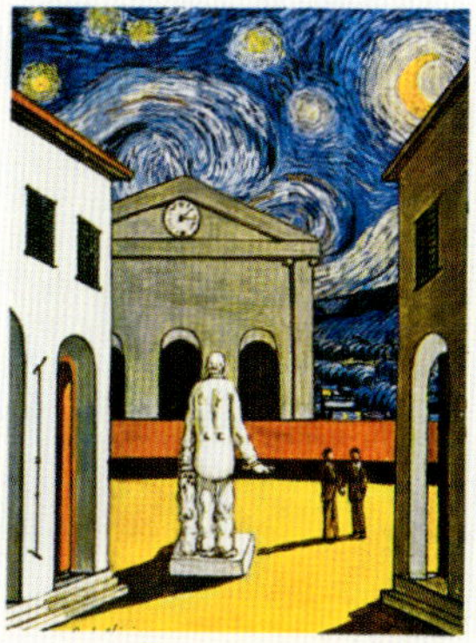

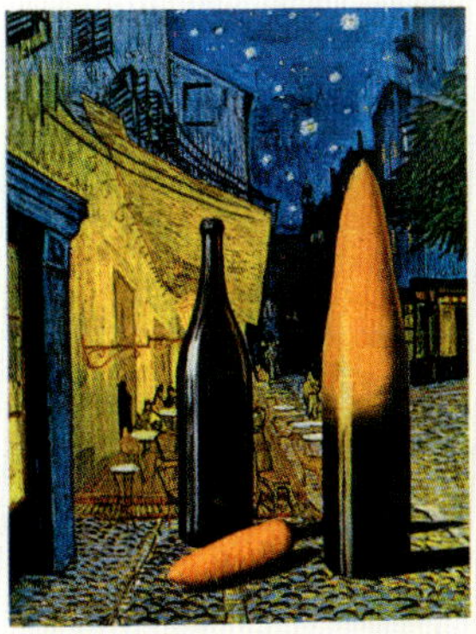

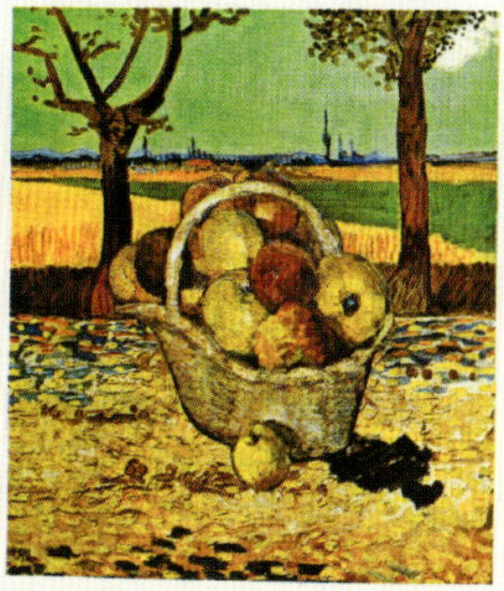

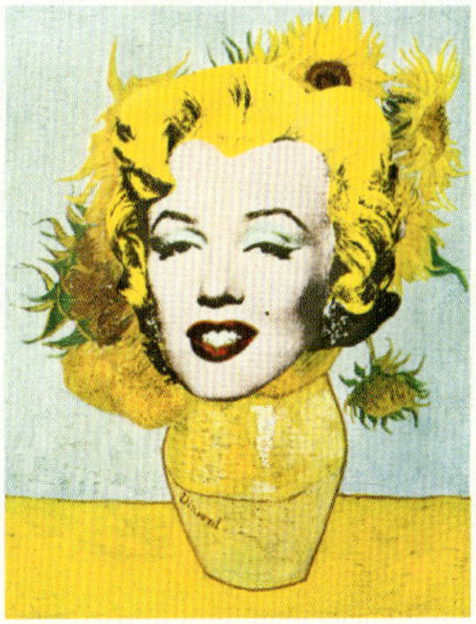

Paul Uhlmann
Eng 1987

This is a creation story simply told in words and given complexity through accompanying images. Eng is a character who is taken through a journey from 'nowhere to somewhere'. This might be the creative process, the work of the artist or the experience of the reader, or all three.

The story begins with the closed book. Smallish, about one centimetre thick and bound in black, cloth-covered boards, with the title and some forms and marks above it pressed into the cover, *Eng* feels like a standard book. The first pages confirm this impression, but as the pairing of words and images begins to unfold, the book starts to combine text and images with some subtlety.

The story is told through ten double-page spreads, with a few lines of text on the left-hand page and a single, full-page image on the right-hand page: white paper on the left, black paper on the right; apparent simplicity on the left, apparent complexity on the right. The text also has a symmetry to it – the first five pages plot the journey to 'nothing', the second five pages describe a vision that takes Eng to 'something … [a] new kind of sleep'. The text is conventional in that, once read, its physicality can be ignored.

The etchings, on the other hand (on the other side), play two roles. At first, you look into them via the adjacent words, as if the text contained the titles for the etchings, but then, because of their suggestive qualities, the etchings begin to evoke other responses. The etchings start working as 'titles' to the text, suggesting how the words might be played with.

Every illustrated book of 'image-plus-caption' works towards this condition. In *Eng*, the interaction is helped by the poetic nature of the story. In its text format, the story takes ten sentences to describe a single event, and the text has a unified narrative structure; in its visual format, the story is told in ten etchings that are surprisingly different in composition, each of which demands a slow reconnaissance.

At the end of the story, the last double-page spread says simply 'The End', with a small etching as a memory on the right-hand side page. Then come the cream endpapers and the black back cover closes the book to the left-hand side, whereupon you turn the book over the right-hand side to begin again.

One day ENG went
Northeast.
Over the sea.
In a boat.

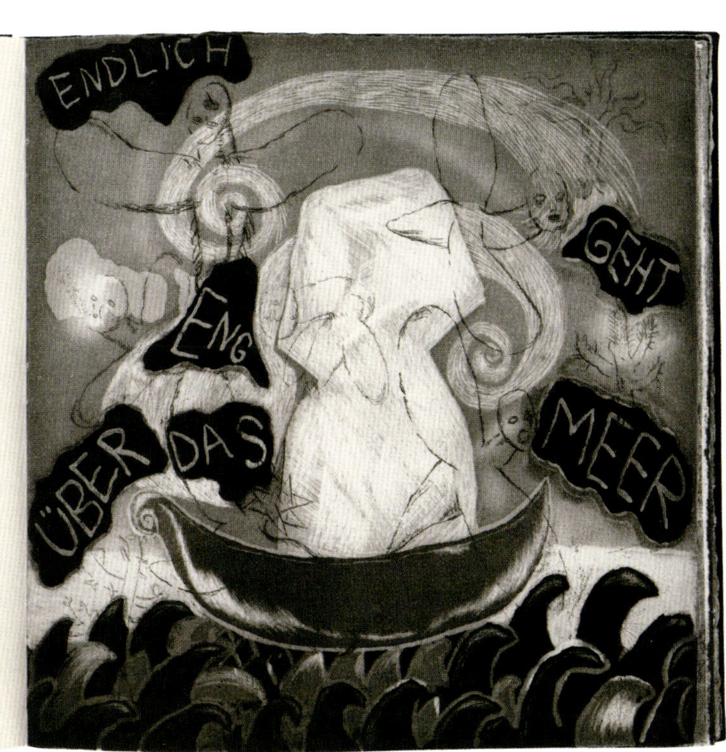

Murray Walker
Black rubber stamp syndrome 1983

Unlike most artists books, which use the cover as only one element beginning the composition of the book, this work has a cover that is complex, fascinating and, as it turns out, an apt summary of the book and sundry items contained therein. *Black rubber stamp syndrome*'s cover is the lid of a box of the sort that handkerchiefs or lingerie might come in. Walker uses the lid in its portrait format, encrusting it with rubber-stamped work, paper, found printed ephemera, erotic texts and paint.

When you take the lid off, you are confronted with a tableau of boxes, small objects and samples of materials. Two smaller boxes of the same proportion as the outer one have been stuck in the larger box, creating three open boxes, one inside the other. In a symmetrical overall composition, the outer zones are filled with a plastic wolf, bits of black fur, matches, plastic shoes and boots, some rubber. There is also a loose strip of shiny black fur. Nested in the smallest box is a small book.

This book is covered with more collage (like the outside lid), but it is also covered with red fish-net stocking material. More matches are found under the book, stuck to the box. On flipping through the book quickly, you are bombarded with page upon page of rubber-stamped images. These images range from legs (glamorous, stocking-advertisement type of legs), animal stamps, body parts such as heads, torsos and hands, 'happy hearts' (outline hearts with sentimental wishes written in them), cars, men in uniform, female office secretaries and women in seductive poses. The latter are taken from advertisements for fetish rubber-wear. The mixture of enhanced sex, office routine and humour is disarming.

There is a serious undercurrent in this ambience of amusement. The constant repetition of the stamps, both humorous and sexy, leads you to consider the interplay of 'male' and 'female' as socially defined roles; the use of layers and coverings that these roles require; and to face the suspicion that, while engaged in sex at least, we are closest to our animal nature. But there's more: the drawings taken from rubber-wear catalogues reveal a desire for formal purity, with the garments and accessories promising to transform real, 'misshapen' bodies into ensembles of near-Platonic spheres and cones. Here again, humour intervenes: page 47 of the book has the stamped image of a woman with particularly spherical breasts, under the caption 'My bosoms are absolutely unbelievable!' Silliness and the desire for transcendence mix together to show that there is also a ludicrous aspect to sex.

When you put the book back in its place, you notice that the objects and materials are three-dimensional bits and pieces relating to the book. When you put the lid back on, the puns in the work's title take hold of you, and suggest that the work is a kind of Pandora's Box.

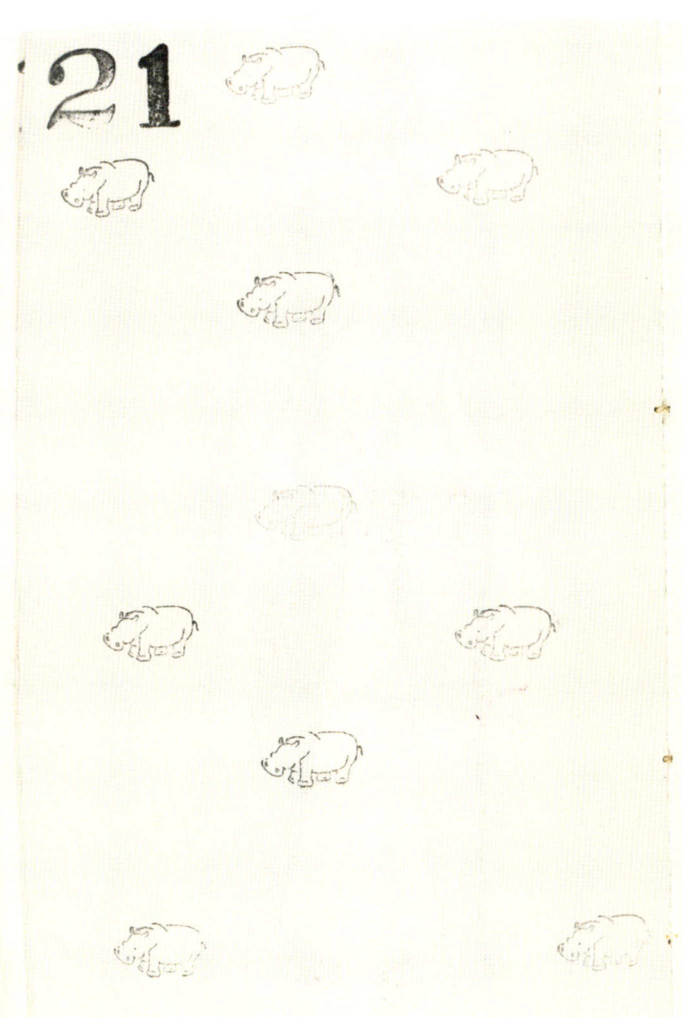

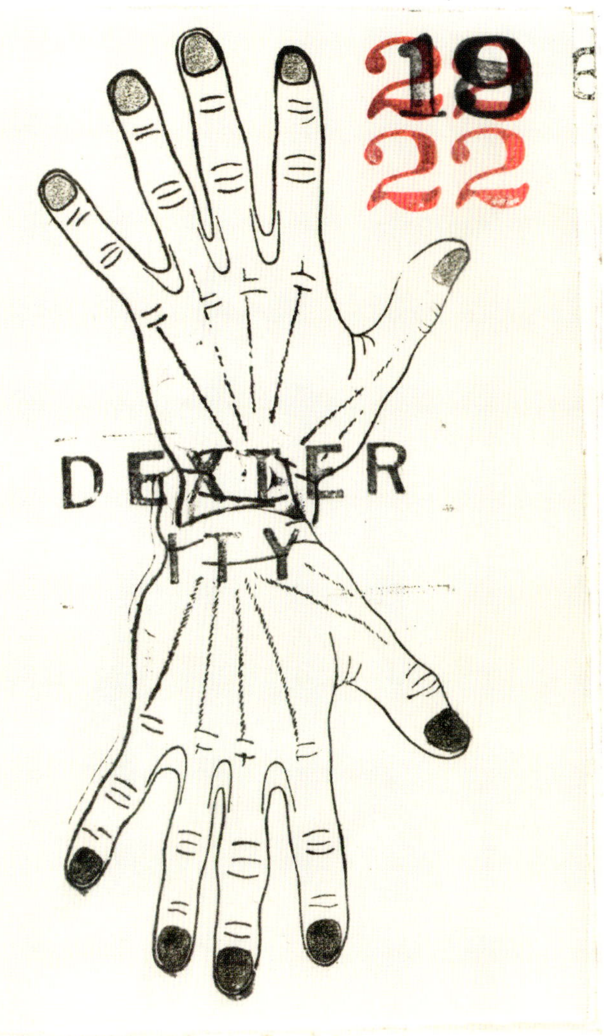

21

19
22

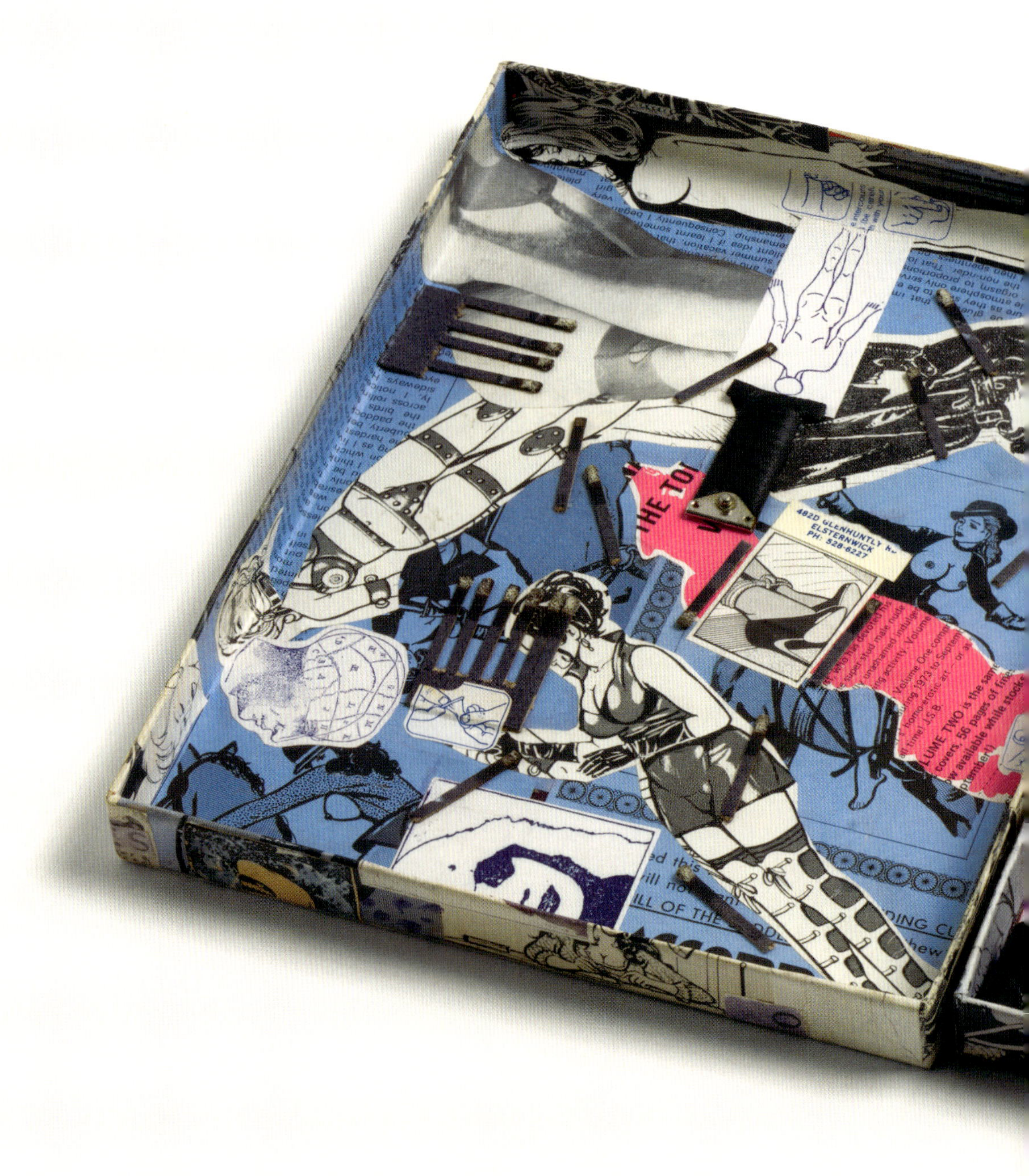

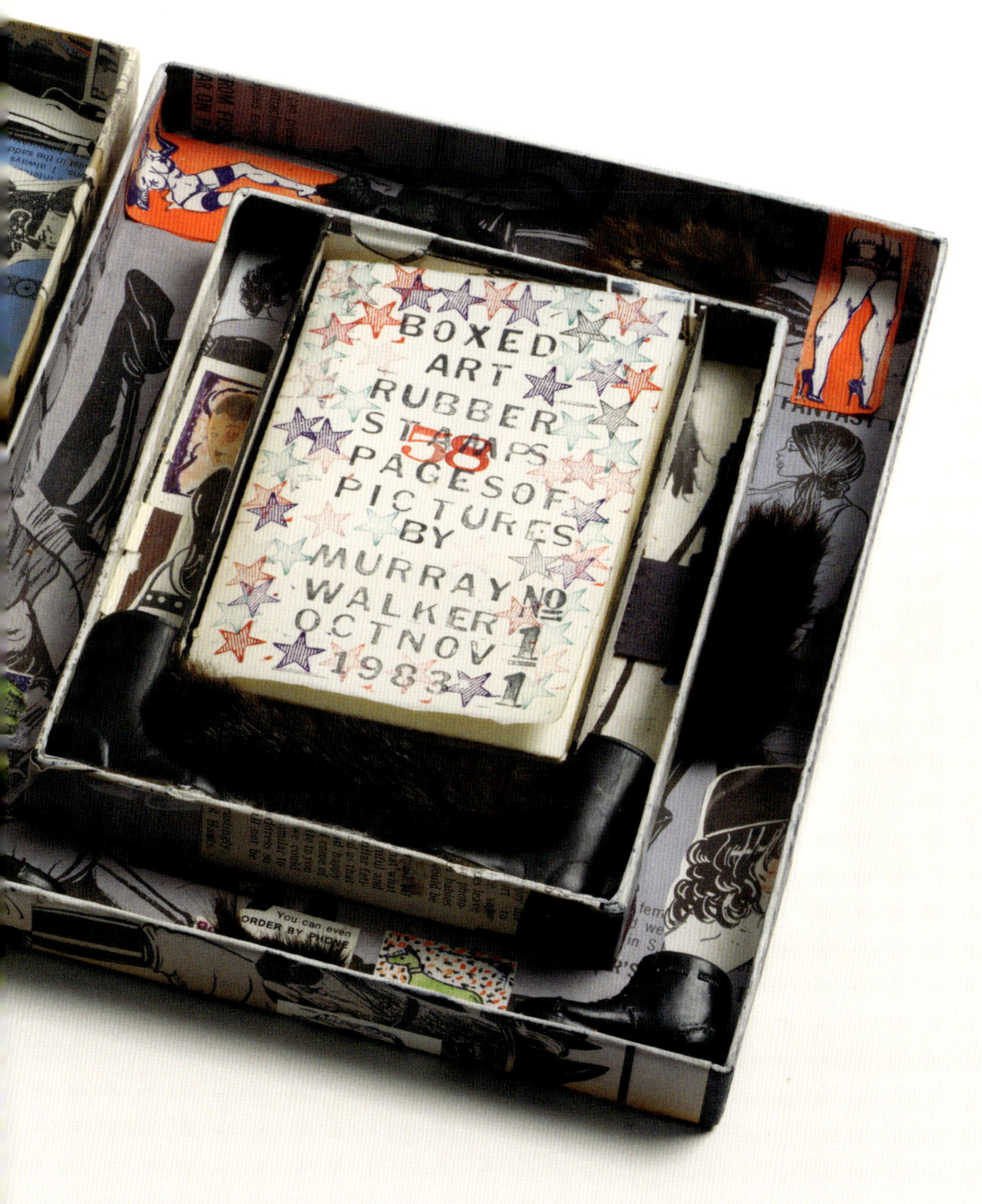

BOXED
ART
RUBBER
STAMPS
58
PAGES OF
PICTURES
BY
MURRAY N?
WALKER 1
OCT NOV
1983 1

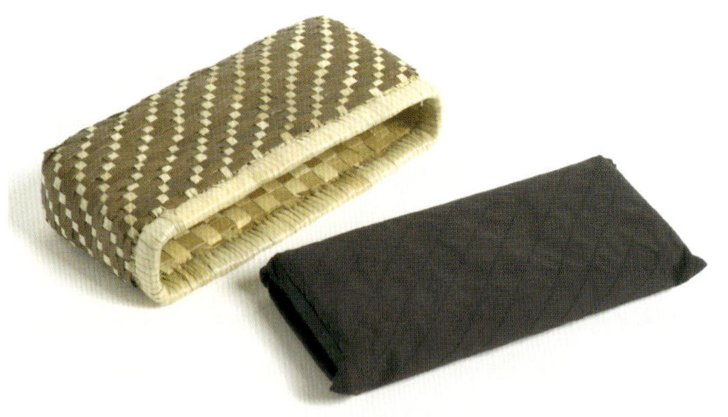
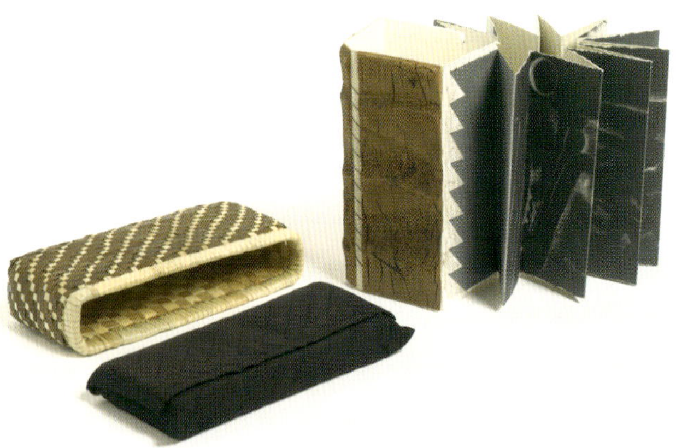
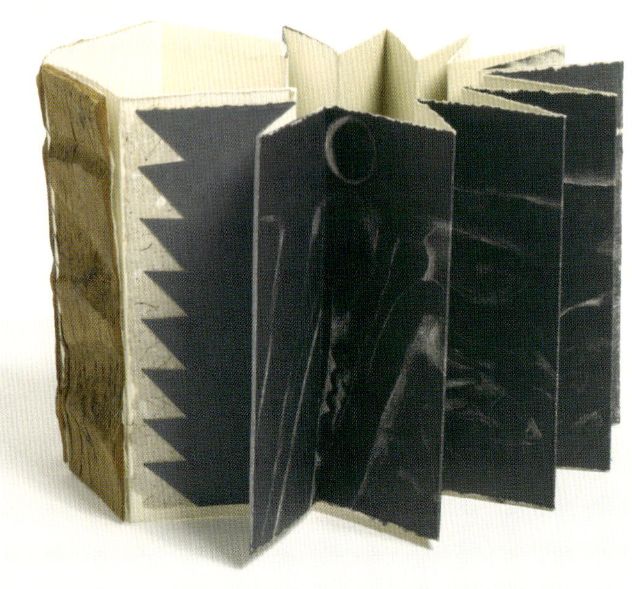
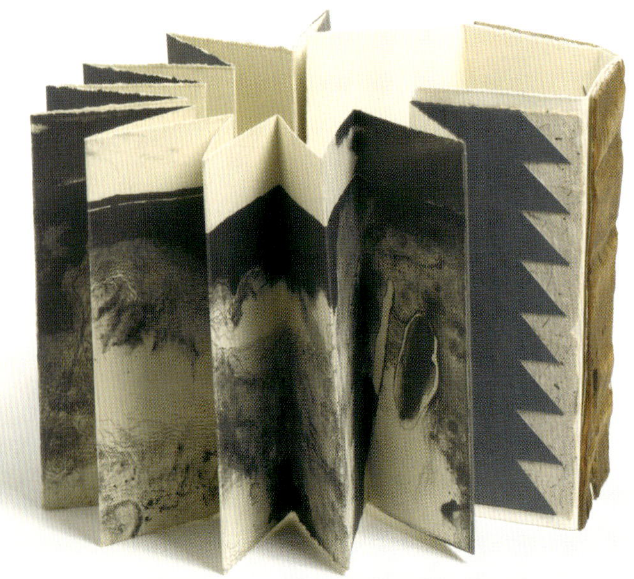

Robin White
Walking to Tebuatarawa 1991

This book begins as a purse-like object, easy to hold in one hand: a black cloth bag inside a slip-case woven from grass. On removal, the cloth bag opens like a satchel, and reveals diagonal and zigzag stitching, echoing the diagonal weave of the slip-case. Inside the satchel there is a bark-covered object: a book with very thick rough covers. Twelve stitches of grey thread, like hatching, are visible on the spine's edge, and draw attention to the thick paper covers under the bark.

On opening the book, you find that it is a long accordion fold of paper, held in the book by grey end papers. You can either look through the book fold after fold, or push it out into a long, zigzag landscape that billows out from the covers and returns. On the first page, fifteen placenames are listed, from 'Buota' to 'Tebuatarawa'. Then follows a long landscape, or rather seascape, which takes you from night-time at one end, to dawn halfway along the folds, then to daylight at the right-hand end. Because the accordion fold is glued at both ends to the covers, it cannot be seen as a long flat panorama, but only as a curved bow out from the spine of the book. On the last page, the placenames are listed again, but in reverse order, implying a walk back or maybe a memory of the walk.

The journey – the walk implied in the book's title – is not only given a visual image in the list of names and the panorama, but is also acted out through the step-by-step continuity of the folds and through the resistance of the whole to being spread out flat. When handling the book, you easily slip from the considerations of one fold (a single pace) to the length of the entire accordion fold (the whole journey). The book is a sculpture of time, using the walk as the example of linear time, and daytime as a counterpoint of cyclical time. Then there is also the walk back ...

The seascape drawn over the accordion folds looks out to sea from the land, with the horizon line drawing together the black-ink of night-time at the beginning (left) of the panorama and the white paper of the daytime at the end (right) of the panorama. No indication is given of the distance between the placenames, nor is it clear from the book that they are places (although Tabiteuea appears in the Kiribati Islands in the *Macquarie world atlas*, 1984, page 79).

The book is easy to repack: doing this, you note that it uses materials associated with books (wood, paper, grass, cloth, thread, string) separated out and exposed in their strongest and most individual way.

LIST OF BOOKS BY THE FEATURED ARTISTS

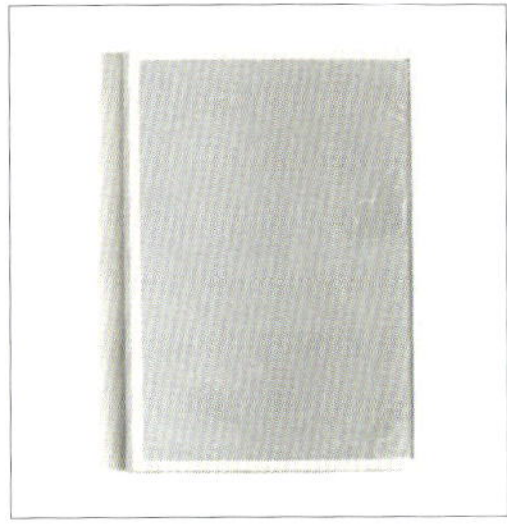

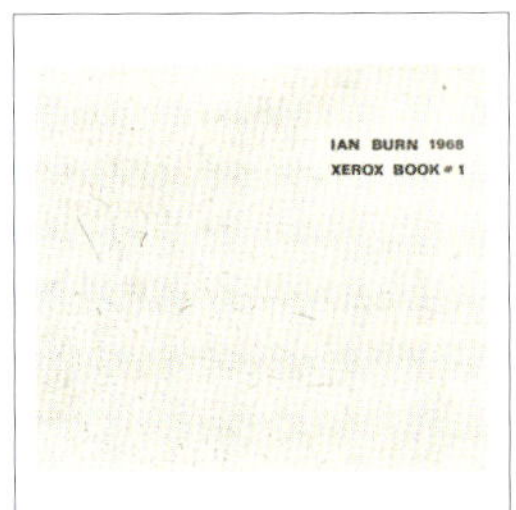

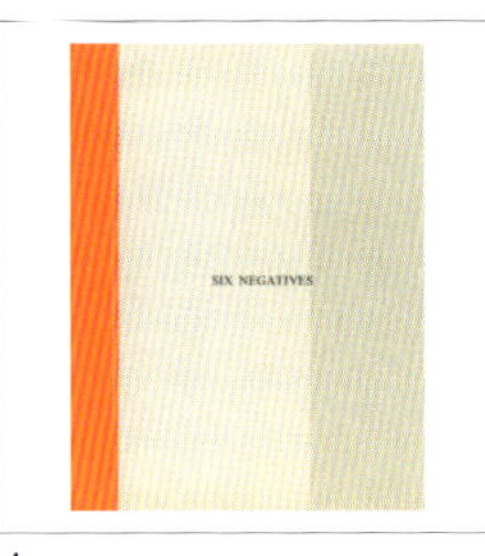

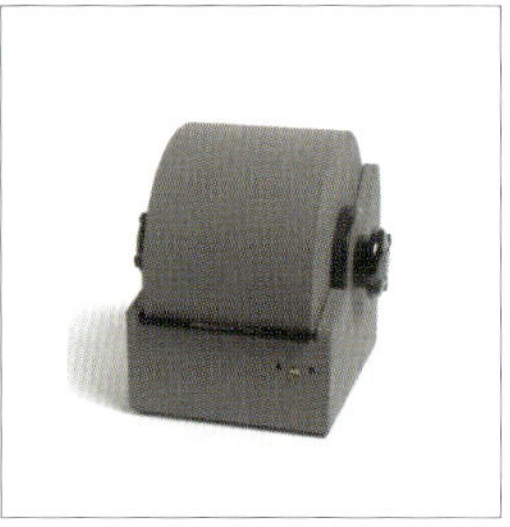

1   2   3   4   5

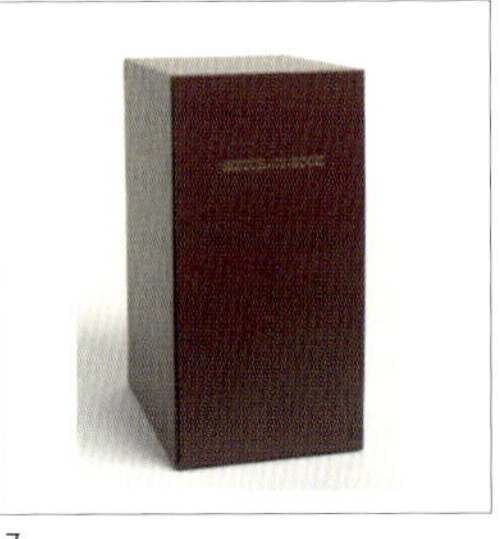

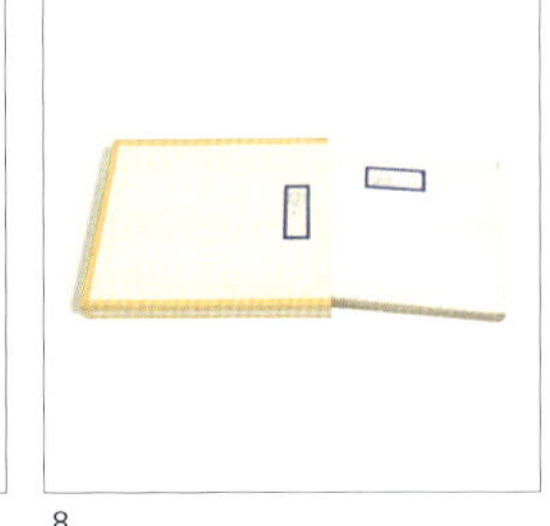

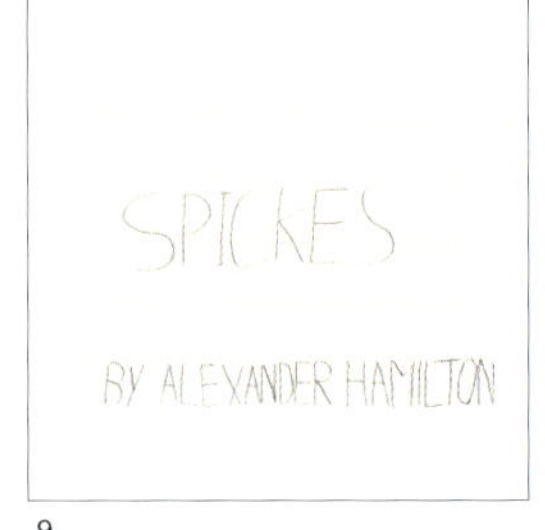

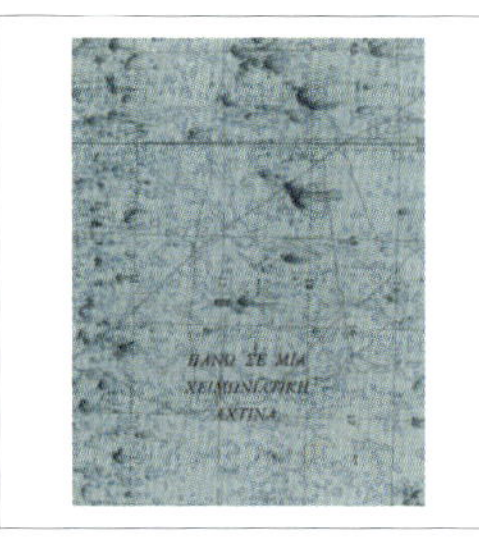

6   7   8   9   10

Ian BURN
Australia, 1939–1999

1   *MIRROR PIECE*, Melbourne, Victoria, 1967
mirror and glass on a wood support; printed instructions
for installation
frame: 52.8 x 37.5 x 2.8 cm; installation: 52.8 x 330.7 cm
sheet (each): 27.5 x 21.4 cm
Purchased 1978 78.844A–B

2   *XEROX BOOK #1*, Melbourne, Victoria, 1968
photocopies, printed in black ink
book (closed): 21.2 x 27.6 cm
book (open): 21.2 x 50.7 cm
Purchased 1978 78.847

3   *ABSTRACTS OF PERCEPTION #2*,
Melbourne, Victoria, 1968–69
typewritten text, black-and-white photographs
in plastic sleeves in folder
book (closed): 31.5 x 24.3 cm
book (open): 31.5 x 48.8 cm
Purchased 1978 78.848

Ian BURN
Australia, 1939–1999

Mel RAMSDEN
England, born 1944

4   *SIX NEGATIVES*, Melbourne, Victoria, 1968–69
offset lithographs, printed in black ink, in plastic sleeves
folio (closed): 31.0 x 23.6 cm; binder: 28.0 x 21.6 cm
sheet (each): 27.8 x 21.4 cm
Purchased 1978 78.851

5   *(INDEX (MODEL (…)))*, Melbourne, Victoria, 1970
typed statements collaged onto 12 file cards
in metal rotary card file
object: 23.0 x 23.0 x 21.8 cm; card (each): 7.6 x 12.6 cm
Purchased 1978 78.850

Gaynor CARDEW
Australia, 1951–1999

6   *REQUIEM TO AN EPIDERMIS*, Canberra,
Australian Capital Territory, 1984
unique book, 18 pages
handmade paper, pencil diagrams
book (closed): 43.8 x 30.6 x 2.8 cm
book (open): 43.8 x 62.0 cm
Purchased 1985 85.1477

Christopher CROFT
Australia, born 1947

7   *SKETCH-OF-BOOK*, Melbourne, Victoria, 1983
copy 3 of edition of 5
etchings, printed in red ink, on handmade paper;
accordion folded, fixed in wooden, hinged frame
in cloth-covered slip-case
case (closed): 30.5 x 20.2 x 15.7 cm
frame (closed): 28.5 x 20.6 cm
frame (open): dimensions variable
Purchased 1986 86.1229.1–6
© Christopher Croft. Licensed by VISCOPY,
Australia, 2007.

Ross GROUNDS
Australia, 1949–1998

8   *FIRE-GRID*, East Brunswick, Victoria, 1970
unique book
photographs and typed notes on 12-sheet
accordion fold in card, in cardboard slip-case
slip-case: 30.8 x 38.2 x 3.6 cm
book (folded): 27.6 x 36.4 x 3.3 cm
book (unfolded): 27.6 x 439.2 x 0.1 cm
Purchased 1972 72.138

Alexander HAMILTON
Australia, born 1958

9   *SPICKES*, Melbourne, Victoria, c. 1986
copy 13 of edition of 100
bound book, 14 pages
black cloth-covered board covers, drawings
and handwritten text, photocopy on paper
book (closed): 27.3 x 39.2 x 1.0 cm
book (open): 27.0 x 76.0 cm
Purchased 1987 87.830

Petr HEREL
Czechoslovakia, born 1943

10   *ON A RAY OF WINTER SUN*, Canberra,
Australian Capital Territory, 1988
copy 12 of edition of 13
etchings, printed in colour; letterpress text in
3 folios of folded paper in paper folder with cover
book (closed): 19.4 x 14.8 x 0.3 cm
book (open): 19.4 x 30.4 cm
Gordon Darling Fund 1989 89.362
© Petr Herel.

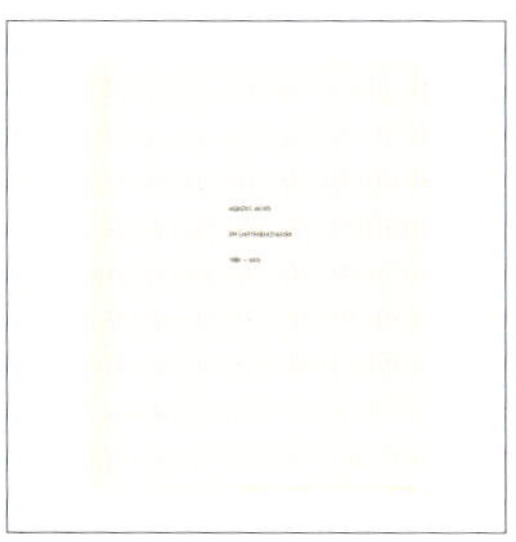  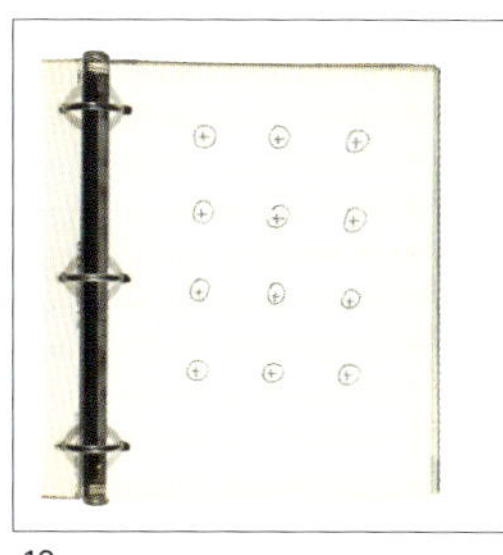 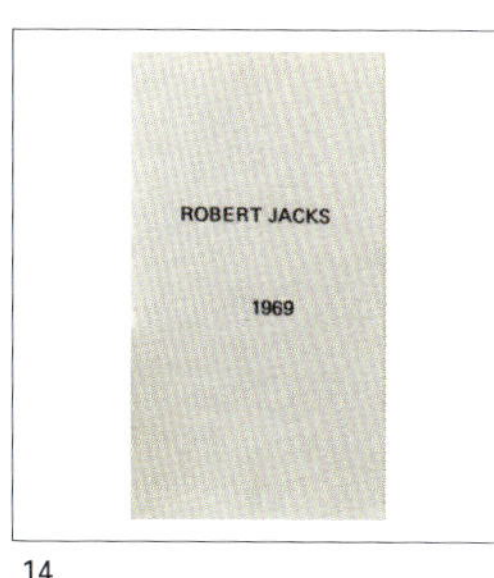 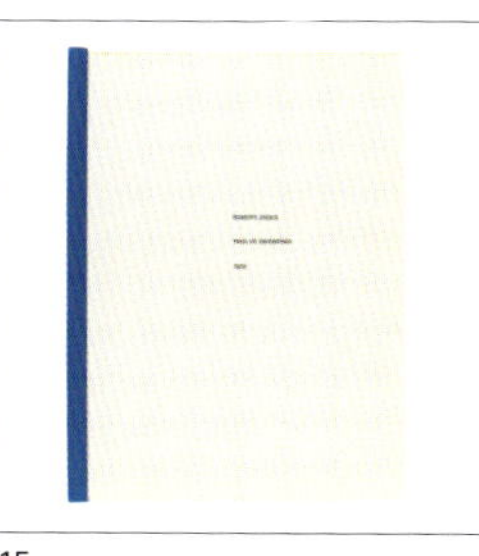

11   12   13   14   15

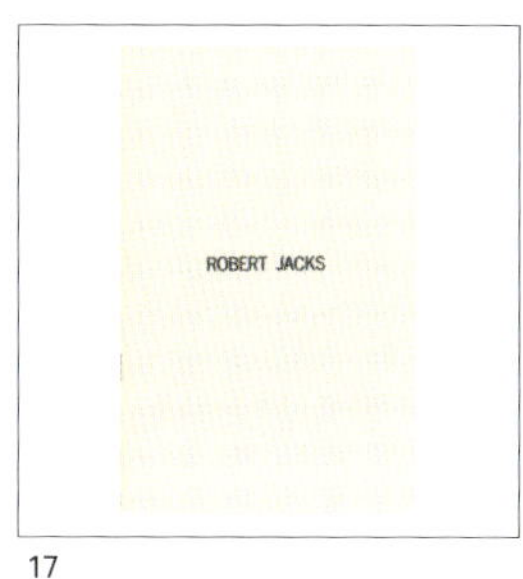 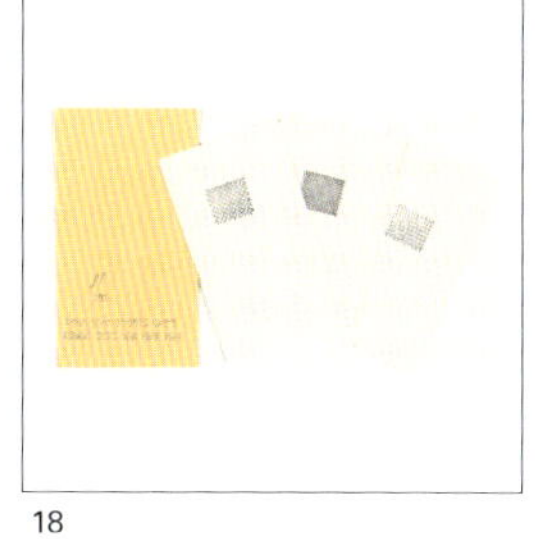 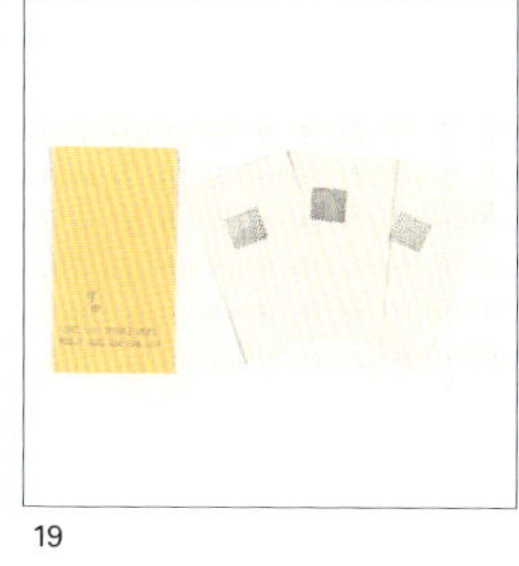 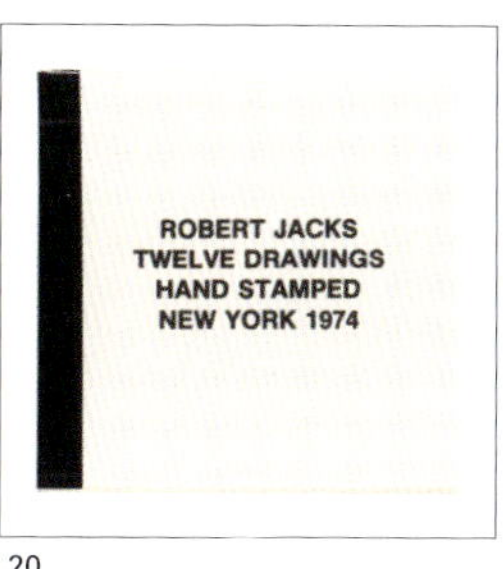

16   17   18   19   20

Robert JACKS
Australia, born 1943

11   *AN UNFINISHED WORK*, New York,
United States, 1966–71
photocopies, printed in black ink, in plastic cover
book (closed): 28.0 x 22.7 x 0.3 cm
book (open): 28.0 x 42.8 cm
Purchased 1977   77.1032

12   *AN UNFINISHED WORK VOLUME I. Specifications for
works exhibited at Whitney Museum Artists Resource
Centre*, New York, United States, 1966–71
photocopies, printed in black ink; pencil
and black-and-white photographs
folder: 28.8 x 26.8 x 5.8 cm
sheet (each): 28.0 x 21.7 cm
Purchased 1979   79.2647

13   *AN UNFINISHED WORK VOLUME II. Specifications for
works exhibited at Whitney Museum Artists Resource
Centre*, New York, United States, 1966–71
photocopies, printed in black ink; pencil, crayon
and black-and-white photographs
folder: 28.8 x 26.8 x 5.8 cm
sheet (each): 28.0 x 21.7 cm
Purchased 1979   79.2648

14   *1–12*, New York, United States, 1969
offset printed booklet, printed in black ink
book (closed): 9.2 x 5.6 x 1.0 cm
book (open): 9.2 x 10.8 cm
Purchased 1977   77.1031

15   *TWELVE DRAWINGS*, New York, United States, 1970
photocopies, printed in black ink, in plastic cover
book (closed): 28.5 x 22.2 x 0.3 cm
book (open): 28.5 x 41.2 cm
Purchased 1977   77.1028

16   *TWELVE RED GRIDS*, New York, United States, 1973
hand-stamped rubber stamps, printed in red ink;
red taped spine
book (closed): 4.0 x 12.8 x 0.2 cm
book (open): 11.4 x 12.8 x 0.2 cm
Purchased 1977   77.1037

17   *INSTALLATIONS. 1971–1973*, New York,
United States, 1974
offset lithographs, printed in black ink
book (closed): 21.4 x 14.0 x 0.2 cm
book (open): 21.4 x 28.0 cm
Purchased 1977   77.1040

18   *THREE HAND STAMPED GRIDS*, New York,
United States, 1974
hand-stamped rubber stamps, printed in black ink
envelope: 15.4 x 8.6 cm; sheet (each): 12.8 x 7.6 cm
Purchased 1977   77.1047
Edition 89 of 100

19   *THREE HAND STAMPED GRIDS*, New York,
United States, 1974
hand-stamped rubber stamps, printed in black ink
envelope: 15.3 x 8.6 cm; sheet (each): 12.7 x 7.6 cm
Purchased 1977   77.1048
Edition 90 of 100

20   *TWELVE DRAWINGS*, New York, United States, 1974
hand-stamped rubber stamps, printed in black ink;
black taped spine
book (closed): 11.4 x 12.8 x 0.2 cm;
book (open): 11.4 x 25.6 cm
Gift of the Philip Morris Arts Grant, 1982   83.2825

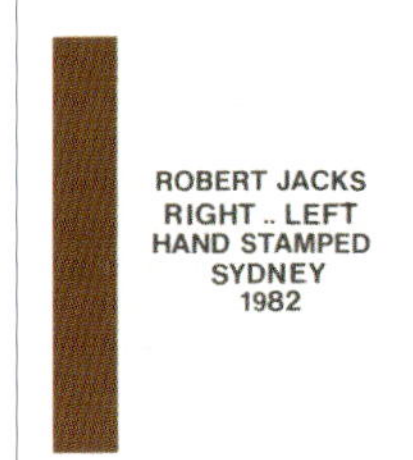

21

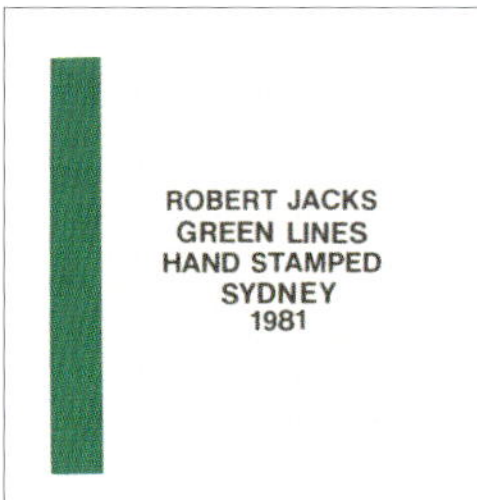

22

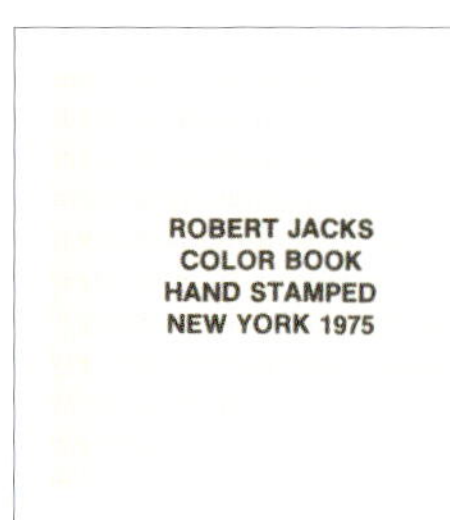

23

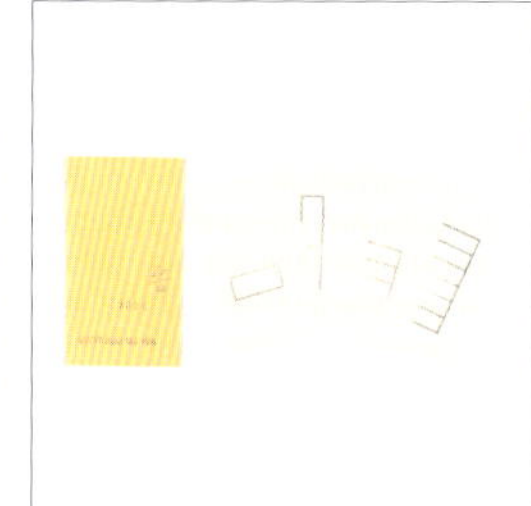

24

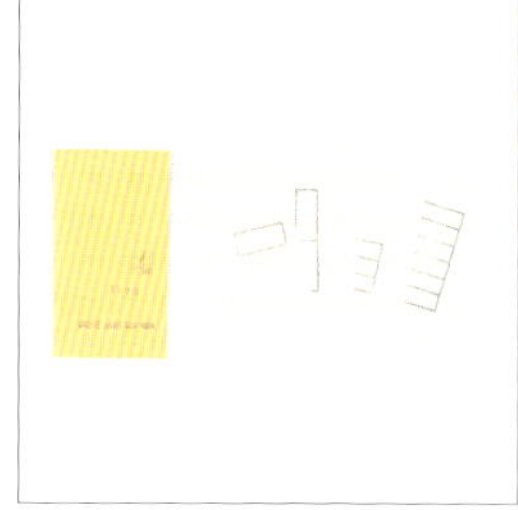

25

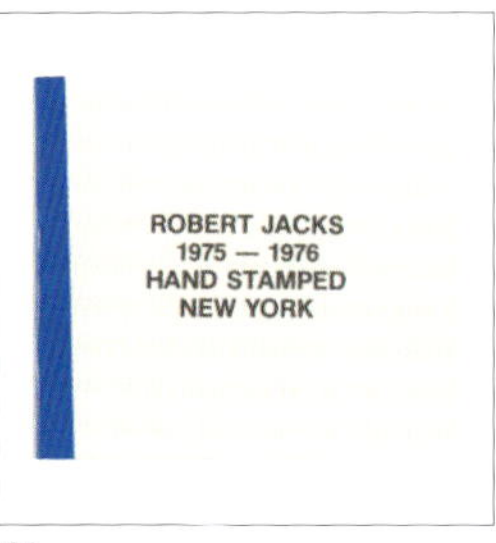

26

27

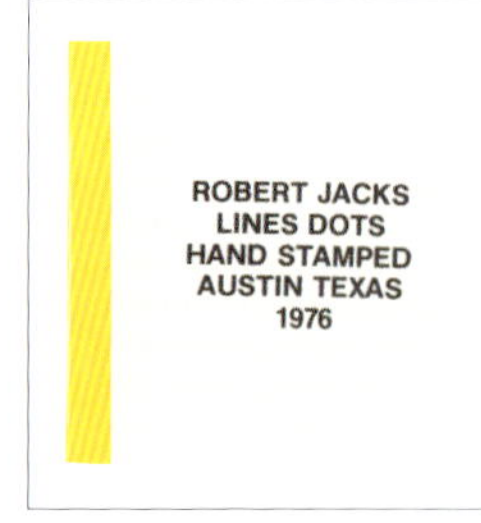

28

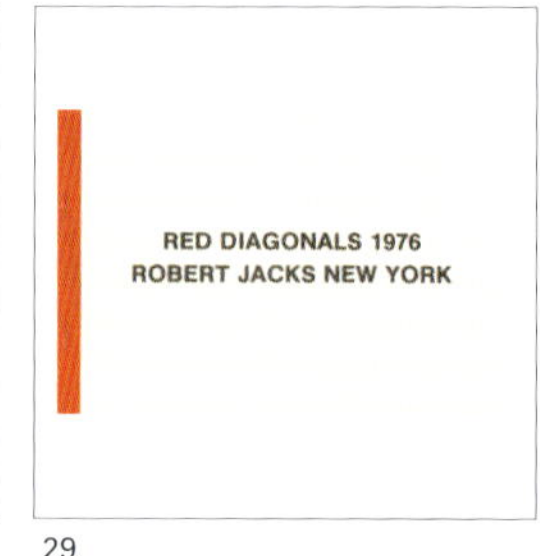

29

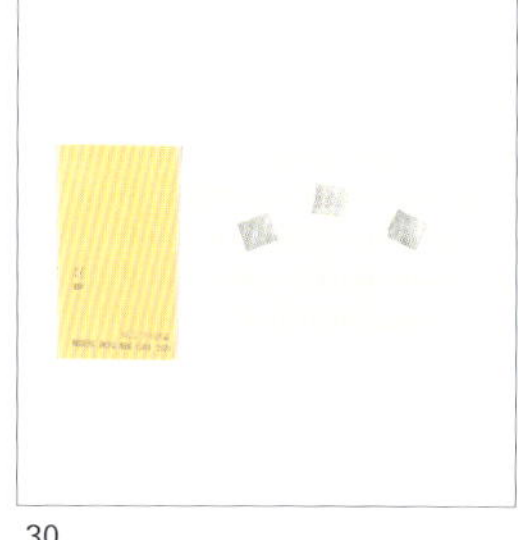

30

21 *RIGHT .. LEFT*, New York, United States, 1975
hand-stamped rubber stamps, printed in colour;
brown taped spine
book (closed): 11.4 x 12.8 x 0.2 cm
book (open): 11.4 x 25.6 cm
Gift of the artist, 2006 2006.835.3

22 *GREEN LINES*, New York, United States, 1975
hand-stamped rubber stamps, printed in green ink;
green taped spine
book (closed): 11.4 x 12.8 x 0.2 cm
book (open): 11.4 x 25.6 cm
Gift of the artist, 2006 2006.835.4

23 *COLOR BOOK*, New York, United States, 1975
hand-stamped rubber stamps, printed in colour;
white taped spine
book (closed): 11.4 x 12.8 x 0.2 cm
book (open): 11.4 x 25.6 cm
Gift of the Philip Morris Arts Grant, 1982 83.2826

24 *[Four hand stamped grids]*, New York,
United States, 1975
hand-stamped rubber stamps, printed in black ink
envelope: 15.4 x 8.6 cm; sheet (each): 12.8 x 7.6 cm
Purchased 1977 77.1049.A–D
Edition 60 of 100

25 *[Four hand stamped grids]*, New York,
United States, 1975
hand-stamped rubber stamps, printed in black ink
envelope: 15.4 x 8.6 cm; sheet (each): 12.8 x 7.6 cm
Purchased 1977 77.1050.A–D
Edition 61 of 100

26 *HAND STAMPED NEW YORK*, New York,
United States, 1975–76
hand-stamped rubber stamps, printed in colour
book (closed): 11.5 x 12.8 cm; book (open): 11.5 x 25.6 cm
Purchased 1977 77.1038 (unbound); 77.1039 (bound)

27 *40 STAMPED PRINTS*, New York, United States, 1976
rubber stamps, printed in colour
sheet (each): 12.6 x 11.4 cm
Gift of Anonymous Donor, 1990 90.1108.399 1–40

28 *LINES DOTS*, Austin, Texas, United States, 1976
hand-stamped rubber stamps, printed in colour;
yellow taped spine
book (closed): 11.6 x 12.8 x 0.2 cm
book (open): 11.6 x 25.6 cm
Gift of the Philip Morris Arts Grant, 1982 83.2827

29 *RED DIAGONALS*, New York, United States, 1976
offset printed book, printed in red ink
book (closed): 14.1 x 21.7 cm
book (open): 14.1 x 43.4 cm
Purchased 1977 77.1045 (unbound)
Gift of an Anonymous Donor, 1990 90.1108.400 (bound)

30 *HAND STAMPED NEW YORK*, New York,
United States, 1976
hand-stamped rubber stamps, printed in black ink
envelope: 15.4 x 8.6 cm; sheet (each): 12.7 x 7.6 cm
Purchased 1977 77.1052.A–C

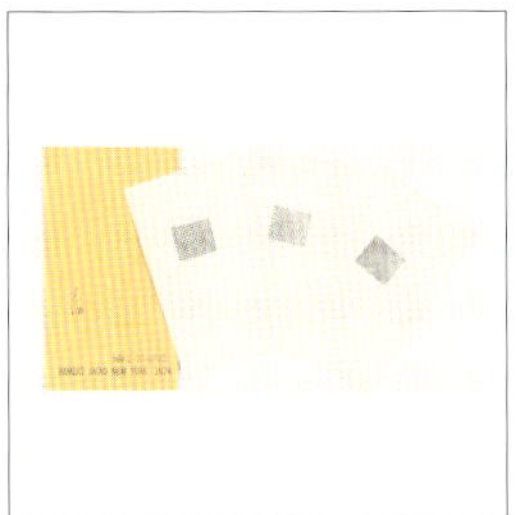

31

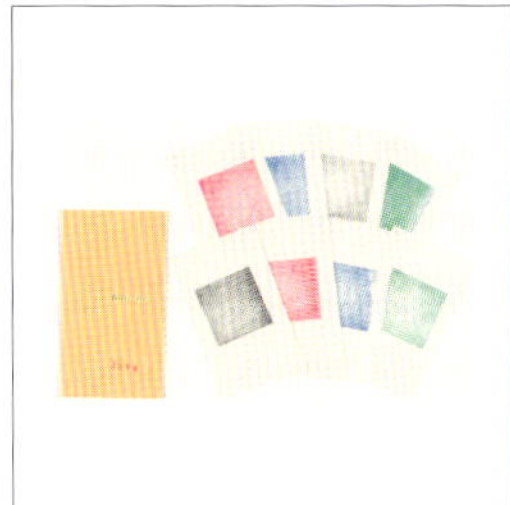

32

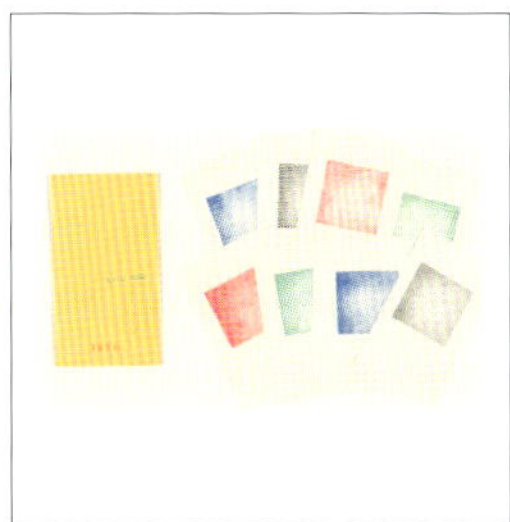

33

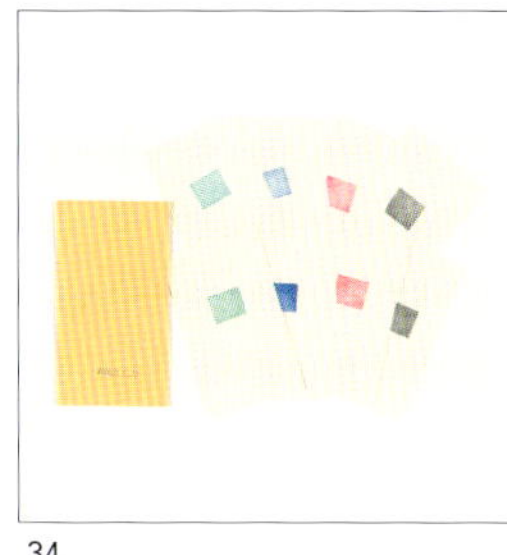

34

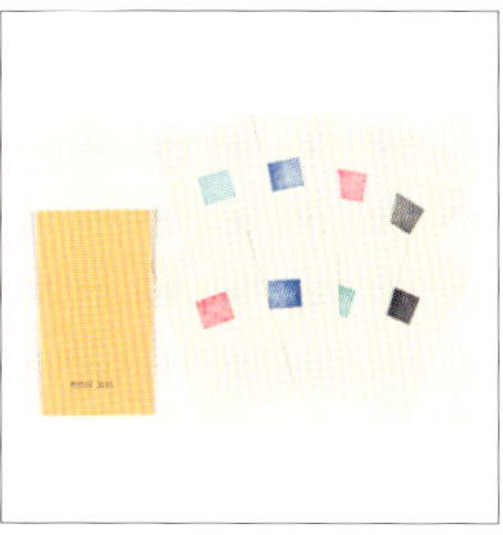

35

36

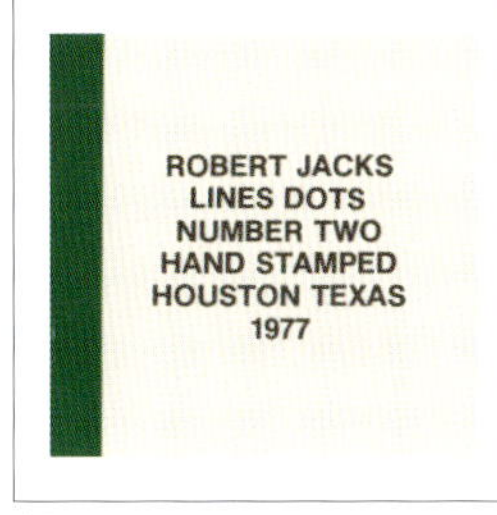

37

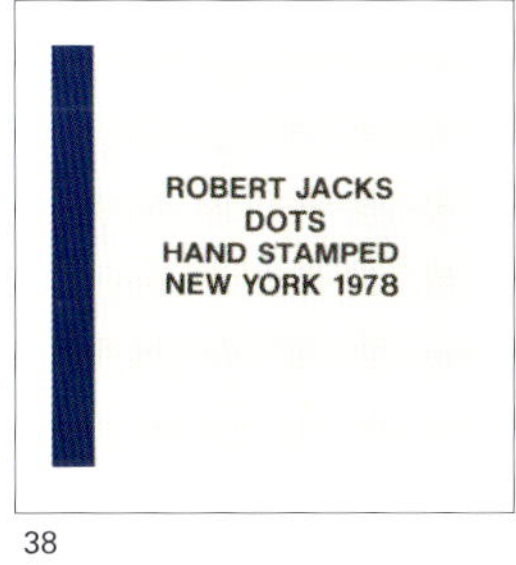

38

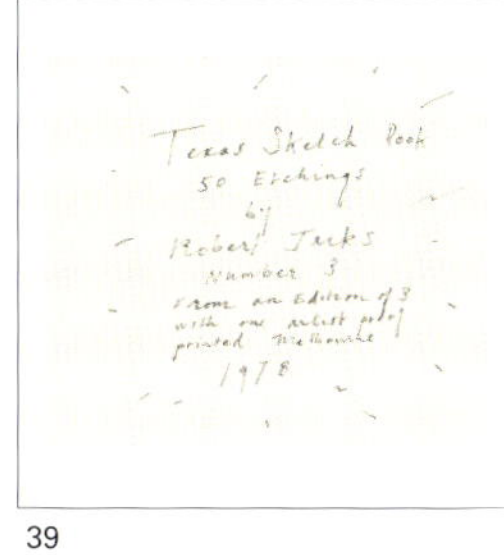

39

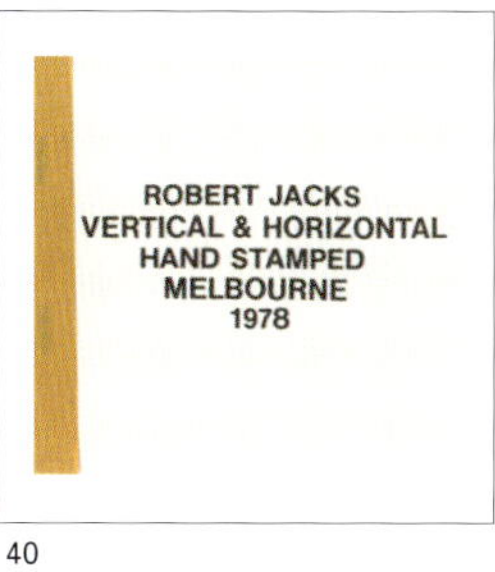

40

31 *HAND STAMPED NEW YORK*, New York,
United States, 1976
hand-stamped rubber stamps, printed in black ink
envelope: 15.4 x 8.6 cm; sheet (each): 12.7 x 7.6 cm
Purchased 1977 77.1053.A–C
Edition 18 of 100

32 *[Eight hand stamped prints]*, New York,
United States, 1976
hand-stamped rubber stamps, printed in colour
envelope: 15.4 x 8.6 cm; sheet (each): 12.7 x 7.6 cm
Purchased 1977 77.1024.A–H

33 *[Eight hand stamped prints]*, New York,
United States, 1976
hand-stamped rubber stamps, printed in colour
envelope: 15.4 x 8.6 cm; sheet (each): 12.7 x 7.6 cm
Purchased 1977 77.1025.A–H

34 *[Eight hand stamped prints]*, New York,
United States, c. 1976
hand-stamped rubber stamps, printed in colour
envelope: 15.3 x 8.7 cm; sheet (each): 12.8 x 7.6 cm
Purchased 1977 77.1046.A–H

35 *[Eight hand stamped prints]*, New York,
United States, c. 1976
hand-stamped rubber stamps, printed in colour
envelope: 15.3 x 8.7 cm; sheet (each): 12.8 x 7.6 cm
Purchased 1977 77.1051.A–H

36 *TWO FOUR-PART DRAWINGS*,
New York, United States, 1977
hand-stamped images, printed in green ink
book (closed): 15.2 x 11.4 cm
book (open): 15.2 x 22.8 cm
Gift of the artist, 2007 2007.354

37 *LINES DOTS NUMBER TWO*, Houston, Texas,
United States, 1977
hand-stamped rubber stamps, printed in colour;
green tape
book (closed): 11.5 x 12.8 x 0.2 cm
book (open): 11.5 x 25.6 cm
Purchased 1977 77.1027

38 *DOTS*, New York, United States, 1978
hand-stamped rubber stamps, printed in colour;
dark-blue taped spine
book (closed): 11.6 x 12.8 x 0.2 cm
book (open): 11.6 x 25.6 cm
Gift of the Philip Morris Arts Grant, 1982 83.2829

39 *TEXAS SKETCH BOOK*, Melbourne, Victoria, 1978
title page handwritten in felt-tip pen; etchings printed in
black ink on paper; bound in black leather with gilt title
book (closed): 26.0 x 34.5 x 4.4 cm
book (open): 26.0 x 68.0 cm
Purchased 1980 80.3796.1–51

40 *VERTICAL & HORIZONTAL*, Melbourne,
Victoria, 1978
hand-stamped rubber stamps, printed in colour;
brown taped spine
book (closed): 11.6 x 12.8 x 0.2 cm
book (open): 11.6 x 25.6 cm
Gift of the Philip Morris Arts Grant, 1982 83.2828

41 *RED DOTS*, Sydney, New South Wales, 1979
hand-stamped rubber stamps, printed in red ink;
red taped spine
book (closed): 11.6 x 12.8 x 0.2 cm
book (open): 11.6 x 25.6 cm
Purchased 1981 81.1669

42 *BLACK LINES*, Sydney, New South Wales, 1980
hand-stamped rubber stamps, printed in black ink;
black taped spine
book (closed): 11.3 x 12.6 x 0.2 cm
book (open): 11.3 x 25.2 cm
Purchased 1981 81.1663

Carol BRUNS (coordinator)
United States, born 1943

Robert JACKS (coordinator)
Australia, born 1943

43 *SEVENTY-SIX PAGES*, New York, United States, 1977
photocopies, printed in black ink
book (closed): 28.0 x 21.6 x 1.0 cm
book (open): 28.0 x 43.2 cm
Gift of an anonymous donor 1990 90.1108.407

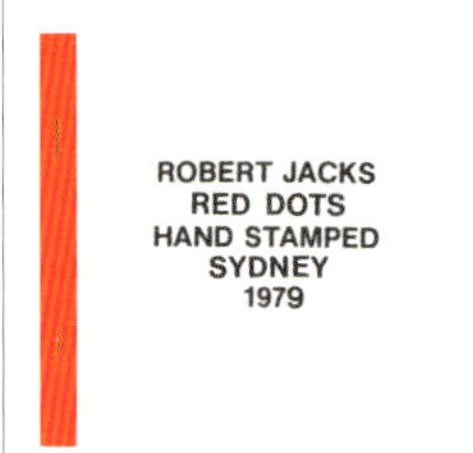

41

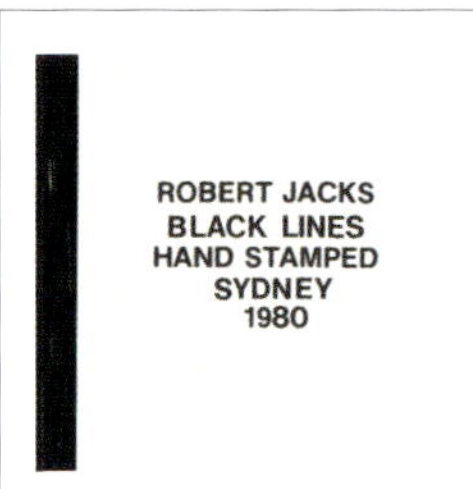

42

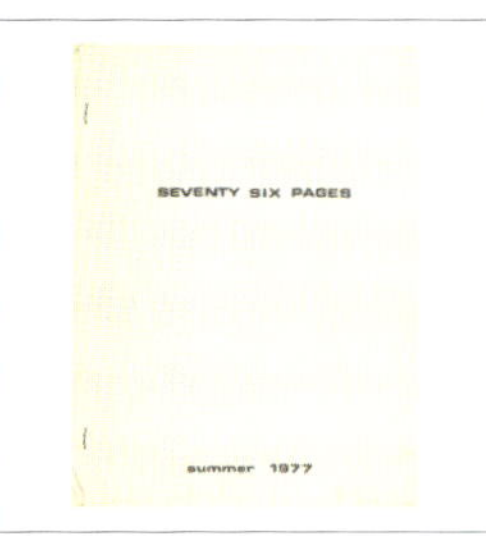

43

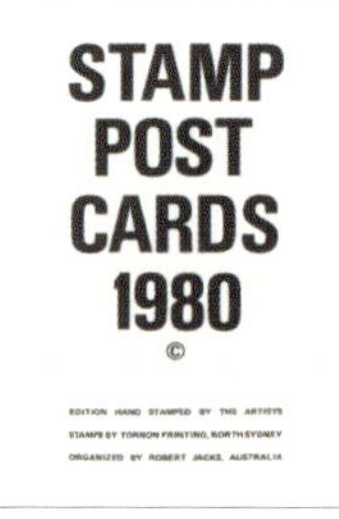

44

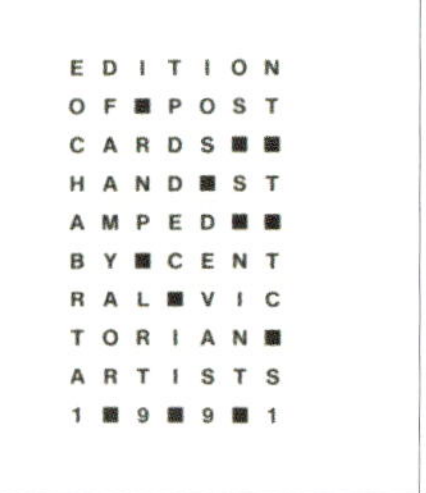

45

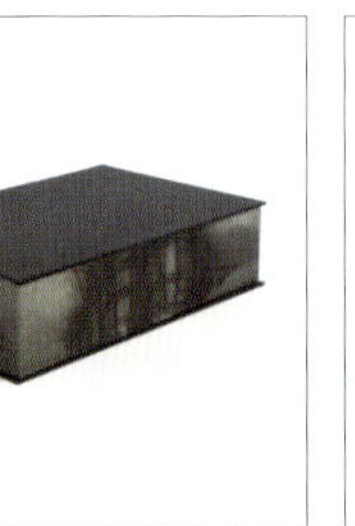

46

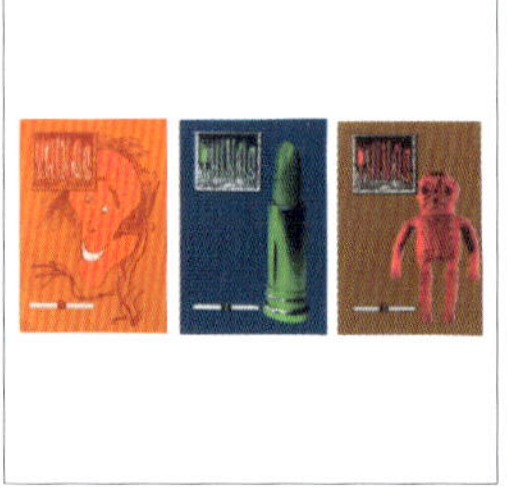

47

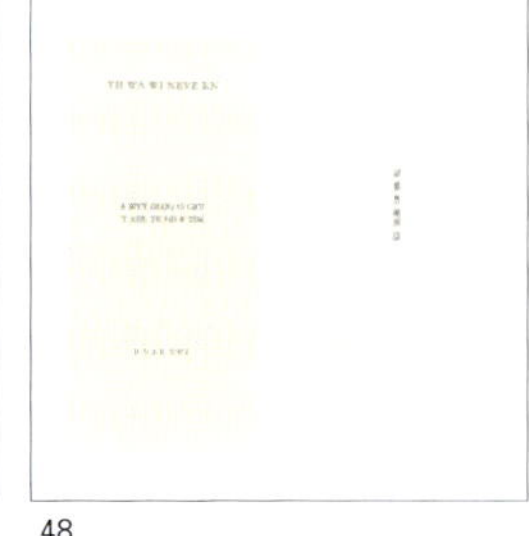

48

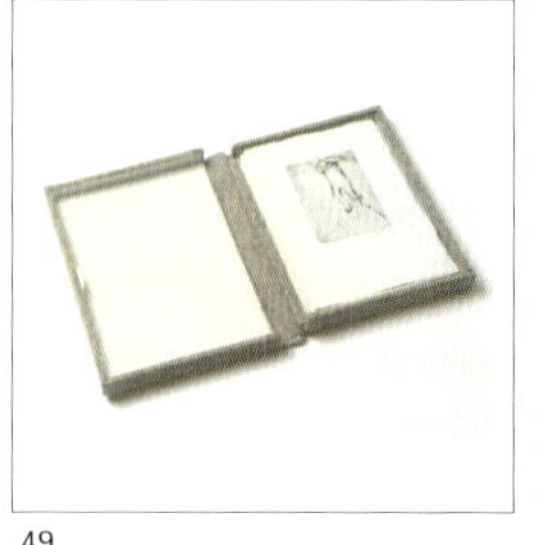

49

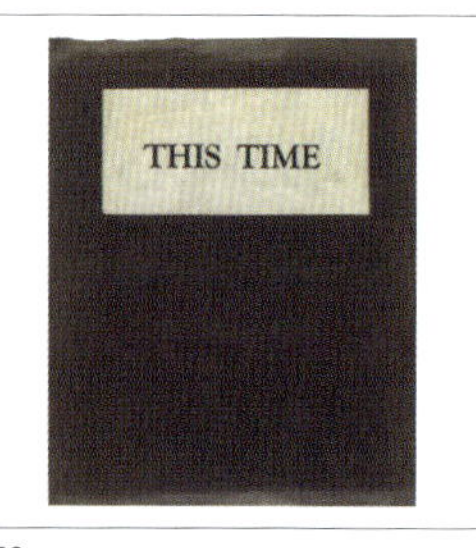

50

Robert JACKS

(coordinator) Australia, born 1943
Suzanne ARCHER, Tom ARTHUR, Tony COLEING,
John FIRTH-SMITH, Robert JACKS, Arthur LEYDEN,
Jennifer MARSHALL, Michael C. McMILLEN,
Robert OWEN, Peter POWDITCH, Gary SHEAD,
Tim STORRIER, Ann THOMSON, David van NUNEN
and Guy WARREN

44 *STAMP POST CARDS*, Sydney,
New South Wales, 1980
hand-stamped rubber stamps, printed in colour
folio (closed): 15.7 x 10.0 x 0.8 cm
sheet (each): 14.8 x 8.8 cm
Gift of Brian McHugh, 1980 81.229.1–15

Robert JACKS

(coordinator) Australia, born 1943
Peter D. COLE, Filomena COPPOLA,
Russell DREVER, Stanley FARLEY, Craig GOUGH,
Robert JACKS, Jennifer MARSHALL, Bernard OLLIS,
John ROBINSON, Wendy STAVRIANOS and
Stephen TURPIE

45 *EDITION OF POST CARDS HAND STAMPED
BY CENTRAL VICTORIAN ARTISTS*, Bendigo,
Victoria, 1991
hand-stamped rubber stamps, printed in colour
folio (closed): 15.3 x 9.1 x 0.5 cm
sheet (each): 14.8 x 8.8 cm
Gift of Robert Jacks, 1992 92.1275.1–11

Ruth JOHNSTONE

Australia, born 1955

46 *Untitled (panoramic boxed set)*, Melbourne,
Victoria, 1991
edition 1 of 4
four books (2 with fold-outs, 2 with accordion folds)
in a fold-out box; etchings, printed in colour, in books;
etching on fold-out box edges
box (closed): 35.0 x 23.8 x 8.6 cm
box (open): 35.0 x 55.8 x 8.2 cm
book 1 (closed): 32.8 x 21.4 x 1.0 cm
book 1 (open): 32.8 x 44.0 cm
book 2 (closed): 21.9 x 32.7 x 1.0 cm
book 2 (open): 21.9 x 66.4 cm
book 3 (closed): 21.9 x 32.7 x 1.0 cm
book 3 (open): 21.9 x 66.4 cm
book 4 (closed): 32.2 x 21.4 x 1.3 cm
book 4 (open): 32.2 x 44.0 cm
Gordon Darling Australasian Print Fund 1992 92.455.1–4

Maria KOZIC

Australia, born 1957

47 *THINGS 1*, Melbourne, Victoria, 1988
THINGS 2, Melbourne, Victoria, 1988
THINGS 3, Melbourne, Victoria, 1988
unlimited, unnumbered edition
three bound books, 54, 56 and 48 pages respectively
offset lithograph, printed in black ink, with screenprinted
covers, printed in colour
books (closed): 29.7 x 21.0 x 0.2 cm
books (open): 29.7 x 42.4 cm
Gift of Michael Desmond, 1989
89.1559, 89.1560, 89.1561
© Courtesy of the artist and Anna Schwartz Gallery.

Ruark LEWIS

Australia, born 1960

48 *TH WA WI NEVE EN*, Sydney, New South Wales, 1991
copy JJ/ZZ of edition of 150
uncut copy, 16 pages
bound book in envelope, letterpress text,
printed in black ink, with frontispiece drawing
envelope: 12.0 x 23.6 cm
book (closed): 23.3 x 11.0 x 0.4 cm
book (open): 23.3 x 22.0 cm
Gordon Darling Australasian Print Fund 1994 94.1485

Bea MADDOCK

Australia, born 1934

49 *MELBOURNE SERIES*, Melbourne, Victoria, 1964–81
drypoints, printed in black ink, in artist-made box
box (closed): 24.5 x 18.2 x 2.9 cm
sheet (each): 19.6 x 14.8 cm
Gift of the artist, 1984 84.2822–2839

50 *THIS TIME*, Launceston, Tasmania, 1967–69
linocuts, printed in black ink
folio (closed): 25.3 x 20.5 x 1.8 cm
sheet (each): 22.7 x 18.8 cm
Purchased 2000 00.169.A–Z

51 *BEING AND NOTHINGNESS BY JEAN-PAUL SARTRE*,
Macedon, Victoria, 1982
handwritten text on 27 sheets of handmade paper,
impregnated with beeswax, in artist-made box
box (closed): 33.0 x 24.6 x 3.5 cm
sheet (each): 29.2 x 21.2 cm
Gift of the artist, 1984 84.2840.A–AA

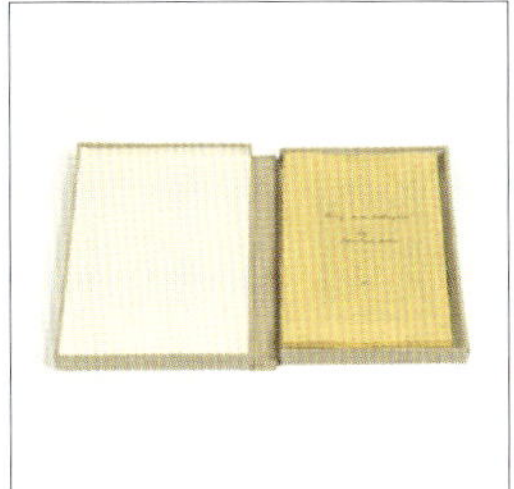

51

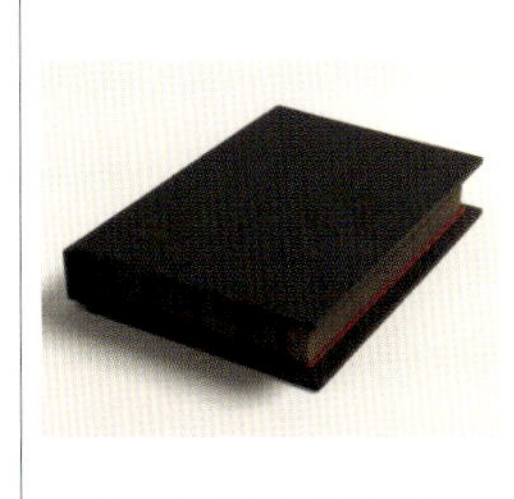

52

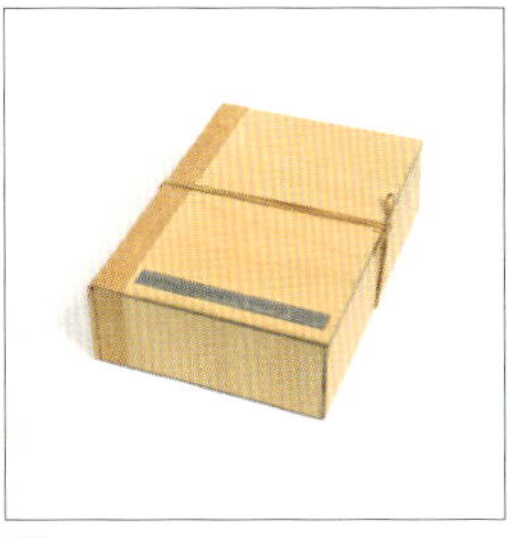

53

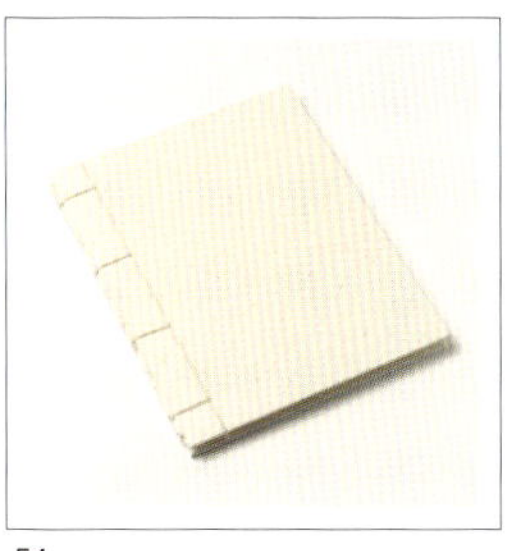

54

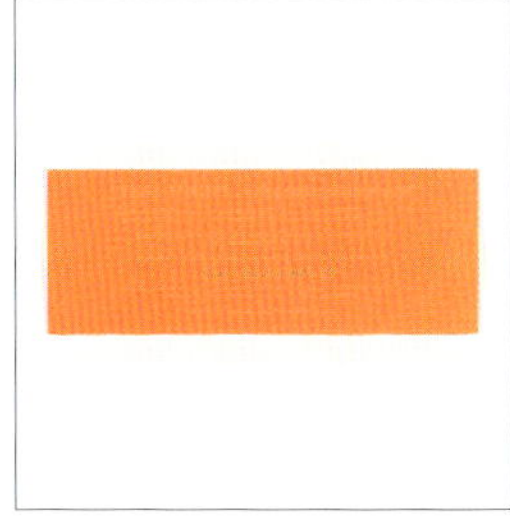

55

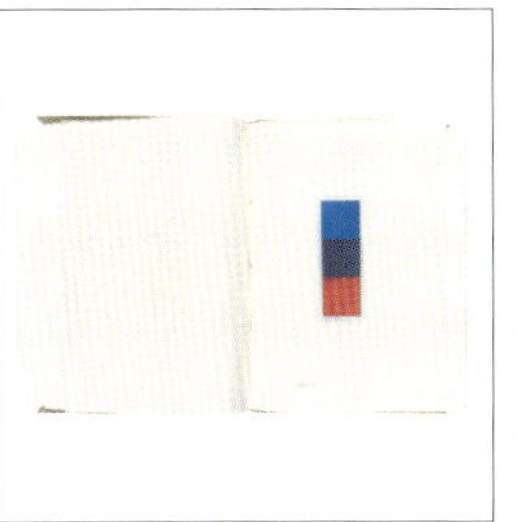

56

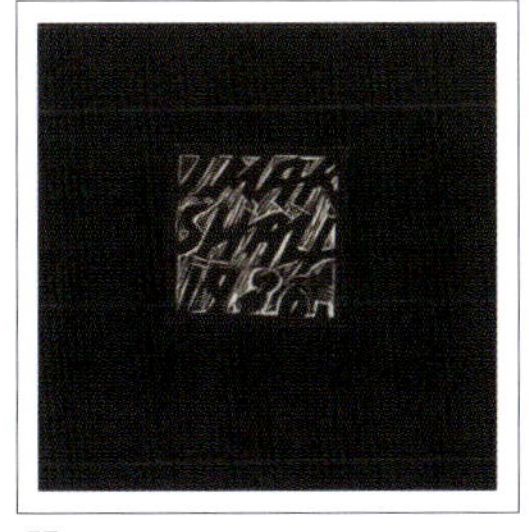

57

58

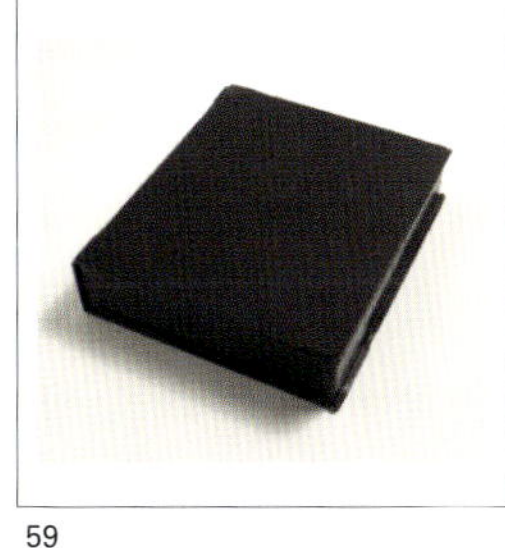

59

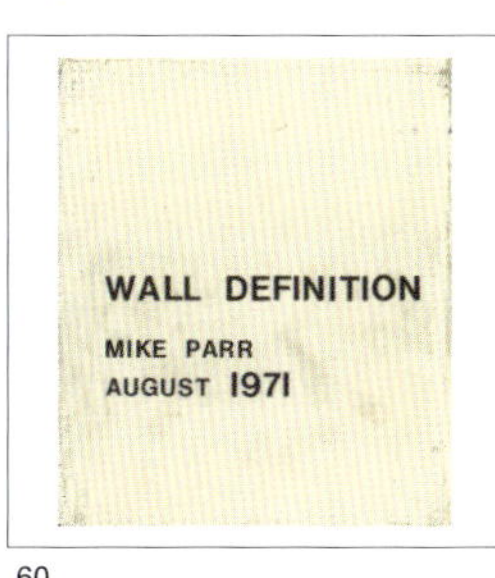

60

52 *THE DIVINE COMEDY*, Launceston, Tasmania, 1984–88
graphite, conté crayon over printed paper
in artist-bound found book
book (closed): 33.0 x 24.2 x 6.0 cm
book (open): 33.0 x 48.4 cm
Purchased 1988 88.2263

53 *IMPRESSIONS OF FORTY WORKING DAYS*,
Launceston, Tasmania, 1985
embossing on artist-made paper (from pulped
newspaper), in wooden box with leather tie
box (closed): 33.3 x 23.8 x 9.3 cm
sheet (each): 30.0 x 21.6 cm
Gordon Darling Australasian Print Fund 1989 89.53

54 *ARTEFACTS FROM TROMEMANNER*, Launceston,
Tasmania, 1990
etching, engraving, monotype, printed in colour;
letterpress text
book (closed): 24.6 x 21.4 x 1.4 cm
book (open): 24.6 x 36.4 cm
printed image (each): 14.8 x 12.4 cm
Gordon Darling Australasian Print Fund 1991 91.851

55 *TERRA SPIRITUS ... WITH A DARKER SHADE OF
PALE*, Launceston, Tasmania, 1993–98
stencil print, printed in hand-ground Launceston ochre,
from multiple hand-cut Mylar stencils; letterpress text
blind-printed and handwritten script
printed image (each): 28.4 x 76.0 cm
sheet (each): 28.4 x 76.0 cm
printed image (overall): 28.4 x 3952.0 cm
Gordon Darling Australasian Print Fund 1998
98.149.1–52

Bea MADDOCK
Australia, born 1934

David MARSDEN (printer)
Australia, born 1949

Ilme SIMMUL (book-binder)
Australia, born 1951

56 *COLOUR*, Macedon, Victoria, 1979
etching, aquatint, embossing and letterpress,
printed in colour
book (closed): 29.4 x 22.4 x 2.4 cm
book (open): 29.4 x 44.8 cm
Purchased 1980 80.86

Jennifer MARSHALL
Australia, born 1944

57 *FLICK BOOK*, Adelaide, South Australia, 1986
copy 3 of edition of 5, signed
bound book in a cardboard slip-case; linocuts,
printed in black ink, on paper
slip-case: 20.4 x 20.2 x 1.4 cm
book (closed): 19.8 x 21.0 x 1.0 cm
book (open): 19.8 x 38.8 cm
Purchased 1987 87.427

Ian MILLISS
Australia, born 1950

58 *Not titled* [*twenty-six concepts*], Sydney,
New South Wales, 1970
unlimited, uneditioned copy, 23 pages
photocopies of typed signed pages, printed in black ink,
in card folder with handwritten letter
folio (closed): 40.4 x 29.6 cm
sheet (each): 33.8 x 21.0 cm
Gift of Daniel Thomas, 1980 80.1499.1–2

Mike PARR
Australia, born 1945

59 *WORD SITUATIONS 1 & 2*, Sydney,
New South Wales, 1970–71
typewritten text, in black and red ink
box (closed): 30.6 x 27.7 x 6.9 cm
sheet (each): 25.2 x 20.2 cm
Purchased 1973 73.561.1

60 *WALL DEFINITION*, Sydney,
New South Wales, August 1971
typewritten text, black ink
box (closed): 31.4 x 27.5 x 7.0 cm
sheet (each): 25.0 x 20.4 cm
Purchased 1973 73.561.2

61 *ONE HUNDRED PAGE BOOK*, Sydney,
New South Wales, 1971
photocopies, printed in black ink
book (closed): 24.7 x 20.2 cm
book (open): 24.7 x 36.8 cm
Purchased 1973 73.1217

62 *4 SLIDE WORKS*, Sydney, New South Wales,
1971 and 1972
1. *Excerpts from notebooks* 1971 and 1972 (167 slides)
2. *Earth book* 1972 (55 slides)
3. *Blacked-out book* 1972 (129 slides)
4. *Three weeks annual leave* 1971 and 1972 (67 slides)
35 mm slides in wooden slide case
box (closed): 21.0 x 29.0 x 5.6 cm
Purchased 1973 73.561.3, 73.561.5, 73.561.6, 73.561.7

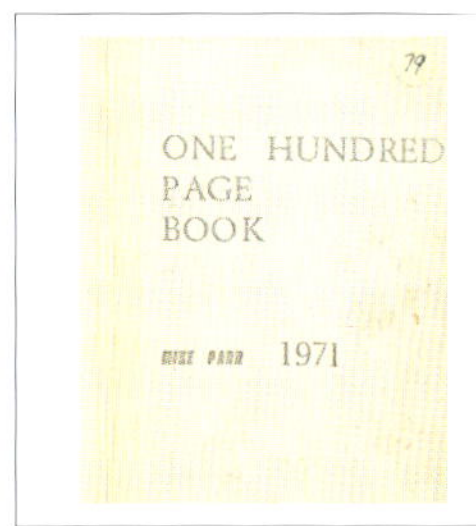
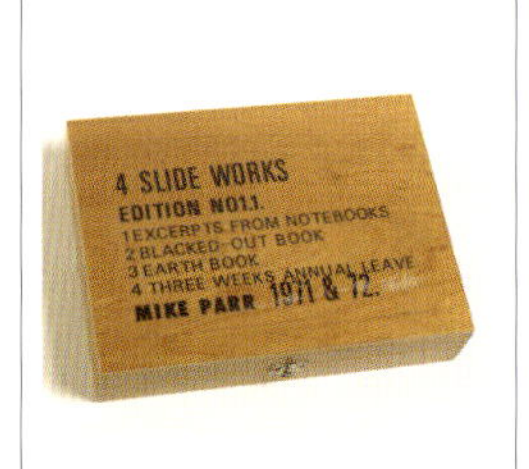

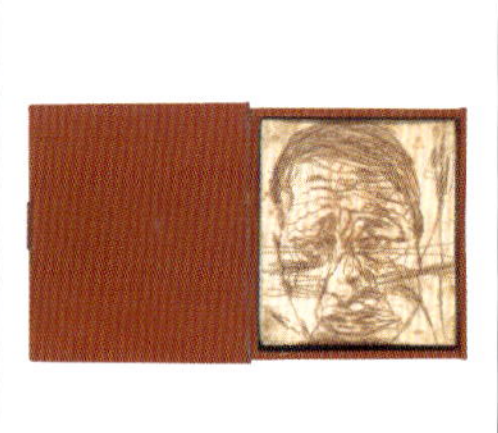
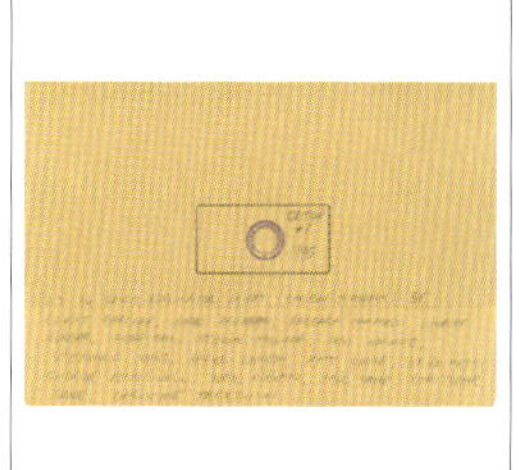

61   62   63   64   65

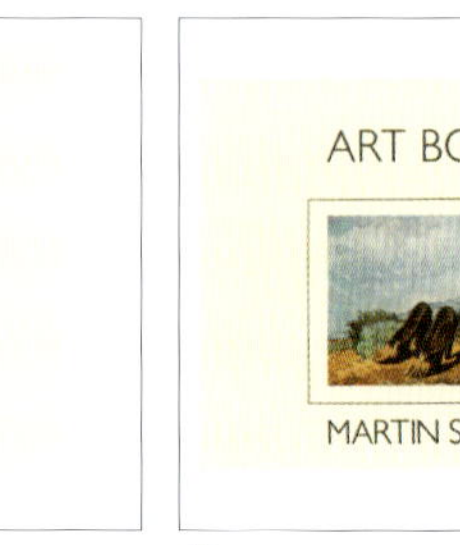
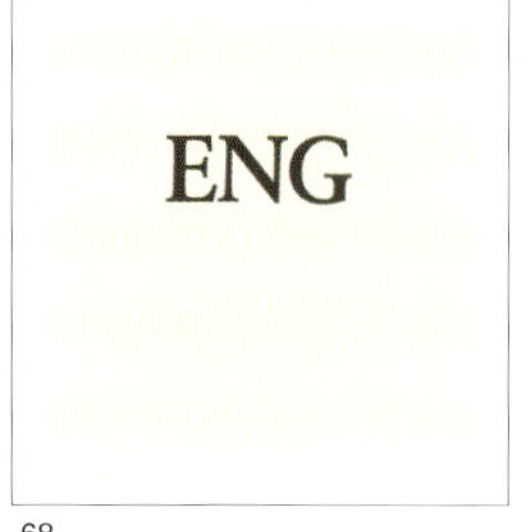
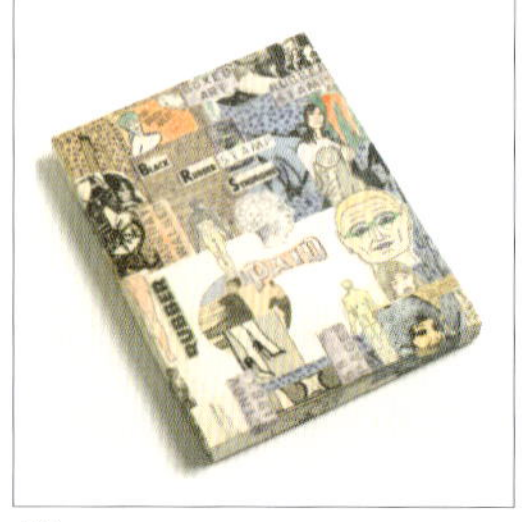
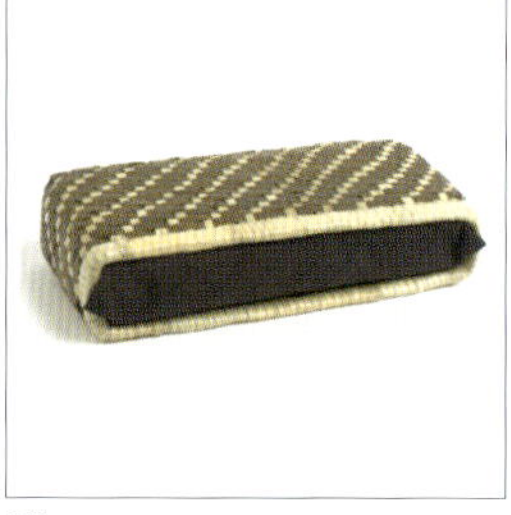

66   67   68   69   70

63 *COMMUNICATION 4–6*, Sydney,
New South Wales, 1973
from *Literary works in space and time*: a weekly
mail-out to 56 arts professionals commencing 5/11/1973,
including this sequence of 3, posted to James Mollison
at the National Gallery of Australia; typewritten text,
each printed in black ink
card (each): 10.1 x 15.2 cm
envelope: 10.1 x 15.2 cm
Purchased 2000 00.244, 00.245, 00.246, 00.247

Mike PARR
Australia, born 1945

John LOANE (printer)
Australia, born 1950

64 *ALPHABET/HAEMORRHAGE*, Olinda, Victoria, 1996
101 etchings, printed in red ochre ink
printed image and sheet (each): 27.4 x 24.0 cm
box (closed): 31.7 x 27.7 x 7.5 cm
Purchased 1996 96.1057.1–101

Neil ROBERTS (coordinator)
Australia, 1954–2002
Claire BARCLAY, Anne BRENNAN,
Barbara CAMPBELL, Lindsay DUNBAR, Fiona
HALL, Steven HOLLAND, Tess HORWITZ, Stephanie
JONES, Nigel LENDON, Kate LOHSE, eX de MEDICI,
George POPPERWELL, Neil ROBERTS, Paul SAINT,
Christopher SNEE, Christine TARKOWSKI

65 *MULTIPLE CONSTANTINOPLES*,
Queanbeyan, New South Wales, 1995
copy 2 of edition of 10, signed by all individual artists
spirit duplicator prints by 16 artists, printed in purple ink,
with sample blank duplicator sheet
loose packed between two sheets of boxboard
in standard office file wallet
folio (closed): 23.4 x 34.6 cm
sheet (each): 29.6 x 21.0 cm
Gordon Darling Australasian Print Fund 1997
97.1446.1–23

Bruce SEARLE
Australia, born 1949

66 *SUB-STATIONS*, Sydney, New South Wales, 1985
copy 4, unknown edition
(signed in pencil, with 4/85)
bound book; introductory text with
3 fold-out/pop-up photographs
book (closed): 20.0 x 15.0 x 0.3 cm
book (open): 20.0 x 29.2 cm
KODAK (Australasia) Pty Ltd Fund, 1986 87.896

Martin SHARP
Australia, born 1942

67 *ART BOOK*, London, United Kingdom, 1972
unspecified (commercial) edition, Matthews Millar
Dunbar Ltd., London (publishers)
hardback bound book with colour illustrations;
36 images plus 2 (front and back cover)
book (closed): 13.3 x 16.0 x 1.0 cm
book (open): 13.3 x 31.8 cm
Gift of Tony Twigg, 1980 81.1910

Paul UHLMANN
Australia, born 1962

68 *ENG*, Braunschweig, Germany, 1987
copy 8 of edition of 10
bound book, cloth board cover, etching and relief,
printed in black ink
book (closed): 24.8 x 25.0 x 0.8 cm
book (open): 24.8 x 49.8 cm
Purchased 1989 89.374.1–12

Murray WALKER
Australia, born 1937

Ilme SIMMUL (book-binder)
Australia, born 1951

69 *BLACK RUBBER STAMP SYNDROME*, Melbourne,
Victoria, October/November 1983
unique copy
hand-stamped bound book, 58 pages, set in larger
cardboard box with object/rubber stamp/printed paper
collage, inside and outside of box
box (closed): 28.0 x 22.0 x 2.4 cm
book (closed): 14.1 x 9.6 cm; book (open): 14.1 x 19.3 cm
Purchased 1993 93.193
© Murray Walker.

Robin WHITE
New Zealand, born 1946

70 *WALKING TO TEBUATARAWA*, Kiribati, Oceania, 1991
copy 2 of edition of 5
lithograph on paper in accordion fold,
coconut bark covers, in black loose cloth bag
in woven pandanus satchel
satchel size: 17.4 x 8.2 x 4.0 cm
book (closed): 15.0 x 6.8 x 2.0 cm
book (open): dimensions variable
Gordon Darling Australasian Print Fund 1991 91.1255

Alexander, Charles (ed). *Talking the boundless book: art language & the book arts*, Minneapolis, Minnesota: Minnesota Center for Book Arts, 1995.

Anselmi, Paola. *Ian Burn minimal – conceptual work 1965–1970*, exhibition catalogue, Perth: Art Gallery of Western Australia, 1992.

Arts Council of Great Britain. *Artists' books*, London: Arts Council of Great Britain, 1976.

Burke, Janine. 'Portrait of the artist: Bea Maddock', in *Survey 11, Bea Maddock*, exhibition catalogue, Melbourne: National Gallery of Victoria, 1980.

Bury, Stephen. *Artists' books, the book as a work of art, 1963–1995*, United Kingdom: Scolar Press, 1995.

Castelman, Riva. *A century of artists books*, New York: The Museum of Modern Art, 1994.

Catalano, Gary. *The bandaged image: a study of Australian artists' books*, Sydney: Hale & Ironmonger, 1983.

Coulter-Smith, Graham. *Mike Parr: the self portrait project*, Melbourne: Schwartz City, 1994.

Drucker, Johanna. *The century of artists' books*, New York: Granary Books, 1995.

Gates, Merryn. *Artists make books*, exhibition catalogue, curated and introduction by Christine Johnson, St Kilda, Victoria: Linden Gallery St Kilda Centre for Contemporary Arts, 1991.

Gates, Merryn and Parr, Mike. *Mike Parr artist-in-residence 1990/91*, Melbourne: University of Melbourne Museum of Art/Ian Potter Gallery, 1991.

Glasmeier, Michael. *Die Bücher der Künstler: publications and editions from the sixties in Germany*, Germany: Edition Hansjorg Mayer and Institute for Foreign Cultural Relations, 1989.

Grahame, Noreen (ed). *Beware, books by artists, artists books fair 94*, catalogue, Milton, Qld: Numero Uno Publications, 1994.

Grahame, Noreen (ed). *Artists' books + multiples fair 1996; 1998; 2001*, catalogues, Milton, Qld: Numero Uno Publications; 1996; 1998; 2001.

Graphic Investigation Workshop. *Artists books and limited editions*, exhibition catalogue, Canberra: Canberra School of Art, 1992.

Graphic Investigation Workshop. *Fragile objects*, exhibition catalogue, Canberra: Canberra School of Art, 1994.

Graphic Investigation Workshop. *Artists books and limited editions 3*, 1995–98, Canberra: Canberra School of Art, 2001.

Guest, Tim and Celant, Germano (eds). *Books by artists*, Toronto: Art Metropole, 1981.

Isselbacher, Audrey. *Iliazd and the illustrated book*, New York: The Museum of Modern Art, 1987.

Johnson, Robert Flynn and Stein, Donna. *Artists' books in the modern era 1870–2000: the Reva and David Logan collection of illustrated books*, exhibition catalogue, San Francisco: Fine Arts Museums of San Francisco, 2001.

Kaldor, John et al. *An Australian accent: three artists, Mike Parr, Imants Tillers, Ken Unsworth*, exhibition catalogue, John Kaldor curator, John Kaldor Art Project 7, PS1, New York, 1984, Sydney: John Kaldor, 1984.

Kirker, Anne and Butler, Roger. *Being and nothingness: Bea Maddock, works from three decades*, exhibition catalogue, Brisbane/Canberra: Queensland Art Gallery/Australian National Gallery, 1991.

Kronenberg, Simeon. *Robert Jacks, on paper 1958–1990*, Melbourne: The University of Melbourne Museum of Art, 1990.

Lauf, Cornelia and Phillpot, Clive. *Artist/author: contemporary artists' books*, exhibition catalogue, New York: Distributed Art Publishers Inc and The American Federation of Arts, 1998.

Loney, Alan. 'Bruno Leti's artists books', in *Bruno Leti, survey artists books 1982–2003*, curated by Brian Hubber, with an introductory essay by Alan Loney, exhibition catalogue, Geelong: Geelong Art Gallery, 2003, pp 9–13.

Lyons, Joan (ed). Artists' books: *a critical anthology and sourcebook*, Rochester, NY: Visual Studies Workshop Press, 1985.

McGregor, Ken. *Robert Jacks, Past Unfolded*, Sydney: Craftsman House, 2001.

Paper plus, artist books and designer bookbinding, curated by Anne Virgo, with an essay by Nola Anderson, exhibition catalogue, Canberra: Crafts Council ACT, 1987.

Rothenberg, Jerome and Clay, Steven (eds). *A book of the book*: some works and projections about the book and writing], New York: Granary Books, 2000.

Rowell, Margit and Wye, Deborah (eds). *The Russian avant-garde book 1910–1934*, exhibition catalogue, New York: The Museum of Modern Art, 2002.

Salzmann, Siegfried. *Das Buch, Künstlerobjekte. The book, art in book form*, exhibition catalogue, Germany, Institute for Foreign Cultural Relations, 1989.

Selenitsch, Alex. 'Unique copies', *Imprint*, vol 28, no 2, winter 1993, Melbourne: Print Council of Australia, pp 6–8.

Selenitsch, Alex (ed). *Imprint*, vol 34, no 2, winter 1999, (special issue on artists' books), Melbourne: Print Council of Australia.

The book garden: contemporary Russian artists' books, exhibition catalogue, Bristol, UK: Off-centre Gallery, c 1995.

Spector, Buzz. *The book maker's desire*, Pasadena, CA: Umbrella Editions, 1995.

Stephen, Ann (ed). *Artists think: the late works of Ian Burn*, Sydney: Power Publications in association with Monash University Gallery, Melbourne, 1996.

Tonkin, Steven. 'Australian artists' books in the National Gallery's collection', *artonview*, issue 24, summer 2000–01, Canberra: National Gallery of Australia, pp 50–1.

Turner, Silvie and Tyson, Ian (eds). *British artists' books 1970–1983*, exhibition catalogue, London: Atlantis Paper Company, 1984.